ECONOMIC PERSPECTIVES

ECONOMIC PERSPECTIVES

An Annual Survey of Economics

Edited by David W. Pearce and Nicholas J. Rau
University College, London

ECONOMIC PERSPECTIVES

An Annual Survey of Economics

Edited by David W. Pearce and Nicholas J. Rau
University College, London

Volume 4
1986

Routledge
Taylor & Francis Group
LONDON AND NEW YORK

First published 1986 by Harwood Academic Publishers

Published 2021 by Routledge
2 Park Square, Milton Park, Abingdon, Oxon OX14 4RN
605 Third Avenue, New York, NY 10017

Routledge is an imprint of the Taylor & Francis Group, an informa business

The Library of Congress has catalogued the second issue of this serial as follows:

HB1
.E2516 **Economic perspectives.** v.2 1981
Chur [Switzerland] New York, Harwood Academic Publishers.
v.I1l. 23 cm.
Annual.
"An annual survey of economics."
Key title: Economic perspectives, ISSN 0142-5900
1. Economics–Periodicals
HB 1.E2516 330'.05 80-642162
ISBN 3-7186-0362-4

ISBN 13: 978-3-7186-0362-6 (hbk)

Contents

Preface to the Series

New avenues for the communication of research and ideas are needed in a discipline growing in number, specializations and outside recognition. It is important, however, that such communications be conducted at levels of abstraction that are accessible to all who conscientiously claim economics as a vocation. Graduate students, business economists, government specialists and academicians alike, should have at hand a means whereby they can be informed of the state-of-the-art not only in their own particular corner of the discipline, but elsewhere in presentations that are written to be widely understood. Furthermore, as the rapidity of developments in some areas threatens to outdate research even before work is published, it is desirable that the time between final manuscript completion and publication be reduced as much as possible.

Economic Perspectives: An Annual Survey of Economics is designed to meet these and other requirements of economists. Contributions are generally solicited on the advice of members of the editorial board and reflect the viewpoints of their respective authors on recent developments, current issues, current research and prospective progress.

We would like to thank Helen G. Nichols for her assistance in the preparation of this volume.

Foreword

Starting with this volume, *Economic Perspectives* comes under new editors. We hope to maintain the standard set by our predecessor in publishing clear, accurate and useful surveys of recent developments in economics, written by experts for graduate students and working economists.

The first two articles in Volume 4 are concerned with applied welfare economics. The paper by George McKenzie and David Ulph is addressed to the problem of deriving an indicator of welfare from observable behaviour as specified by Marshallian demand functions. This problem has a long history, as is evident from what a leading advanced textbook calls the "large and not very edifying literature" on consumer surplus (A. Deaton and J. Muellbauer, *Economics and Consumer Behaviour*, Cambridge, Cambridge University Press, 1980, p. 190). However, real progress has been made in recent years, which McKenzie and Ulph summarize and extend. After a survey of work by others on consumer surplus as an approximation, the authors present a numerical solution procedure for an *exact* welfare measure, applicable to single or multiple price changes. The method of solution is simple to implement on a low-cost micro-computer, and the authors provide a Pascal program in an appendix.

The use of numerical algorithms as a tool of microeconomic analysis is also a central feature of the article by Christopher Heady and Pradeep Mitra. Their work can be regarded as a synthesis of two of the most important developments in economic theory during the past two decades: applied general equilibrium analysis as pioneered by Scarf and his students, and the optimal tax theory of Diamond and Mirrlees. In a series of papers published during the last five years, Heady and Mitra have developed procedures for computing optimal taxes, tariffs and shadow prices in models of increasing complexity, with special reference to developing economies. Their article in this volume is an introduction to an overview of all this important work, relating it to its antecedents and suggesting future developments.

One of our aims in this series is to provide relatively non-technical surveys of recent developments in econometrics, with a view to their applications. The third and fourth papers in this volume are of this nature. John Mullahy's article is an extensive exploration of limited-dependent-variable models, illustrated by a common field of application: the economics of participation in recreational activities. The main classes of models studied and compared are the analysis of truncation and censoring (building on the work of Tobin, Cragg and Heckman), recent work on count data and models with grouped dependent variables. The article also discusses predictions using such models.

Malcolm Pemberton's article provides a concise survey of econometric disequilibrium models. After an exposition of the simplest single-market model under alternative price adjustment rules, Pemberton discusses various extensions, with special reference to the problem of testing the hypothesis of continuous market-clearing. The models are illustrated by reference to ongoing research by Pemberton and his collaborators on the housing market and the labour market in the United Kingdom.

Aspects of the United Kingdom labour market also form the subject of each of the next three papers. The emphasis on these issues in this volume reflects not so much any Anglocentric views the editors may hold, but our belief that some of the best work on the problem of mass unemployment happens to have used UK data.

Martyn Andrews' contribution assesses the state of the cost of econometric modelling of the aggregate labour market in the United Kingdom. He focusses on models that *jointly* determine real wages, employment and possibly unemployment and are estimated using time-series data. Four models are examined in some detail which can be described as market-clearing, market-clearing with a unionized sector, a fully unionized model and finally a non-market-clearing model. Andrews shows that these models lead to quite similar specifications in the equations estimated: salient differences result not so much from clashes of theoretical paradigm as from pragmatic considerations at the estimation stage. There is, however, too little consensus between the models for them to be regarded as anything other than illustrative and descriptive; Andrews warns against their use for policy purposes.

Tim Hatton provides a comprehensive survey of the considerable amount of recent work by himself and others on the causes of British unemployment between the two world wars. The main impetus behind this research was the remarkable article by Benjamin and Kochin claiming that the high unemployment of the later 1930s was largely benefit-induced, and the subsequent controversy in the *Journal of Political Economy*. Hatton summarizes this work and its subsequent extensions using structural models and less aggregated data. Again, issues of model specification become central: Hatton argues that "using a static market-clearing model strains credibility as well as doing violence to the observed facts". He also discusses in detail recent research on the institutional aspects of British labour markets between the wars, the effects of collective bargaining on wages, the consequences for different regions of changes in demand and the factors affecting and attenuating mobility of labour.

With Peter Hart's paper we return to more recent labour market behaviour in the United Kingdom, and to an important topical question. The unemployment rate of teenagers has risen since the early 1970s, even relative to a rising adult unemployment rate: to what extent can this be attributed to a rising relative price of labour services of youths? Hart contributes a critical survey of six econometric studies using different approaches. He concludes that all the studies support the hypothesis of a relative price effect but that "the precise importance of relative labour costs compared with all the other determinants of youth unemployment has not been established".

The last article in this volume, by Ben Lockwood, is theoretical in nature but potentially fruitful in application to many brands of empirical economics, both micro and macro. The theory of games of strategy has been with us for many decades, but it is only recently that game theorists have conducted detailed formal analysis of issues of timing and credibility in strategic behaviour. Lockwood's paper explains Selten's important concept of perfect equilibria, with special reference to strategic precommitment and credible preemption. The theory is illustrated with examples of wage bargaining and oligopoly. The article concludes with a survey of research on repeated games.

Nicholas J. Rau
David W. Pearce

EXACT WELFARE MEASURES

GEORGE MCKENZIE
University of Southampton
DAVID ULPH
University of Bristol

I. INTRODUCTION

One of the classic problems in both theoretical and applied welfare economics has been that of deducing consumer's valuations of commodities from their observed consumption behaviour. For well over a century economists have debated what it is that we should be measuring and the nature of the assumptions underlying particular computational procedures, in particular those involving the concept of consumer surplus.

It is not our objective here to survey the vast and very diverse literature in this area[1]. Rather we shall concentrate on a relatively small number of recent contributions which we believe now effectively provides the basis for modern applied welfare analysis. The common factor underlying these works is that they all involve exploiting duality theory to retrieve information about the expenditure function from the parameters of ordinary demand equations[2]. The significance of this is that the expenditure function enables the calculation of the compensating and equivalent variations, measures which have traditionally formed the basis of cost-benefit analysis. Although applied welfare analysts have generally focused on the former indicator, the equivalent variation possesses the property of being an ordinal welfare metric. Hence duality theory also provides us with a basis for recovering a representation of consumer preferences which is denominated in monetary units. As a consequence it enables ease of interpretation and presentation by lay economists and policy makers.

As stated above, the problem we are addressing is that of deriving a welfare indicator from observable consumer behaviour as specified by Marshallian demand equations. It may be asked why this is any longer a problem. For it is now a fairly widespread practice when estimating consumer demand behaviour to exploit duality theory directly by specifying an explicit functional form for either the indirect utility function of expenditure function, deriving the associated Marshallian demand functions by straightforward differentiation, and then fitting these demand functions to the data so as to effectively determine the parameters of the expenditure or indirect utility function[3]. From these functions the welfare evaluation of different price/income situations is immediate. An exposition of this approach is given in King (1983).

There are, however, two problems that remain for the applied welfare analyst. First, he or she may simply be presented with a system of demand equations which has already been estimated without using the dual approach and for which it is impossible to recover the expenditure function in closed form. This is the dilemma which arises most often in cost-benefit analysis and is frequently handled by resort to consumer surplus triangles. Second, even if it is possible to estimate well-behaved expenditure or indirect utility functions, there may be some features of consumer behaviour which are better represented by a particular class of demand equation for which there is no corresponding closed form of utility or expenditure function. Indeed, there is a virtual infinity of such systems, many of which will be less restrictive than those currently popular in econometric demand research. The problem then becomes one of numerically evaluating the expenditure function from the parameters of the demand equations without knowledge of the explicit form of that expenditure function.

Of course, the advantage of being able to capture consumer behaviour more exactly by specifying demand equations directly could be largely dissipated if there were no subsequent method for deriving precise calculations of welfare gains and losses from these demand equations. However, drawing upon recent work by McKenzie (1982), Hausman (1981) and Vartia (1983), we will present a simple procedure for deriving an exact measure of consumer welfare from any well-defined system of demand equations.

The method which we propose is in essence the same as that developed by Vartia although the actual solution procedure is different. Since our procedure is based on the traditional consumer surplus framework it has, we believe, considerable padagogic advantages for convincing practitioners to abandon their theoretically inexact surplus methods.

One point to stress is that the technique does not produce a formula for calculating welare measures, but an algorithm which will, in principle, generate a number representing an exact welare measure. It is therefore designed precisely for practitioners who have to produce such numbers rather than for theorists who wish to investigate the properties of the measure. Standard duality techniques will suffice for this latter problem.

The method proposed involves obtaining solutions to simple first-order ordinary differential equations. These are simple enough that the calculations can be carried out on a calculator or low-cost home computer. (A simple algorithm written in Pascal is provided in Appendix B). Errors of approximation inevitably must be considered and, in principle, these are the same as those that will arise from numerical integration in the standard consumer surplus calculation. The advantage of our method is that the approximation is of an exact formula and not the inexact formula of the consumer surplus method. As a consequence, it provides the applied economist, who has been presented with a demand equation from which to derive a welfare measure, with a technique which is soundly based in theory and, as our examples will show, can provide extremely accurate calculations of the true measure.

For the practitioner who has to obtain estimates of the demand system in question, it leaves open the choice of either specifying the demand system directly, as we do here, or of utilizing duality techniques. There is now no significant drawback to the former approach from the point of view of deriving accurate welfare measures.

The plan of the paper is as follows. In the next section, we briefly survey some of the recent work based upon the expenditure function. The analysis is confined to the case of a single price variation. In Section III, the solution procedure for the exact welfare indicator is explained in detail, again for the case of a single price change. Then, in Section IV, the solution procedure for the general case is explained. This enables evaluation of the welfare effects associated with changes in consumer income and multiple price variation. In Section V, we illustrate how to specify very general demand systems which satisfy all the standard properties of economic theory yet do not possess a closed for representation of either the associated utility or expenditure functions. In the final section, we discuss some practical issues in addition to the meaning of "measurable utility".

II. RECENT DEVELOPMENTS

Much has been written about expenditure functions and applied welfare analysis over the past fifteen years, starting with the work of Mohring (1971), Bergson (1975) and Hause (1975). In what follows we shall concentrate on four papers which form a logical progression towards the ultimate development of an exact welfare indicator: McKenzie and Pearce (1976), Willig (1976 a, b) Seade (1978), and Hausman (1981). All involve use of the expenditure function and hence enable calculation of both the equivalent and compensating variations. For ill-ustrative purposes we shall concentrate only on the equivalent variation (sence it is a welfare metric). In addition, we shall initially consider only the case of evaluating the effects of a single price change. This appears to be the case involved in most applied welfare analysis although it is not difficult to conceive of projects or policies which will not induce variations in several prices. As we shall argue, focus on the case of a single price change is most likely a pragmatic one reflecting the difficulty which researchers have previously encountered in constructing welfare metrics enabling the analysis of multiple price variations.

Throughout this paper, we shall assume that there exists a set of "well-behaved", non-stochastic demand functions for each individual consumer. That is, the demand functions are homogeneous of degree zero, satisfy the budget constraint and generate a symmetric, negative semi-definite Slutsky matrix. No additional restrictions are required on the functional form of the demand equations to guarantee the existence of a preference ordering. We shall write the <u>direct</u> preference function as

$$U = U(X_1, \ldots, X_n) \tag{1}$$

where X_i is the quantity of the ith commodity consumed. This preference ordering may be presented in its <u>indirect</u> form as

$$\psi = \psi\ (Y, p_1, \ldots, p_n) \tag{2}$$

where p_i is the price of commodity i and Y represents consumer income.

Associated with the preference systems (3) or (4) is the expenditure function:

$$C = C\ (\psi, p^*) \tag{3}$$

where C indicates the minimum amount of money required to support the level of satisfaction ψ defined by Y and p but given the alternative price vector p*. The equivalent variation (EV) and the compensating variation (CV) may then be represented as follows. Let us suppose that in the base or initial period expenditure and prices are denoted by the vector (Y^o, p^o) whereas in the current period they are (Y^1, p^1). Then

$$EV = C(\psi\,(Y^1,p^1),p^o) - C(\psi\,(Y^o,p^o),p^o) \quad (4)$$

$$= C(\psi\,(Y^1,p^1),p^o) - Y^o$$

$$= C(\psi\,(Y^1,p^1),p^o) - C(\psi\,(Y^1,p^1),p^1) + (Y^1 - Y^o) \quad (5)$$

and

$$CV = C(\psi\,(Y^o,p^o), - C(\psi\,(Y^o,p^o),p^o) - (Y^1 - Y^o) \quad (6)$$

$$= C(\psi\,(Y^o,p^o),p^1) - Y^1$$

$$= C(\psi\,(Y^o,p^o),p^1) - C((Y^1,p^1),p^1) \quad (7)$$

That is, the equivalent and compensating variations are formally symmetric in the sense that the equivalent variation associated with a move from the base to the current period is identical to the compensating variation associated with a move from the current to the base period (compare (4) with (7) or (5) with (6)).

a) The McKenzie-Pearce Taylor Series Representation

Let us assume that the expenditure function is analytic over the region of price and income variation being considered. Thus this function can be represented by a Taylor series expansion that is convergent as its order approaches infinity.

Let M represent the money metric $C(\psi\ (Y,p),p^o)$, that is, the cost of achieving the level of satisfaction generated by $\psi\ (Y,p)$ but given initial prices p^o. If the Taylor series for M is expanded around initial prices then the equivalent variation can be written exactly as the infinite series:

$$EV = \Delta M = \frac{\partial M}{\partial p_i} \Delta p_i + \frac{1}{2} \frac{\partial^2 M}{\partial p_i^2} (\Delta p_i)^2 + \frac{1}{6} \frac{\partial^3 M}{\partial p_i^3} (\Delta p_i)^3 + \ldots \tag{8}$$

This expansion can be transformed so as to incorporate only the parameters of ordinary observable demand functions. This can be achieved by making use of the following properties of the monly metric:

(i) Given initial prices

$$\frac{\partial M}{\partial Y} (Y,p^o) = \lambda(Y,p^o) \equiv 1 \tag{9}$$

$$\frac{\partial^r \lambda}{\partial Y^r} (Y,p^o) \equiv 0 \quad r = 1,2,\ldots \tag{10}$$

(ii) Since M is an ordinal welfare metric Roy's Identity is satisfied, i.e.

$$\frac{\partial M}{\partial p_i} = -\lambda X_i \tag{11}$$

Equations (9) - (11) can then be used to calculate the various derivatives contained in the Taylor series expansion (8) with the following result:

$$\frac{\partial M}{\partial p_i} = - X_i \tag{12}$$

$$\frac{\partial^2 M}{\partial p_i^2} = - \frac{\partial X_i}{\partial p_i} + X_i \frac{\partial X_i}{\partial Y} \tag{13}$$

$$\frac{\partial^3 M}{\partial p_i^3} = - \frac{\partial^2 X_i}{\partial p_i^2} + 2 \frac{\partial X_i}{\partial Y} \cdot \frac{\partial X_i}{\partial p_i}$$

$$-X_i \left[\left(\frac{\partial X_i}{\partial Y} \right)^2 \frac{\partial^2 X_i}{\partial Y \, \partial p_i} + X_i \frac{\partial^2 X_i}{\partial Y^2} \right] \quad \text{etc.} \tag{14}$$

If the above expansion were truncated at the second-order terms then we would obtain Hicks' (1946) second-order approximation to the equivalent variation. This formulation also enables us to appreciate the errors of approximation involved in utilizing tne consumer surplus integral

$$A = - \int X_i dp_i \tag{15}$$

which can be written as an infinite Taylor series

$$A = - X_i \, \Delta p_i - \frac{\partial X_i}{\partial p_i} (\Delta p_i)^2 - \frac{\partial^2 X_i}{\partial p_i^2} (\Delta p_i)^3 + \ldots \tag{16}$$

The difference between M and A therefore consists of all terms involving a derivative of X_i with respect to total income Y.

<u>Comments</u>

i) The McKenzie-Pearce Taylor series representation showed that a welfare metric expressed in monetary units could be

expressed exactly in terms of the parameters of ordinary demand functions, that is, price and income effects.
ii) Such a representation could be achieved without resort to the Marshallian consumer surplus integral or approximation based upon it.
iii)Practical calculations based upon the McKenzie-Pearce representation can be made by truncating the Taylor series at an arbitrary point. This is problematic in that, in principle, the remainder error could be important.
iv)The Taylor series representation can be extended to allow for any number of price variations as well as changes in total expenditure. [cf. McKenzie and Pearce (1976)]. A general approximation method for this more general case is contained in McKenzie (1982, Ch.3).

b) Willig's Error Bounds

Despite the well-known problems associated with the consumer surplus integral A, it has continued to act as a focal point for much of the applied welfare analysis. Given the pedagogic simplicity of (15) it is easy to appreciate why this is the case. It is thus not surprising that attempts should be made to preserve it as a corner-stone for applied work by examining its ability to approximate the expenditure function and, more specifically, to approximate the equivalent and compensating variations. The approach taken by Willig (1976a) is to identify error bounds.

Following Mohring (1971), Willig exploits the relationship between the ordinary and compensated demand functions. From Shephard's lemma, the derivative of the expenditure function with respect to the price of the ith commodity is simply the compensated demand function

$$X_i^c = \frac{\partial C(\psi(Y' , p'), p)}{\partial p_i} \tag{17}$$

This compensated function can then be recast as an ordinary demand function

$$X_i^c = X_i[p, C(\psi(Y',p'), p)]$$

$$= X_i[p, C(\psi',p)] \tag{18}$$

If we denote by η_{iu} and $\eta_{i\ell}$ the upper and lower bounds for the income elasticity of demand associated with commodity i over the range of price and income variation, then it can be shown (Willig, 1976b) that

$$\left[\frac{C(\psi', p)}{Y^o}\right]^{\eta_{i\ell}} \leq \frac{X_i(p, C(\psi', p))}{X_i(p, Y^o)} \leq \left[\frac{C(\psi', p)}{Y^o}\right]^{\eta_{iu}} \tag{19}$$

$$X_i(p, Y^o).(Y^o)^{-\eta_{i\ell}} \leq \frac{\partial C(\psi', p)}{\partial p_i} \left[C(\psi', p)\right]^{-\eta_{i\ell}} \tag{20}$$

and

$$X_i(p,Y^o).(Y^o)^{-\eta_{iu}} \geq \frac{\partial C(\psi', p)}{\partial p_i} \cdot \left[C(\psi', p)\right]^{-\eta_{iu}} \tag{21}$$

Integration of (20) and (21) then enables the construction of the following "error bounds" for the consumer surplus measure A as an approximation to the equivalent variation EV:

$$\frac{[(A/Y^o)\ (1-\eta_{i\ell}) + 1]^{1/(1-\eta_{i\ell})} - 1 - A/Y^o}{|A|/Y^0} \geq$$

$$\frac{EV-A}{|A|} \geq \frac{[(A/Y^o)(1-\eta_{iu}) + 1]^{1/(1-\eta_{iu})} - 1 - A/Y^o}{|A|/Y^o} \qquad (22)$$

Willig argues that provided that $\eta_{i\ell}$ and η_{iu} are fairly close in value and

$$1 + (1-\eta_{i\ell})\ A/Y^o > 0 \qquad (23)$$

$$1 + (1-\eta_{iu})\ A/Y^o > 0 \qquad (24)$$

then the Marshallian measure will serve as a good representation of the equivalent variation. Similar bounds can be set for the compensating variation.

Comments

i) The method is not general, requiring a fairly tight bound on the range of variation of the income elasticities.

ii) Like the exact methods to be discussed later in the paper, Willig's approach makes use of the relationship between Shephard's lemma and the compensated and ordinary demand schedules. In other words, an exact valuation of the equivalent variation can be obtained utilizing the same information that Willig uses to construct his error bounds.

iii) In general, the consumer surplus integral cannot be evaluated as a closed form and hence numerical methods will be required.

iv) Identification of error bounds in the case where several prices vary is extremely difficult and is realistically possible only in special cases such as when all price changes are small or when they all vary in the same direction or when preferences are homothetic (Cf. McKenzie (1982), pp.116-122).

c) Seade's approch involving linear Engel curves

The money-metric form of any preference system exhibiting linear Engel curves is

$$M = \frac{Y-a(p)}{b(p)} b(p^o) + a(p^o) \tag{25}$$

where a(p) and b(p) are functions homogeneous of degree one in prices. Utilizing Roy's Identity to calculate the associated system of demand functions and then differentiating with respect to income, we obtain the income effect

$$\frac{\partial X_i}{\partial Y} = \frac{\partial b}{\partial p_i} \frac{1}{b(p)} \tag{26}$$

Seade notes that these income effects can be directly related to the marginal (money-metric) utility of total expenditure. From (25) we obtain

$$\lambda(p) = \frac{\partial M}{\partial Y} = \frac{b(p^o)}{b(p)} \tag{27}$$

which can easily be rewritten as

$$\lambda(p) = \exp\left[-\int_c \Sigma \frac{\partial X_i}{\partial Y} dp_i \right] \tag{28}$$

Equation (28) can then be utilized as an integrating factor to evaluate the money-metric exactly from the following line integral

$$M = - \int_c \Sigma\lambda X_i \, dp_i \tag{29}$$

Since a(p) and b(p) are both homogeneous of degree one it should be a fairly easy matter to retrieve M in closed form. Curiously, Seade does not opt for this general approach but instead constructs an approximation within which the consumer surplus integral can be explicitly identified.

In the case of a single price change we can write the integrating factor

$$\begin{aligned} \lambda(p) &= \exp\left[- \int_c \frac{\partial X_i}{\partial Y} \, dp_i \right] \\ &= \exp\left[- \int_c \frac{1}{Y} \eta_i \, X_i dp_i \right] \\ &= \exp\left[- \frac{\tilde{\eta}_i}{Y} \int_c X_i dp_i \right] \\ &= \exp\left[\frac{\tilde{\eta}_i}{Y} A \right] \end{aligned} \tag{30}$$

where the income elasticity $\tilde{\eta}_i$ is evaluated at $\tilde{p}_i$ where $p_i^1 > \tilde{p}_i > p_i^o$. Equation (30) is then introduced into (29) to obtain Seade's approximation to the equivalent variation:

$$EV \sim \frac{Y}{\tilde{\eta}_i} \left| \exp\left[\frac{\tilde{\eta}_i A}{Y} \right] - 1 \right| \tag{31}$$

Comments

Seade's approach shares three things in common with that of Willig:

i) It represents an attempt to justify continued use of the Marshallian consumer surplus integral (15).

ii) It involves assumptions about the nature of income

effects where, in this case, the Engel curves are linear. iii) It does not make full use of the information contained in observable consumer demand functions.

III. AN EXACT SOLUTION FOR A SINGLE PRICE CHANGE

Independently, Hausman (1981) and Vartia (1983) have presented essentially identical methods for recovering the expenditure function from ordinary demand functions. Hausman considers only the case of a single price change and bases his presentation on an example where the expenditure function can be retrieved in closed form. Vartia's presentation is more general in that multiple price changes are directly evaluated even in circumstances where the expenditure function cannot be expressed in closed form. Both authors develop their analysis in terms of the compensating variation. However, our approach will continue to focus upon the equivalent variation since this is an ordinal welfare metric.

In principle the method is straightforward and starts from the well known results that

$$\frac{\partial C(\psi,\ p)}{\partial p_i} = X_i^c\ (\psi,p) = X_i[C(\psi,p),\ p] \tag{32}$$

This is the differential equation noted by Mohring and exploited by Willig (see above discussion). This simply says that the compensation the consumer needs for a small price change is equal to the amount demanded of the good whose price has changed.

Equation (32) cannot be exploited immediately since it contains the unobservable utility level ψ. The essence of our procedure for overcoming this problem and obtaining an exact welfare measure can be explained intuitively as follows.

We start with the consumer having a given income and facing a vector of prices. There is a large change in the price of, say, the first commodity and we wish to calculate the equivalent variation associated with this price change.

Break the overall price change into a large number of small steps. Although we cannot observe the consumer's utility either before or after the price change we do know the consumer's income. Hence the change in income which would be equivalent to the first small price change can be read off the Marshallian demands using the consumer observed income and the appropriate prices. To calculate the change in income which is equavalent to the second small price change we again exploit (32) evaluating the Marshallian demand at the prices prevailing after the first small price change has been made, and at a level of income adjusted by the equivalent variation of the first small price change (which we have just calculated). The equivalent variation of the third small price change is read off the Marshallian demand for the first commodity evaluated at the prices prevailing after the first two changes and at the level of income adjusted by the equivalent variations of these two changes (which again will have been calculated). Proceeding sequentially in this fashion one can calculate an approximation to the overall equivalent variation of the price change.

How good an approximation this is will depend on how large the price changes are at each step - for this will determine how accurately the Marshallian demands measure the welfare effects of price changes. In the limit as the price steps go to zero this algorithmic method reduces to solving a differential equation, the solution to which is, by construction, exactly the equivalent variation we require.

It is possible to illustrate what is involved by considering Figure 1. Here we break the price change from p_1^0 to p_1^1 into two steps. p_1^0 to p_1^2 and p_1^2 to p_1^1.

In the diagram HH is the compensated demand curve for utility level ψ^1 and the equivalent variation we wish to calculate is the area $p_1^0\ S^0\ S^1\ p_1^1$. To calculate this, we begin with the price p_1^1. Since we are at utility level ψ^1, the compensated demand at price p_1^1 will coincide with the Marshallian demand at price p_1^1 given the initial income level $Y_1^0 = Y_1^1$ This is shown by the intersection of the

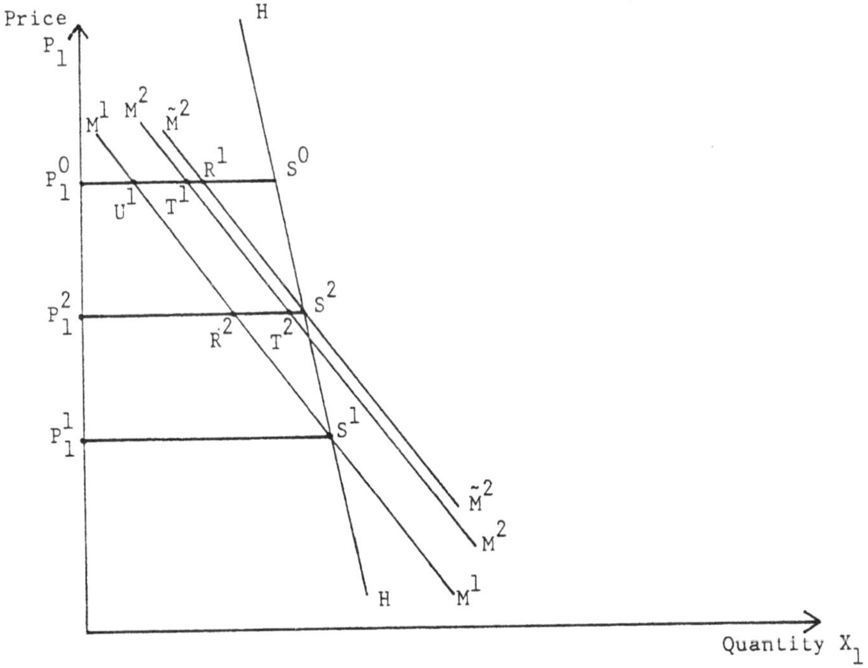

FIGURE 1

Marshallian curve M^1M^1 with HH at p_1^1. We use this Marshallian demand curve to calculate a consumer surplus approximation $p_1^2\ R^2\ S^1\ p_1^1$ to the true equivalent variation $p_1^2\ S^2\ S^1\ p_1^1$ of the rise in price from p_1^1 to p_1^2. We then pay this to the individual and shift the Marshallian demand curve accordingly. Had the compensation been exact the resulting demand curve $(\tilde{M}^2\ \tilde{M}^2)$ would have intersected HH at p_1^2. Since there was undercompensation for the price increase the resulting Marshallian curve will lie below $\tilde{M}^2\ \tilde{M}^2$ as shown by the curve $M^2\ M^2$. We now use the Marshallian curve $M^2\ M^2$ to calculate an approximation p_1^0 $T^1\ T^2\ p_1^2$ to the true equivalent variation $p_1^0\ S^0\ S^2\ p_1^2$ of the price increase from p_1^2 to p_1^0. The total approximation we therefore have is

$$p_1^0\ T^1\ T^2\ p_1^2 + p_1^2\ R^2\ S^1\ p_1^1$$

While this is clearly better than the traditional consumer surplus approximation $(p_1^0\ U^1\ S^1\ p_1^1)$ with only two steps there is still an error involved. As we increase the number of steps the components $R^1\ S^0\ S^2$ and $R^2\ S^2\ S^1$ of the error get smaller, and as this occurs $\tilde{M}^2\ \tilde{M}^2$ moves closer to $M^2\ M^2$ reducing the component $T^1\ R^1\ S^2\ T^2$ of the error as well.

Turning to the formal presentation we wish to calculate the following equivalent variation:

$$\begin{aligned} EV = -\ G_1 &= C(\psi(Y^1,p^1),p_1^1,p_2^1,\ldots,p_n^1) \\ &\quad - C(\psi(Y^1,p^1),p_1^0,p_2^1,\ldots,p_n^1) \end{aligned} \tag{33}$$

In order to evaluate this, we define the function

$$\begin{aligned} g_1(p_1) &= C(\psi(Y^1,p^1),p_1^1,p_2^1,\ldots,p_n^1) \\ &\quad - C(\psi(Y^1,p^1),p_1,p_2^1,\ldots,p_n^1) \end{aligned} \tag{34}$$

i.e.

$$g_1(p_1) = Y^1 - C(\psi(Y^1,p^1),p_1,p_2^1,\ldots,p_n^1) \tag{35}$$

Then, in terms of the compensated demand function

$$\frac{dg_1}{dp_1} = - X_1^c(\psi(Y^1,p^1),p_1,p_2^1,\ldots,p_n^1) \tag{36}$$

While using (32) this can be related to the observable Marshallian demand function by:

$$\frac{dg_1}{dp_1} = - X_1[C(\psi(Y^1,p^1),p_1,p_2^1,\ldots,p_n^1),p_1,p_2^1,\ldots,p_n^1] \tag{37}$$

Substitution of (35) then yields

$$\frac{dg_1}{dp_1} = - X_1[Y^1 - g_1(p_1),p_1p_2^1,\ldots,p_n^1] \tag{38}$$

Equation (38) is the fundamental equation of our model, for to calculate the equivalent variation, in this case $G_1 = g_1(p_1^0)$, all we need to do is to solve the first-order ordinary differential equation (in g_1 and p) using the initial condition $g_1(p_1^1) = 0$ and evaluate the solution at p_1^0.

Of course, it will not always be possible to solve this differential equation to obtain an analytical form for $g_1(p_1)$. There are, however, many numerical procedures for solving differential equations of the simplicity that (38) will normally have (given the kinds of functional forms used in demand studies) to very high degrees of accuracy. This essentially explains the algorithmic approach outlined above and such a sequence of calculation could easily (if somewhat tediously) be performed on a calculator.

IV. AN EXACT METHOD FOR THE EVALUATION OF ECONOMIC WELFARE: THE GENERAL CASE

Let us suppose that there are n commodities and that all prices as well as total expenditure vary. If we adopt Hausman's approach, the problem then becomes one of solving n differential equations of the form given by (32). Unfortunately, even if the resulting expenditure function can be expressed in closed form, finding the correct solution is by no means a simple task. Indeed, in most cases, it will be simpler and quicker to allow the computer to process all desired numerical calculations. The procedure which we propose represents a generalization of the method discussed in the previous section and is based on an analogy with the path of integration utilized by McKenzie (1982) and suggested by a number of consumer surplus theorists (e.g. Harberger (1964), Mohring (1971), Willig (1979)). Because the equivalent variation is a true, ordinal welfare metric, its value is independent of the path of calculation. Thus we can repeat in recursive fashion the procedure of the previous section for each of the n price changes. That is, calculate the area under the compensated demand curve, starting from the "new" level of satisfaction and varying p_1 by steps from its "new" to "original" position. Then begin with the resulting vector of prices. Vary p_2 by steps from its "new" to its "original" position. This results in the calculation of the area under a compensated demand curve for commodity 2. Repeat this process until the effects of all prices have been calculated. The sum of all resulting "areas" will be the equivalent variation associated with the shift from the "original" to the "new" price vector.

That this is the case is ensured by the matrix of Slutsky price effects is symmetric.

This path of calculations can also be easily related to the underlying preference ordering as shown in figure 3. The initial pattern of consumption is indicated by point 1 and generates the level of satisfaction ψ^1. The price of X_1 rises generating the relative price line CB and an equivalent variation equal to the change in expenditure from AB to ED. This equals the area measured in figure 2a. The fall in the price of X_2 shifts the price line from CB to CH which is equivalent to the change in expenditure from ED to FG. This equals the area measured in figure 2b. The net change or total equivalent variation is thus the difference between the budget lines AB and FG.

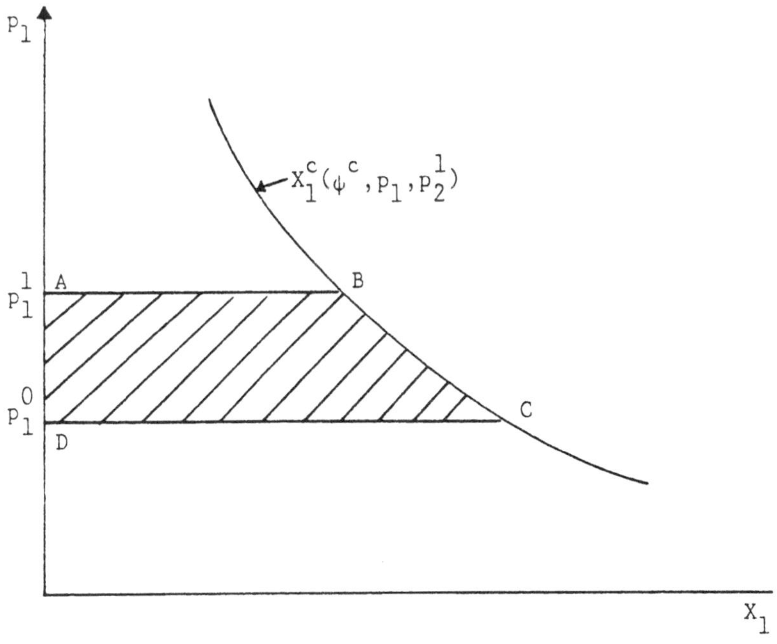

FIGURE 2a

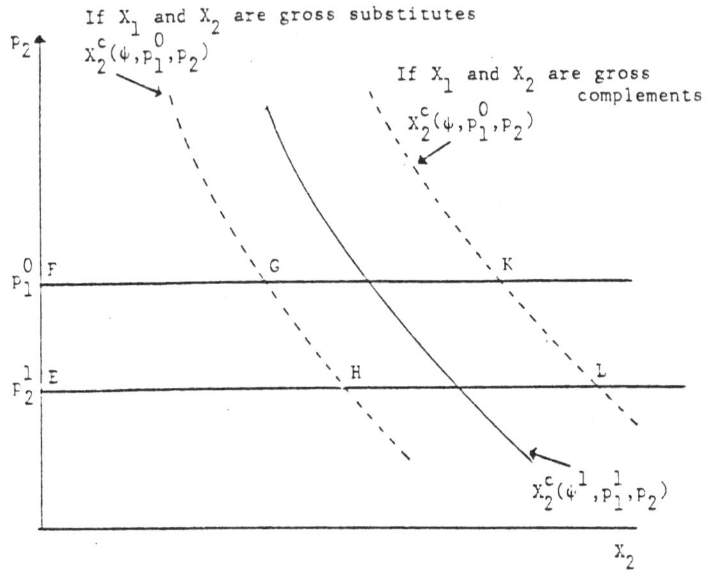

FIGURE 2b

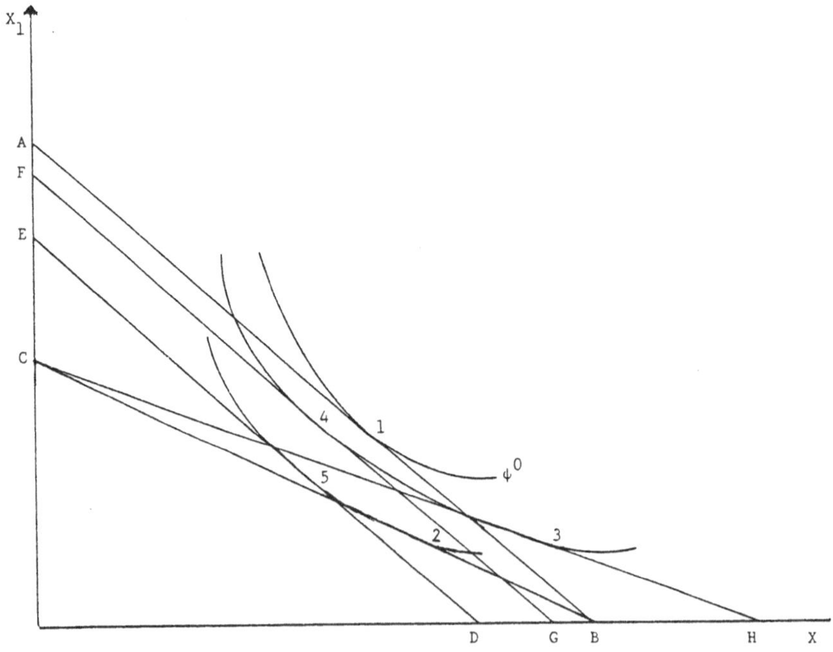

FIGURE 3

This method can be formalized as follows. From equation (4) we can write the equivalent variation in general as

$$EV = Y^1 - Y^0 - G \tag{39}$$

where

$$G = C(\psi(Y^1,p^1),p^0) - C(\psi(Y^1,p^1),p^1) \tag{40}$$

Letting ψ^1 represent $\psi(Y^1,p^1)$ we can write

$$G = \sum_{i=1}^{n} G_i \tag{41}$$

where

$$G_1 = C(\psi^1,p_1^1,p_2^1,\ldots p_n^1) - C(\psi^1,p_1^0,p_2^1,\ldots p_n^1) \tag{42}$$

$$G_i = C(\psi^1,p_1^0,\ldots,p_{i-1}^0,p_i^1,p_{i+1}^1,\ldots p_n^1) -$$

$$C(\psi^1,p_1^0,\ldots,p_i^0,p_{i+1}^1,\ldots,p_n^1) \qquad i=2,\ldots n-1 \tag{43}$$

$$G_n = C(\psi^1,p_1^0,\ldots p_{n-1}^0,p_n^1) - C(\psi^1,p_1^0,\ldots p_n^0) \tag{44}$$

Analogous to the case of a single price change we define

$$g_i(p) \equiv C(\psi^1,p_1^0,\ldots p_{i-1}^0,p_{i+1}^1,\ldots p_n^1)$$

$$- C(\psi^1,p_1^0,\ldots p_{i-1}^0,p_i,p_{i+1}^1,\ldots p_n^1)$$

i.e.

$$g_i(p) = Y^1 - \sum_{j=1}^{i-1} G_j - C(\psi^1,p_1^0,\ldots p_{i-1}^0,p,p_{i+1}^1,\ldots p_n^1) \tag{45}$$

Then $g_i(p)$ satisfies the differential equation

$$\frac{dg_i(p)}{dp_i} =$$

$$(- X_i[Y^1 - \sum_{j=1} G_j - g_i(p), p_1^0, \ldots p_{i-1}^0, p_i, p_{i+1}^1, \ldots p_n^1]) \quad (46)$$

and in order to calculate $G_i = g_i(p_i^0)$ all we need to do is to solve the first-order ordinary differential equation (46), using initial condition $g_i(p_i^1) = 0$, and evaluate the solution at p_i^0. The only information that is required for this is the Marshallian demand for commodity i, and the solutions G_j, j=1, ...i-1, of the previous i-1 problems.

Thus we have reduced the problem of calculating the equivalent variation to that of solving <u>in sequence</u> a series of first-order ordinary differential equations. The number of such equations that need to be solved depends solely on the number of prices that are changed. For if $p_i^0 = p_i^1$ for some i, then trivially, $G_i = 0$, and we can proceed to the calculation of G_{i+1}. From a pedagogic point of view, the virtue of this procedure is clear since it is analogous (but not identical) to the measurement of consumer surplus utilizing a <u>ceteris paribus</u>, ordinary demand schedule. However, although it does preserve both the ordinary and compensated demand functions in an identifiable form throughout the solution procedure, the ultimate formula generates an exact, ordinal welfare metric.

It should be noted that the only difference between the solution procedure just explained and that proposed by Vartia is the path of calculation. For Vartia the path is defined by the variable t where

$$p(t) = p^1 + t(p^0 - p^1) \tag{47}$$

where t is the amount by which each individual price changes in the solution procedure. The relationship between the expenditure function C and the ordinary demand functions can thus be expressed in terms of this variable as follows:

$$\frac{dC(t)}{dt} = \sum_i X_i(p(t), C(t)) \frac{dp_i(t)}{dt} \tag{48}$$

Vartia's solution procedure therefore involves calculating the compensation required to keep satisfaction constant while varying <u>all</u> prices simultaneously, rather than sequentially as in our method.

At a conceptual level, Vartia's method has the advantage that it is algebraically more compact. On the other hand, our method enables a better understanding of the structural relationships between consumer demands and preferences and thus affords greater ease in its economic interpretation.

V. THE CONSTRUCTION OF WELL-BEHAVED DEMAND FUNCTIONS

As indicated in the introduction to this paper, the primary motivation for seeking to derive welfare implications from information contained in ordinary demand functions is that it enables us to analyse a wider range of consumer behaviour than would otherwise be the case. That is, there will exist well-behaved demand systems in closed form for which it is impossible to express the expenditure or preferences function in closed form.

The orthodox textbook procedure of first stating an

explicit functional form for an expenditure or preference function and then deriving an estimable system of demand equations thereby actually acts as a limit to the range of consumer behaviour which can be analysed.

The question then arises: how should we go about specifying suitable demand functions? In much applied welfare analysis, there has been a preference for utilizing linear or log-linear demand functions. However, unless great care is taken such systems will be inconsistent with the theory of consumer behaviour. That is they will not satisfy the condition that the matrix of Slutsky substitution terms be symmetric. In cases such as the linear expenditure system or indirect addilog system where the theory is satisfied, the resulting preference function is fairly restrictive. However, in actual practice it is possible to construct a very wide range of well-behaved demand systems. Two broad classes of systems will be considered.

i) the ordinary or direct form

$$X_i = X_i\ (Y,\ p_1, \ldots p_n) \tag{49}$$

and ii) the inverse form

$$p_i = p_i(Y, X_1, \ldots, X_n) \tag{50}$$

In general it will not be possible to express in closed form both the direct and inverse forms associated with a particular preference function. For example, it is possible to express the system of inverse functions associated with Houthakker's direct addilog utility function as such but not the ordinary demand functions or the expenditure function. However, because of its linearity, the linear expenditure system can easily be written in both direct and inverse forms.

Actual functional forms for (49) or (50) can be constructed as follows:

i) the direct form

$$X_i = \frac{Y \cdot a_i(p,Y)}{\sum_j p_j \cdot a_j(p,Y)} \tag{51}$$

where $a_i(p,Y)$ is the derivative of the indirect preference function with respect to price, i.e. $\partial\psi/\partial p_i$

ii) the inverse form

$$p_i = \frac{Y \cdot b_i(X)}{\sum_k X_k \cdot b_k(X)} \tag{52}$$

where $b_i(X)$ is the derivative of the direct preference function with respect to quantity, i.e. $\partial U/\partial X_i$ (cf. Pearce (1964)).

A myriad of well-behaved demand systems can now be constructed by the suitable choise of a_i or b_i. This choice, however, is not unlimited since these functions must satisfy Young's Theorem. That is, the matrices of second-order derivatives $\partial a_i/\partial p_j$ and $\partial b_i/\partial X_j$ must be symmetric. This ensures the symmetry of the matrix of Slutsky substitution effects.

For example, let

$$a_i = \frac{\partial\psi}{\partial p_i} = -\frac{1}{p_i}\,[\alpha_i + \beta_i \cot^{-1} \frac{p_i}{Y}] \tag{53}$$

which from (5) gnerates the system of direct demand functions

$$X_i = \left[\frac{\alpha_i + \beta_i \cot^{-1}\left(\frac{p_i}{Y}\right)}{\sum_j \alpha_j + \sum_j \beta_j \cot^{-1}\left(\frac{p_j}{Y}\right)}\right] \tag{54}$$

To many readers the choice of an inverse cotangent function as the basis for developing a system of demand functions may appear to be somewhat farfetched. However, on purely a priori grounds there is no reason to adjudge apparently more straightforward linear or log-linear formulations as being superior. More to the point of our analysis, however, is that (54) represents a system of simple demand functions whose preference ordering cannot be expressed in closed form.

Given a set of demand functions of either type, the classic strategy has been to seek an integrating factor with the aim of retrieving the underlying preference function in closed form. However, in large measure this approach is ill-conceived. If the system of demand functions is correctly specified as above, then an integrating factor in the form of a marginal utility of money λ is easily obtained for both direct and inverse forms, viz.

direct form

$$\lambda = - \sum_j \frac{p_j}{Y} \frac{\partial \phi}{\partial p_j} = - \Sigma \frac{p_j}{Y} a_j \tag{55}$$

inverse form

$$\lambda = \sum_j \frac{X_j}{Y} \frac{\partial U}{\partial X_j} = \sum_j \frac{X_j}{Y} b_j \tag{56}$$

Although not as widely discussed as their ordinary counterparts, inverse demand functions have been used in a variety of ways. In his attempt to formalize the concept of consumer surplus Marshall made use of them (1890, pp.841-42). In 1964 Pearce suggested they could form the basis for economic planning. Having determined total expenditure and the quantities to be produced, inverse demand functions could be solved for the prices required to clear markets. More recently, inverse demand functions have been widely used in econometric demand analysis.

We now demonstrate how well-behaved inverse demand functions can be utilized to generate numerical values of the money-metric. First, we express the expenditure function in terms of quantities consumed:

$$\gamma = \gamma(U^1, X, Y) \tag{57}$$

where γ indicates the minimum amount of money required to support the level of satisfaction U^1 defined by the quantity vector X^1 but given some alternative quantity vector X and income level Y. Recall that a set of ordinary inverse demand function expresses market clearing prices as a function of income and a given vector of quantities. (cf. equations 50 and 52). If following a change in the quantity available of one commodity X_i, income is varied so as to maintain a constant level of satisfaction, then we can construct a compensated inverse demand function

$$p_i^c = p_i(X\ ;\ Y^c) \tag{58}$$

where Y^c is the income level following compensation and may be calculated from the cost function (57). Hence

$$p_i^c = p_i(X\ ;\ \gamma(U(X'), X, Y)) \tag{59}$$

That is $\{p_i^c\}$ is the price vector associated with a quantity vector X but with income varied from Y so as to achieve the level of satisfaction generated by X^1. It can be shown that this inverse compensated demand function is the derivative of the cost function with respect to X_i (e.g. Deaton and Muellbauer (1980), pp. 56-57). That is

$$\frac{\partial\gamma}{\partial X_i} = p_i^c \tag{60}$$

It is then possible to calculate the equivalent variation in a manner completely analogous to that associated with the ordinary demand functions. We confine ourselves here to the simple case where the supply of commodity one is varied from X_1^0 to X_1^1 and total expenditure remains constant at Y^1. Thus

$$EV = - G_1^* \tag{61}$$

where

$$G_1^* = \gamma(U^1, X_1^1, X_2^1, \ldots, X_n^1, Y^1) - \gamma(U^1, X_1^0, X_2^1, \ldots, X_n^1, Y^1) \tag{62}$$

To evaluate this we define the function

$$g_1^*(X_1) = Y^1 - \gamma(U^1, X_1, X_2^1, \ldots, X_n^1, Y^1) \tag{63}$$

where

$$\frac{dg_1^*}{dX_1} = 1 - p_1^c(U^1, X_1, X_2^1, \ldots, X_n^1, Y^1) \tag{64}$$

Rewriting (64) in terms of the ordinary inverse demand function, we obtain

$$\frac{dg_1^*}{dX_1} = - p_1^c(U^1, X_1, X_2^1, \ldots, X_n^1, Y^1 - g_1^*(X_1)) \tag{65}$$

which can now be solved for G_1^* and hence the equivalent variation associated with this quantity change. The more general case involving several quantities simply involves the step-wise calculation of (65) in much the same way as we utilized the ordinary direct demand functions.

VI. FINAL THOUGHTS

Although our price objective in this paper has been the technical one of examining recent literature relating duality theory to applied welfare analysis, it is important to comment upon conceptual issues in order to place the practical methods into perspective. Hence we shall confine ourselves to two such points, one arising from the unavailability of suitable data and the second concerning whether or not the expenditure function actually "measures" utility.

i) The Lack of Suitable Data

The fundamental law of economics that "there is no such thing as a free lunch" applies just as much to the research activities of economists as to the operation of the global economy. Unfortunately, this point is frequently neglected.

The above analysis assumed, as a prerequisite of applied welfare analysis, that we should possess statistical estimates of the various parameters of the system of demand equations. However, if such estimates are unavailable then the sorts of calculations which we have been describing will not be possible. In such circumstances one possibility is resort to the non-parametric consumer surplus measure suggested by Harberger in his important 1971 article, namely

$$p_i \, \Delta X_i + \frac{1}{2} \Delta p_i \, \Delta X_i \tag{65}$$

He suggests that this formula provides a reasonable second-order approximation to any change in satisfaction. It has the apparent advantage that it requires price and quantity data for only the two situations being compared. However, not surprisingly, something cannot be obtained for nothing. Firstly, as McKenzie and Pearce (1976) argued, (65) is a simple average of the Laspeyres and Paasche quantity variations and hence is subject to the region of ignorance as identified by Samuelson (1950). Secondly, if we enquire into the circumstances under which (65) will be an exact welfare indicator, as Diewert (1976) did, then we learn that this will be the case if consumer preferences are homothetic quadratic.

The only conclusion that can be drawn from these results is that great care must be taken in presenting and especially interpreting results based on (65). A good scientific procedure to follow is to spell out the potential errors that may arise when there is incomplete information. This principle is, of course, also relevant to the methods which we have presented here. The statistical parameter estimates which will inevitably be used are conditional upon the validity of the particular functional form of the demand equations. They are also subject to stochastic errors, which will be unsystematic if valid estimation procedures have been employed.

ii) Measurable Preferences

A cardinal number is one which answers the question "how many?" whereas an ordinal number is one which answers the different question "what order?" The equivalent variation is thus a cardinal measure but only in the sense that it indicates, given initial prices, "how many" pounds or dollars are required to yield the same satisfaction as that generated by an alternative price/quantitiy situation. It is not a cardinal measure of utility. However, since the equivalent variation is an increasing monotonic transformation of an underlying consumer preference function it is an ordinal preference indicator. Finally, as we have seen in this paper, the equivalent variation can be computed from information in ordinary observable demand functions even though equivalent variation cannot be expressed in closed form.

In our opinion, the above three characteristics of the equivalent variations, namely:

a) cardinality

b) ordinality

and c) computability

provide everything that an applied worker could possibly desire in terms of a welfare metric[4]. However, it is necessary to emphasize, as Morey (1984) has recently done, that calculation of the equivalent variation does not imply that we are able to measure the intensity of consumer preferences. Consider the following example. Suppose that relative to some initial situation A feasible situation B is equivalent to a £500 increase in income and that feasible situation C is equivalent to a £750 increase in income.

This calculation unambiguously reveals that situation C is preferred to both B and A and that B is also preferred to A. However, it does not enable us to undertake the following sort of comparisons, as Morey has correctly emphasized:

a) We cannot say that the move from A to B has led to a greater increase in satisfaction than the move from B to C. If preferences exhibited this property, they would be classified as weakly cardinal.

b) We cannot say that the move from A to B generates an increase in satisfaction that is fifty percent greater than the increase in satisfaction from B to C. If preferences exhibited this property, they would be classified as strongly cardinal.

The reason why preferences cannot be either weakly or strongly cardinal is that consumer behaviour is invariant under increasing monotonic transformations of consumer preferences. But what about the equivalent variation? Can it not act as a measure of intensity of preferences? Here again the answer must be "no". The reason for this is that evaluation of the equivalent variation depends upon the initial/base price vector chosen for the computation. In the above example we chose A as the base situation. However, if we started from B our calculation would be different although, of course, the ordering would remain invariant. For example, the move from B to A might be equivalent to a loss of income of £600 whereas the move from B to C might be equivalent to an increase in income of £200. Hence, intensity of preferences cannot even be determined from a metric such as the equivalent variation.

However, this consideration is not important since measurement of the intensity of preferences is not a prerequisite for applied welfare analysis. The primary consideration is the ability to order the various possibilities vis-a-vis the current situation. The fact that we can also evaluate a cardinal metric, the equivalent variation, is the icing on the cake which facilitates a pedagogic presentation to lay economists and policy makers.

APPENDIX A

Since the sum $\sum_{j=1}^{n} G_j$ (from equation (41)) is an exact representation of the equivalent variation, illustrative examples are, in principle, superfluous. However, they do have the merit of giving us a feel for the accuracy of the numerical methods for solving differential equations. Three sets of calculations are presented in Appendix C. These are based on the computer program presented in Appendix B. For the first set we took equation system (46) and calculated the equivalent variation for a uniform percentage increase in all prices. In fact, we doubled all prices.

For the next two sets of calculations we employed the linear expenditure system of demand functions (see for example Deaton and Muellbauer (1980) pp.64-7). The cost-of-utility function associated with this can be expressed analytically, thus enabling an exact calculation of the equivalent variation. In an experiment we doubled all prices as before. For the second experiment with this system, we set all initial prices at one and arbitrarily determined a new set of prices. Arbitrary parameter values were assumed in all cases, and the differential equations used in our procedure were solved by the fourth-order Runge-Kutta method. This solution technique is consistent with the intuitive explanation offered at the beginning of Section III. The Runge-Kutta method involves breaking down each price change into a number of discrete steps. (In our calculations 16 steps were chosen, although this number may be made arbitrarily large). At each step compensation is paid so as to maintain satisfaction at a constant level. This compensation is determined from the relationship between the Hicksian and the ordinary demand functions (cf. equation (32)) where the latter is evaluated at an income level corrected for all compensation which has been paid up to that step.

In all three examples considered, the solution procedure discussed above yielded answers correct to at least six decimal places. Since no points of principle are involved, the details of these simulations are presented in Appendix C. It should be emphasized, however, that while even greater accuracy might be achieved by the use of more sophisticated numerical methods, it is impossible to achieve better results by utilizing consumer surplus techniques. Our procedure is, in principle, exact. In addition, consumer surplus calculations are inferior even in terms of computational simplicity. First, complex numerical procedures are required for integration of the demand functions. Second, calculations undertaken on this basis are not path independent (cf. Silberberg (1972), McKenzie (1982)). In contrast, this procedure (and Vartia's) is path independent since it makes use of the properties of the expenditure function.

APPENDIX B

The results referrred to in Appendix A were calculated by means of a computer program written in the Pascal language.

There were several reasons for utilizing this format. First, Pascal has a modular form which enables users to readily modify programs. Second, Pascal compilers are available on most computers. Third, it is very fast even when implemented on a personal computer.

The program consists of three parts. Program Utility lines 320-610, directs the Runge-Kutta computations. The user could substitute an alternative numerical method. this Program calls two Procedures, Demand and Param. In the procedure Demand, lines 110-200, the functional form for each demand equation are stated. In Param, lines 210-310, the initial and final values of prices and expenditure along with the parameters of the demand system are given. These can be modified without alterations to the computational part of program although all parameter and variable names must be stated at the beginning as is Pascal practice.

Certain constants and variables should be utilized in all programs. These are:

K = number of commodities/or commodity groupings;

N = number of segments into which each price change is divided for Runge-Kutta computation;

P(1) = new price level for the ith commodity;

Z(1) = old or initial price level for the ith commodity;

Y = new level of total expenditure;

Z1 = old level of total expenditure;

The data included in Demand and Param refer to the simulation, case 1, as presented in Appendix B.

```
10  PROGRAM UTILITY;
20  CONST
30        K = 10; N = 16;
40  TYPE
```

```
      INDEX 1 = 1..K;
      AR1 = ARRAY(INDEX1) OF REAL;
VAR
      S,P,B,Z : AR1;
      A,T,X : INTEGER;
      D,Y,Z1,R,P1,F,G,H,K1,K2,K3,K4 : REAL;
PROCEDURE DEMAND;
BEGIN
      R: = 0;
      FOR A: = 1 TO K DO BEGIN
           P1: = P(A)/Z1;
           S(A): = B(A) + B(A) * (D-ARCTAN(P1))
           R: = R + S(A);
      END:
      F: = - Z1 * S(T)/(R * P(T));
END;
PROCEDURE PARAM:
BEGIN
      B(1):=0.22; B(2):=0.18; B(3):=0.14; B(4):=0.12;
      B(5):=0.10; B(6):=0.07; B(7):=0.06; B(8):=0.05;
      B(9):=0.04; B(10):=0.02;
      Y: = 200; Z1
      FOR A: = 1 TO K DO BEGIN
           Z(A): = 1; P(A): = 2;
      END;
      D: = 1.15707963;
END:
BEGIN
G: = 0;
WRITELN:
WRITELN('CALCULATIONS TAKING PLACE');
PARAM
```

```
FOR T: = 1 TO K DO BEGIN
     DEMAND;
     H: = (Z(T) - P(T))/N;
     FOR X: = 1 TO N DO BEGIN
          K1 = H*F
          P(T): = P(T) + H/2;
          Z1: = Y-G-(K1/2);
          DEMAND;
          K2: = H*F;
          Z1: = Y-G-(K2/2);
          DEMAND;
          K3: = H*F;
          P(T): = P(T) + H/2;
          Z1: = Y-G-K3;
          DEMAND;
          K4: = H*F;
          G: = G + (K1+K4*2*(K2+K3))/6;
          Z1: = Y-G;
          DEMAND;
     END;
END;
WRITELN;
WRITELN('ANSWER = ',Z1:6:4);
HALT;
END.
```

APPENDIX C

The numerical simulations based on equation (46) involved the following parameter values:

$\alpha_1 = .22$ $\alpha_6 = .07$

$\alpha_2 = .18$ $\alpha_7 = 0.6$

$\alpha_3 = .14$ $\alpha_8 = .05$

$\alpha_4 = .12$ $\alpha_9 = .04$

$\alpha_5 = .10$ $\alpha_{10} = .02$

$\beta_{ii} = \alpha_i$ $i = 1,\dots,n$

The demand functions associated with the linear expenditure system take on the form

$$X_i = c_i + \frac{b_i}{p_i}(Y - \Sigma\, c_j p_j) \qquad i = 1,\dots,n$$

In our example, we assume that

$b_i = \alpha_i$

and $c_i = -100\ \alpha_i$

The particular configuration chosen was purely for the sake of ease of exposition. All results have been obtained by means of a fourth-order Runge-Kutta method for solving ordinary differential equations.

Case 1: $Y^0 = 200,\ Y^1 = 200,\ p_i^0 = 1,\ p_i^1 = 2$

demand function: equation 29

result: -100

correct answer: -100

Case 2: $Y^0 = 200,\ Y^1 = 200,\ p_i^0 = 1,\ p_i^1 = 2$

demand function: equation A.1

result: -100.00001

correct answer: -100

Case 3: $^{(5)}Y^0 = 200,\ Y^1 = 200,\ p_i^0 = 1,\ p_i^1 = 1 - (-1)^i(0.5)$

demand function: equation A.1

result: -30.798495

correct answer: -30.79849

The Runge-Kutta methods are straightforward to use and economical in terms of programming time where appropriate software is not available (a useful discussion appears in Conte (1965)). Basically, q iterations are required for each step in the process of solving the differential equation system set out above. In the examples presented here q = 16. However, the accuracy of any work can be further increased by increasing the value of q. Thus, as emphasized in the text, the accuracy depends entirely upon the numerical methods utilized and not principles of economic theory.

ACKNOWLEDGMENTS

The authors would like to acknowledge helpful comments from Jan Tinbergen, Ivor Pearce, Peter Wagstaff, Michael Ahlheim and Manfred Rose. All errors remain the authors' responsibility.

FOOTNOTES

1. Most of the key issues are surveyed in Chipman and

Moore (1980), Chipman (1982) and McKenzie (1982). German language readers will wish to consult the more up-to-date survey by Ahlheim and Rose (1984).

2. There are two fundamental problems, in principle. The first, as noted, involves drawing welfare implications from the parameters of ordinary individual demand functions. This has been the objective of traditional consumer surplus analysis. The second involves the procedure for aggregation of the individual measures into a social welfare function. Unfortunately, the actual carrying out of this two-step procedure is thwarted by the unavailability of time series data for individual expenditures. However, Jorgenson et.al (1981, 1984) have introduced auxiliary data which provides a solution to this difficulty and is also amenable to the procedures described in this paper.
3. The standard reference for this procedure is Deaton and Muellbauer (1980).
4. It should be noted that the compensating variation possesses the cardinality and computability characteristics but is not, in general, an ordinal preference indicator.

REFERENCES

A. Ahlheim and M. Rose, Alte and nue Masse individueller Steuerlasten, Finanzarchiv, 42, no.2, (1984).

A. Bergson, A note on consumer's surplus, Journal of Economic Literature, 13, 38-44, (1975).

J.S. Chipman, Samuelson and consumption theory, in Samuelson and Neoclassical Economics, edited by George Feiwel, Amsterdam: Kluwer-Nijhoff, (1980).

J.S. Chipman and J. Moore, Compensating variation, consumer's surplus and welfare, American Economic Review, 70, 933-49, (1980).

S.D. Conte, Elementary Numerical Analysis, New York: McGraw-Hill, (1965).

A.S. Deaton and J. Muellbauer, Economics and Consumer Behaviour, Cambridge University Press, (1980).

W.E. Diewert, Harberger's welfare indicator and revealed preference theory, American Economic Review, 66, 143-152, (1976).

A.C. Harberger, Taxation, resource allocation and welfare, in The Role of Direct and Indirect Taxes in the Federal Reserve System, Princeton University Press, (1964).

A.C. Harberger, Three basic postulates for applied welfare

economics: an interpretive essay, Journal of Economic Literature, 9, 785-97, (1971).

J.C. Hause, The theory of welfare measurement, Journal of Political Economy, 83, 1145-82, (1975).

J.A. Hausman, Exact consumer's surplus and deadweight loss, American Economic Review, 71, 662-76, (1981).

J.R. Hicks, Value and Capital, Oxford University Press, (1946).

D.W. Jorgenson, Efficiency versus equity in economic policy analysis, Harvard Insitute for Economic Research Discussion Paper No.1088, (1984).

D.W. Jorgenson, L. Lau and T. Stoker, Aggregate consumer behaviour and individual welfare, in Macroeconomic Analysis, edited by D. Currie, R. Nobay and D. Peel, London: Croom Helm, (1981).

M.A. King, Welfare analysis of tax reforms using household data, Journal of Public Economics, 21, 183-214, (1983).

G.W. McKenzie, Measuring Economic Welfare : New Methods, Cambridge University Press, (1982).

G.W. McKenzie and I.R. Pearce, Exact measures of welfare and the cost of living, Review of Economic Studies, 43, 465-8, (1976).

A. Marshall, Principles of Economics, London: Mcmillan, (See also Ninth Variorum Edition (1961) with annotations by C.W. Guillebaud, London: Macmillan), (1890).

H. Mohring, Alternative welfare gain and loss measures, Western Economic Journal, 9, 349-68, (1971).

E.R. Morey, Confuser surplus, American Economic Review, 74, 163-73, (1984).

I.F. Pearce, A Contribution to Demand Analysis, Oxford University Press, (1964).

P.A. Samuelson, The problem of integrability in utility theory, Economica, 17, 355-85, (1950).

J. Seade, Consumer's surplus and linearity of Engel curves, Economic Journal, 88, 511-23, (1978).

E. Silberberg, Duality and the many consumer's surpluses, American Economic Review, 62, 942-52, (1972).

Y.O. Vartia, Efficient methods of measuring welfare change and compensated income in terms of demand functions, Econometrica, 51, 79-98, (1983).

R. Willig, Consumer's surplus without apology, American Economic Review, 66, 589-97, (1976a).

R. Willig, Integrability implications of locally constant demand elasticities, Journal of Economic Theory, 12, 391-401, (1976b).

R. Willig, Consumer's surplus without apology: reply, American Economic Review, 69, 469-74, (1979).

THE QUANTITATIVE ANALYSIS OF OPTIMAL TAXATION AND PUBLIC PRODUCTION

CHRISTOPHER HEADY
University College London
PRADEEP MITRA
The World Bank[1]

I. INTRODUCTION

The purpose of this paper is to present an overview of the authors' work on optimal public policy. This work has been concerned with developing a quantitative framework for the analysis of policy both by extending the theory and using numerical analysis to elucidate the theory's implications. We have studied policy issues in the following areas:

(1) Taxation and Pricing

(2) Public Investment

(3) Trade Intervention

The study of policy in these areas is interesting because of the perceived inadequacies of a completely *laissez faire* government. There are of course many such inadequacies stemming from a variety of sources, such as non-competitive markets, externalities, public goods and income inequality. Our work has concentrated on a concern for income inequality as a motive for active government policy and, in order to achieve this concentration, has assumed that no other market imperfections are present. However, our methodology can be readily extended to include other market failures.

This concentration on distributional motives does not imply a lack of interest in the revenue-raising role of taxation. Rather, we regard the revenue-raising role of distortionary taxation as being inescapably linked to its distributional role. The reason for this is that a government which has no concern for inequality could raise any required revenue by non-distortionary poll taxes. Thus an argument for the use of distortionary taxes to raise revenue is essentially an argument against the distributional effect of poll taxes, combined with the observation that it is impossible to achieve redistribution by the use of lump-sum transfers.

This explains our interest in distortionary taxation (including the pricing of nationalised industry outputs above or below marginal cost) but does not necessarily justify government intervention in either investment or international trade. Indeed, Diamond and Mirrlees (1971) have shown that if the government can set optimal taxes on all commodities and if there are not after-tax private sector pure profits then the economy should be productively efficient. This result implies that the government should use private profitability as the criterion for selecting investment projects and that a "small" country (one that cannot influence its terms of trade) should allow free trade. Thus distortionary tax policy should be accompanied by <u>laissez faire</u> investment and trade policy[2].

Despite the significance of this result, it must be emphasised that it rests on strong assumptions. We will leave aside the issue of positive after-tax pure profits as there are no reliable data which can be used to assess their significance. However, much of our work has been concerned with the importance of the other assumption:

optimal taxation of all commodities (including factors of production). In order for this assumption to be satisfied the government must, for example, be able to tax capital income at a different rate from labour income, be able to tax the income of different types of labour at different rates and be able to tax a farm household's consumption of its own products. Also, it must be able to give up the usual practice of taxing consumer goods at only two or three different rates and be prepared to tax each good at a separate rate. We do not believe that all governments have these tax powers and some of our work has explored the policy implications of restricted taxation.

The significance of tax restrictions is that they rob the government of an ability to control consumer prices independently of producer prices. It is this independence that is crucial to the argument for production efficiency because it implies that the organization of production need have no effect of the distribution of income. When taxes are restricted consumer prices depend, to some extent, on producer prices and so some degree of production inefficiency can be desirable if its effect on producer prices alters consumer prices in a way that raises extra revenue or improves the distribution of income. Thus a commercially unprofitable investment project might be socially desirable if it raised the wages for a group of poor workers. Similarly, trade intervention might be justified through its effect on producer, and thus consumer, prices. In this case neither consumer prices nor producer prices are adequate for evaluating government projects. We will therefore have to consider a third set of prices, shadow prices, which can be used in the analysis of public sector projects.

These considerations imply that we should study the following policy instruments. First, taxes (and subsidies) on trade between households and the rest of the economy. These taxes imply that the households face consumer prices which are different from producer prices. The taxes can be levied on the sale of factors as well as on the purchase of goods and services. Thus we include linear income taxation as a possible policy and this can be extended to a negative income tax system if the government can make uniform lump-sum payments to all households. Second, shadow prices for evaluating public sector projects. These shadow prices will equal private sector producer prices if taxes are unrestricted. Third, import and export taxes (and subsidies) which apply to the private sectors transactions with the rest of the world. These will be zero for a small country with unrestricted taxes.

Our work has proceeded by constructing analytical general equilibrium models that capture the essential features of the policies under consideration. These models are used to derive as many general results as possible about the characteristics of optimal government policy. Such results provide valuable insights but they usually are unable to give much idea of the magnitude of optimal taxes, shadow prices or trade taxes. Nor are they able to demonstrate fully the sensitivity of these magnitudes to changes in government objectives, the degree of government control or the general economic environment.

It is in order to overcome this problem that numerical analysis is used. This numerical analysis consists of replacing the general social welfare function, utility functions, production functions and resource endowments of the analytical models with specific functional forms and parameter values for a specific, and usually small, number of households and industries. The optimal policies can then be calculated using numerical optimization routines. This procedure can be repeated for different parameter values and/or different functional forms in order to provide an insight into the sensitivity of the results to the assumptions made.

The parameter values are typically chosen so that the model, before optimization, approximately replicates observed values of outputs, prices and income distribution for a particular country in a particular year. However, it must be stressed that the exploratory models used to date are not meant to provide a strictly accurate description of any economy. Instead, they are designed to deepen our understanding of the theory, and to analyse the sensitivity of policy to different assumptions. The use of actual data in constructing the models provides 'reasonable' parameters values, which can form the central case for a series of sensitivity experiments.

The models are medium-term in that they do not reflect either the short-run difficulties associated with immobility of highly specialised capital and labour or long-run issues of technical progress. Neglect of the long-run follows from the absence of any theory that relates tax policy to technical progress, while neglect of the short-run follows from the fact that governments can only make significant alterations to the tax structure infrequently and so must not compromise longer-run goals for the sake of avoiding short-run difficulties. Such difficulties can often be alleviated by transitional arrangements but their details will depend on the specific circumstances of each particular country and we have not attempted to design them.

We have not used detailed models which accurately describe particular economies for two reasons. First, we believe that a thorough understanding of the theory is essential before practical application is attempted, and such understanding is best obtained by detailed analysis of the properties of simplified models. The understanding that we have gained has allowed us to progress to models that include greater institutional realism and are thus near to practical application. Second, optimal policies often result in sets of relative prices that are significantly different from those that have been observed in practice. Thus any estimates of demand and supply behaviour in the neighbourhood of these prices must be based on extrapolation of relationships well beyond the range of observation. This extrapolation is typically achieved by assuming the constancy of certain key parameters, such as elasticities of substitution or marginal budget shares. While the maintenance of such assumptions does not impair the theoretical value of the results, it would clearly be unwise to base large policy changes on them. However, sensitivity analysis gives us an idea of the range within which optimal policies lie. Moreover, the sensitivity analysis tells us which parameters are particularly significant in the determination of optimal policy and enables econometric work to concentrate in those areas with the highest return for policy making.

Another consequence of the large price changes that can accompany the implementation of optimal policies is that they might encounter strong political opposition and threaten the survival of the government. In such circumstances full implementation will be impossible. However the computed optimal policy can still guide the formulation of a politically acceptable partial reform package by providing an idea of the direction reform should take. However, any proposed partial reform should be analysed to see whether beneficial alterations could be made to it without violating the political constraints. This would proceed by comparing the marginal costs and benefits of politically feasible changes to the reform package, and would be similar in principle to the tax reform work of Ahmad and Stern (1984 and 1985) but would involve looking at small changes to a reform rather than a small reform. An alteration is beneficial when the benefits outweigh the costs, and the reform package will be optimal when the two are offsetting.

The rest of this paper is organized as follows: Section II explains the relationship of our work to other literature in the field of public policy. Section III describes a model that captures many of the issues that we have tackled. Section IV givens an overview of the analytical results we have obtained so far. Section V describes the numerical optimization methods that we have used, while Section VI gives examples of the numerical results we have obtained. Finally, Section VII concludes by considering the shortcomings of the models and the ways in which future research can overcome them.

II. RELATIONSHIP TO THE LITERATURE

Our work is related to several strands of the public finance literature and this Section describes these relationships.

Our first paper (Heady and Mitra: 1980) was directly inspired by the path-breaking theoretical work of Diamond and Mirrlees (1971) on optimal taxation and public production, and represented an attempt to elucidate the quantitative implications of their tax formulae. The work of Diamond and Mirrlees stimulated further theoretical work, recently surveyed by Mirrlees (1985), some of which dealt with the possible consequences of restrictions on the government's tax powers. For example Stiglitz and Dasgupta (1971) and Munk (1980) showed that tax restrictions could make production inefficiency desirable, while Diamond and Mirrlees (1976) showed that private constant returns activities should make zero profits at shadow prices despite such restrictions. Our second paper (Heady and Mitra: 1982) extended the analysis of production inefficiency by introducing intermediate goods and deriving conditions that should be satisfied by the differences between private sector producer prices and shadow prices. It also demonstrated that it may be desirable for public production to eliminate certain private activities and provided numerical examples to illustrate these points. The numerical methods used in that work are explained in Heady and Mitra (1984c). More recently we have extended the application of the theory of restricted taxation to trade policy (Heady and Mitra: 1984a) and to government policy in a dual economy (Heady and Mitra: 1984b and 1985).

The attempt to quantify the implications of theoretical developments in public finance parallels the work on optimal income taxation by Mirrlees (1971) and Stern (1976). There have also been other examples of the quantification of optimal unrestricted commodity taxation. Atkinson and Stiglitz (1972) and Deaton (1977) calculated optimal taxes in models where the structure of the economy had been simplified to enable the use of relatively simple numerical techniques. Both of these papers assumed fixed producer prices and inelastic labour supply in their numerical examples, and Atkinson and Stiglitz assumed identical individuals. Also both papers made assumptions about the demand systems (Atkinson and Stiglitz assumed additive separability while Deaton assumed linear Engel curves) which were essential to their computational methods. Our work has sometimes shared these assumptions, especially with respect to demand systems, because of data limitations, but they are not needed by our computational techniques. This fact permits a much wider range of sensitivity experiments.

This means that we do not have to assume a particular distribution of income or a particular class of demand system in order to obtain results. More significant, in our view, is the fact that we do not have to assume constant producer prices and are therefore able to analyze the interaction between commodity taxes and the production side of the economy[3]. This ability to incorporate flexible producer prices is of great importance in our work on restricted taxes, as is explained in Section III below.

This work on optimal taxation and public production analyzes a situation where the government is simultaneously choosing optimal taxes, optimal public investment and optimal trade policies. In contrast, the literature on project evaluation in underdeveloped countries has concentrated on just one aspect of government policy: public investment. Thus, both Dasgupta, Marglin and Sen (1972) and Little and Mirrlees (1974) are concerned with the position of a project evaluator who has no control over tax policy and only limited control over trade policy. In such a situation it is not appropriate for the project evaluator to assume that tax or trade policy is optimal. Diamond and Mirrlees (1976) argue that this is equivalent to the case of restricted taxes when the restrictions imposed by administrative problems are supplemented by the sub-optimal behaviour of the tax and trade authorities. Thus our analysis of public investment policy in the presence of tax restrictions helps provide an understanding of how shadow prices for project evaluation depend both on the general economic environment and on the degree of suboptimality in the government's tax policies.

A different quantitative anlaysis of government policy is provided by Ahmad and Stern in their work on tax reform in India (1984 and 1985). This involves looking for small tax changes that can improve social welfare without reducing government revenue. This is clearly related to work on optimal policy in that no such tax changes exist at an optimum. However, it has the practical advantage that, as only small changes are considered, it does not involve extrapolation of estimated demand systems so far outside the range of observation.

Another complementary area of work is that of tax and trade policy simulation, recently surveyed by Shoven and Whalley (1984). This work involves no government optimisation but simulates the consequences of alternative policies. A welfare analysis of these consequences can produce useful rankings of specific policies but, as the range of possible policies is so large, it would be impractical to use these techniques to search for optimal policy.

Simulation, of course, uses considerably less computer time than optimization and so the models used in this area typically have much greater detail, with more households and industries. This makes them more useful in practical policy analysis for specific countries. Also, by analyzing specific policy proposals the practitioners of this technique usually restrict themselves to fairly small changes in key variables so that, as with the tax reform literature, they avoid the problems of extrapolation.

III. A TYPICAL MODEL

The purpose of this section is to outline a model that captures the main issues we have studied. This model was used in our first paper on restricted taxes (Heady and Mitra: 1982) and in our paper on trade policy (Heady and Mitra: 1984a). We will also discuss the relationship of this model to the standard model of unrestricted commodity taxation that we analyzed in our first paper (Heady and Mitra: 1980) and to the model we have developed for dual economies (Heady and Mitra: 1984a and 1985).

Households

Each household, indexed by h, has an endowment of goods, such as capital or a particular type of labour. It is the differences in these endowments that generate income inequality. The household sells some or all of its endowment and uses the proceeds to buy consumer goods and services. These transactions can be represented by a vector, x^h, whose positive elements correspond to quantities purchased and whose negative elements correspond to quantities sold. If the total number of commodities (factors, consumer goods and services) is n then x^h is an n-dimensional vector.

All households face an n-dimensional vector of consumer

prices, q. This means that their budget constraint can be written as:

$$q^T x^h = 0 \tag{1}$$

where T denotes the transpose operation.
It should be noted that equation (1) does not allow households to receive pure profits, from non-competitive firms or competitive firms with decreasing returns, although it does allow for a return to capital owned by the household. This is a specification that is shared with much of the theoretical literature[4] and all of the numerical analysis of government policy referred to in Section II. This omission does affect the theoretical results but a practical reason for its maintenance is that there are no data that enable us to distinguish pure profits from the return to capital.

However, equation (1) does allow the possibility of households receiving lump-sum payments from the government. This is simply achieved by including in each household's endowment a good with a positive price that cannot be consumed or used in production: it is simply sold to the government. As lump-sum payments cannot normally be tailored to each individual household this does not remove the distributional motive for distortionary taxation. Our analysis has always assumed that any lump-sum payments are uniform, which together with uniform taxes on factor sales would constitute a negative income tax scheme.

In these circumstances, the transactions and utility of household h will depend on its given endowment and the prices that it faces. It is therefore possible to define a demand function, $x^h(q)$, and an indirect utility function

$v_h(q)$, for each household. These functions will be homogeneous of degree zero in q. It should be noted that the cardinalization of the indrect utility function is significant as the government's objective is assumed to be the maximization of a social welfare function, based on household utility levels:

$$V(q) = W\{v_1(q),\ldots,v_H(q)\} \tag{2}$$

It is this social welfare function that incorporates the government's distributional goals and in the numerical analysis we have used the specific form:

$$\left.\begin{aligned} W &= \frac{1}{\rho}\sum_{h=1}^{H}(v_h)^{\rho}, && \text{when } \rho \neq o \\ W &= \sum_{h=1}^{H}\log(v_h), && \text{when } \rho = o \end{aligned}\right\} \tag{3}$$

Different degrees of aversion to inequality can be obtained by varying the value of ρ, from utilitarianism when $\rho = 1$ to Rawlsian 'maximin' when ρ tends to minus infinity. However, the value of ρ represents the degree of aversion to inequality of <u>utility</u> and so the degree of aversion to inequality of <u>income</u> will depend both on the value of ρ and on the extent to which the indirect utility function displays diminishing marginal utility of income. In most of our numerical analysis we have chosen a cardinalization of the indirect utility function which is linear in income[5]: this would not be possible for some types of preference patterns.

Firms

Private production is assumed to be organized in a series

of industries, indexed by f. They are assumed to operate under constant returns to scale and to behave competitively. Thus, as stated above, they earn no pure profits. In our numerical analysis we have always assumed that each industry produces only one good because of the way that data are presented in input-output tables. However, joint production would not cause any difficulties.

The firms in any one industry are assumed to have access to the same technology and thus behave identically (although each firm's scale of operation is indeterminate). The firms choose production techniques in order to maximise profits at producer prices, p. Because of constant returns, we can represent this choice by a vector, A^f, which describes the inputs (negative elements) and outputs (positive elements) associated with operating the technique at unit level. This vector will depend on producer prices and we therefore have a unit supply function, $A^f(p)$. As we will be interested in the response of private sector activity to tax changes, this supply function is assumed to be continuously differentiable.

The firms in each industry will operate their chosen technique at a total level of y_f. Thus total private sector supply will be given as $A^f(p)y_f$. In order for y_f to be a finite number in equilibrium the industry cannot make a profit. Thus the following conditions must be satisfied.

$$p^T A^f(p) \leqq 0 \qquad \text{for all } f \tag{4}$$

Also, in order for firms to choose a postive y_f the activity must not make a loss. Therefore:

$$\sum_f p^T A^f(p) y_f = 0 \tag{5}$$

Government

The model also allows for government production of some or all of the goods, either as a monopoly or in competition with private producers. In an open economy international trade can also be regarded as a government activity because it is subject to possible government control, either directly or through the use of trade taxes and subsidies.

We have always assumed that government production is subject to constant returns to scale, although the analysis can easily be altered to accommodate either increasing or decreasing returns to scale. In terms of international trade, the constant returns assumption implies that the country is 'small' and thus faces given international prices for its imports and exports.

The public production is described by a matrix G whose columns represent the activities available to the public sector. The levels of each activity are denoted by the vector z so that public sector supply is represented by Gz. The use of a finite number of activities is in contrast to the assumption of smooth substitution made about the private sector and is a reflection of the fact that, as the public sector is directly controlled, we are not concerned with its response to private sector price changes. However, the distinction between a finite number of activities and smooth substitution is more apparent than real because the number of activities can be made very large. Indeed, in most of our numerical analysis the columns of G are chosen to give a very good approximation to a continuous spectrum of techniques.

The model also allows for the government to have a net revenue raising requirement to cover administration and public good provision. As prices are endogenous, it makes sense to represent this as a vector, R, of physical requirements such as labour and different types of goods. In principle, the components of R could be government choice variables to be determined along with taxes and public production. However, this is an unnecessary complication for our purposes and we have not pursued it. Indeed, we have often assumed that there was no such requirement as our main concern has been with redistribution. In an equilibrium supply must be at least as great as demand for each good and this can be represented as:

$$\sum_f A^f(p)y_f + Gz - X(q) - R \geqq 0 \tag{6}$$

where $X(q) = \sum_h x^h(q)$, the vector of aggregate net trades of households. In addition to public production the government controls taxes that produce divergences between private producer prices and consumer prices. However, it has been essential to much of our work that the government does not have unrestricted tax powers and it is important to consider how restrictions should be specified. At first sight it might appear that there are two different types of restriction:

(1) that certain goods must be taxed at the same rate, as in the case of different types of labour;

(2) that certain goods should have a zero rate of tax, as in the case of goods produced and consumed within an agricultural household.

However, it should be noted that the demand and supply functions are homogeneous of degree zero in consumer and producer prices, respectively. Thus, consumer prices (for example) can be scaled up and down without affecting consumer demand or producer prices. This scaling could be manipulated so that the difference between the consumer prices and the producer price (i.e. the tax) on any one good is zero. Thus specifying that any one good should be untaxed would have no effect on the real possibilities open to the government.

To give an example suppose that the government wished to lower the consumer price of capital services below its producer price, and thus raise revenue, but that capital income could not be taxed. The government could instead use taxes to raise the consumer prices of all other goods, with the same effect on relative prices and thus on consumer demands and government revenue.

Note however that this scaling of consumer prices could only make several goods untaxed if their tax rates were the same. Thus a restriction that a group of goods be untaxed is really just like the restriction that the goods should be taxed at the same rate. This means that both types of restriction are of type (1), to the extent that they are restrictions at all, and can be represented by partitioning the set of all commodities into K pre-selected groups, where all elements of group k must be taxed at an <u>ad valorem</u> rate of (t_k-1) common to that group. Thus, for any good i in group k:

$$q_i = t_k p_i \tag{7}$$

It is worth noting that the revenue raised by such a tax on good i in group k will be $(t_k-1)p_i X_i(q)$ (where X_i is the ith element of X). Thus a tax which raises the consumer price of a factor (for which X_i is negative) will result in a loss of revenue, while a tax which lowers it will gain revenue.

Equation (7) enables us to write the vector of aggregate net trades, X, and the social welfare function as functions of p and t. Thus the government problem of maximizing (2) subject to (4), (5) and (6) can be written as:

$$\text{Max} \quad V(t,p) \tag{2'}$$

$$\text{subject to:} \quad \sum_f A^f(p)y_f + Gz - X(t,p) - R \geqq 0 \tag{6'}$$

$$p^T A^f(p) \leqq \quad \text{for all } f \tag{4}$$

$$\sum_f p^T A^f(p) y_f = 0 \tag{5}$$

In practice the government controls only t and z while the market determines p and the y_f. However, in this problem we can regard the government as also choosing p and the y_f because any choice that satisfies the constraints will be a market equilibrium, so long as the government disposes of any goods that are in excess supply. In other words, the government choice of t and z implies (via the contraints) a choice of p and the y_f.[6]

Thus the solution to this problem must satisfy first-order conditions with respect to t, p, z and the y_f:

$$V_t - \lambda X_t^T s \leqq 0 \qquad (t \geqq 0), \tag{8}$$

$$V_p - \lambda X_p^T s + \lambda(\sum_f A_p^f y_f)^T s - \sum_f \mu^t A^f(p)$$

$$+ \nu \sum_f A^f(p) y_f \leqq 0 \qquad (p \geqq 0) \tag{9}$$

$$\lambda s^T A^f(p) + \nu p^T A^f(p) \leqq 0 \qquad (y_f \geqq 0) \tag{10}$$

$$s^T G \leqq 0 \qquad (z \geqq 0) \tag{11}$$

where subscripts denote derivatives and each inequality bears the relationship of complementary slackness with the corresponding variable appearing in parenthesis on the right. s is a vector of shadow prices (corresponding to (6')), λ is a scalar which enables s to be normalized, the μ^t are scalar multipliers corresponding to (4) and ν is a scalar multiplier corresponding to (5).

The results that can be obtained from the analysis of conditions (8) - (11) will be discussed in Section IV below. The rest of this Section will be concerned with the relationship of this model to both the standard model of unrestricted taxation and our more recent work on dual economies.

Looking first at the model of unrestricted taxation, the obvious difference is that each good can be taxed at a separate rate. This implies that the government can choose producer and consumer prices independently and therefore can manipulate private production (via producer prices) without any concern for its effect on consumer prices and welfare. Thus the government has as much control over the private sector as the public sector and in the absence of private sector profits there is no need to distinguish between them. They should therefore face the same prices, p = s. This means that condition (9) is no longer necessary for determining p and condition (10) simplifies to:

$$s^T A^f(s) \leqq 0 \qquad (y_f \geqq 0) \tag{10'}$$

Note that (10'), combined with p = s, means that conditions (4) and (5) are automatically satisfied by an optimal solution and do not have to be imposed. The assumption of unrestricted taxation therefore simplifies the analysis of optimal policy considerably. This analytical simplification is accompanied by a simplification of the computational technique, see Section V below.

In contrast to the relaxation of tax restrictions, the analysis of dual economies introduces additional complications. The basic idea of dual economy models is that agriculture in underdevloped countries is organized in a fundamentally different way from manufacturing. From the point of view of public finance a major difference is that it is typically more difficult to tax agriculture than manufacturing. This is because many farms consume much of their own produce and mainly use their own land and labour in the production process. This means that the returns to labour and land do not correspond to identifiable financial transactions that can be taxed. It is therefore often only practicable to tax agriculture through the transactions it has with the rest of the economy. Thus agricultural land and labour, together with the agricultural sector's consumption of its own output, are nontaxable and this constitutes a significant tax restriction. Moreover, the fact that agriculture can only be taxed through its transactions with the rest of the economy implies that agricultural prices could well be different from both urban producer and urban consumer prices. This means that the government has to choose two sets of taxes: (1) the wedge between urban producer and consumer prices; (2) the wedge between urban producer and agricultural prices. However, the government may not be able to choose these taxes completely independently because of the possibility of arbitrage between the urban and rural sectors. For example, if taxes were set so that the relative prices of food and clothing were different in the rural areas from the urban areas people would be able to make profits by trading between the two sectors. In order to avoid this problem the government must satisfy commodity specific tax restrictions, although it should be noted that they need not apply to all goods. Electricity, for example, can be sold at different prices in different areas without any problems.

The other new feature of the model is the introduction of migration from the rural areas to urban areas. We follow Lewis (1954) in supposing that rural residents only migrate to urban areas if there is a job available and that the wage differential between the two sectors is just enough to offset the difference in the cost of living and in non-pecuniary benefits. Thus there is no unemployment and the utility of a migrant is equal to the utility of an equally endowed non-migrant. One issue that arises in connection with specifying the migration mechanism is whether migrants lose their rights to land. At one extreme one might suppose that migrants can rent or sell their land for its full value, while at the other extreme it could be assumed that migrants give up all rights to their land, which is then distributed to non-migrants. Looking at different countries, one can find examples of both extremes, as well as cases where migrants retain some rights. In order to investigate the sensitivity of optimal policy to this issue we have analysed both extreme cases. The results of this analysis are given in Heady and Mitra (1984b)

In summary, the analysis of a dual economy involves the

introduction of a second set of taxes, a non-taxable sector and an additional equilibrium condition (that the utility of migrants should equal that of equally endowed non-migrants).

IV. ANALYTIC RESULTS

The purpose of this Section is to outline the analytic results that we have obtained (Heady and Mitra: 1982, 1984a, 1984b, 1985). We deal first with the results from the model of restricted taxation as set out in Section III, and then with the extension of these results to the dual economy model. The analytic results of the model of unrestricted taxation are set out in Diamond and Mirrlees (1971) and Atkinson and Stiglitz (1976).

The analytic results on restricted taxation are derived from conditions (8) - (11). Condition (11) is the standard condition that constant returns government sector projects should not make profits at shadow prices. Equation (10) implies that any private activity that is in operation, and thus breaks even at producer prices, must also break even at shadow prices. This result was originally demonstrated by Diamond and Mirrlees (1976).

Our work has mainly been concerned with conditions (8) and (9), as they provide conditions for the choice of taxes and the divergence between shadow prices and producer prices. The analysis of these conditions is simplified if we regard the tax on a good (the difference between its consumer price and producer price) as being the result of two divergences: the difference between the consumer price and the shadow price, τ_i, and the difference between the producer price and the shadow prices, ω_i. Thus:

$$\tau = q - s; \qquad \omega = p - s \tag{12}$$

We will call the vector τ "shadow consumer taxes" and the vector ω "shadow producer taxes". However, it must always be remembered that the actual tax paid, $(t_k-1)p_i$ is the difference between the two taxes $(\tau_i-\omega_i)$ and it is this that is subject to the restrictions.

This enables us to rewrite equation (8) and (9) as (disregarding the inequalities):

$$-\frac{\sum_{i\epsilon k}\sum_h\sum_j p_i x_{ij}^{ch}\tau_j}{\sum_{i\epsilon k} p_i X_i} = 1 - \frac{\sum_{i\epsilon k}\sum_h b^h p_i x_i^h}{\lambda \sum_{i\epsilon k} p_i X_i} \tag{13}$$

$$-\frac{\sum_f \sum_j w_j a_{ij}^f y_f}{\sum_f A_i^f y_f} = \frac{\nu}{\lambda}\;\frac{\sum_f \mu^f A_i^f}{\lambda \sum_f A_i^f y_f} \tag{14}$$

$$-\frac{t_i X_i}{\sum_f A_i^f y_f}\left[\frac{\sum_h \sum_j \tau_j x_{ij}^{ch}}{X_i} + 1 - \frac{\sum_h b^h x_i^h}{\lambda X_i}\right]$$

where k is the group index and x_{ij}^{ch} is the derivative of household h's compensated net demand for good i with respect to the price of good j;

A_i^f is the output of the ith good from the unit activity chosen by industry f;

a_{ij}^f is the derivative of A_i with respect to the price of good j;

b^h is the net social marginal utility of income for household h

$$(b^h = \frac{\partial W}{\partial v_h} \frac{\partial v_h}{\partial I} + \lambda \sum_j \tau_j \frac{\partial x_j^h}{\partial I}$$

where I is the (possibly zero) lump-sum income of household h; the first term represents the social value placed on the extra utility of the household; while the second term represents the social value of the extra taxes that the household will pay).

Equation (13) is similar to the unrestricted tax rule in Atkinson and Stiglitz (1976), except that both sides have been averaged over the goods within each tax group. The reason for this averaging is that the government is restricted to set a uniform tax for all goods in the group. Thus the left-hand side represents the proportionate reduction in value, at producer prices, of compensated demand for the goods in tax group k that would result from a small equi-proportional intensification of shadow consumer taxes if shadow prices were constant. The right-hand side is smaller for groups of goods that are mainly consumed by households with high net social marginal utility of income (typically the poor). Thus equation (13) tells us that the proportionate reduction is smaller for such groups.

The left-hand side of equation (14) is similar to the left-hand side of equatoin (13) but is measuring the distortionary effect of shadow producer taxes, rather than consumer taxes. Also, the effect is not averaged over tax groups because the government can use trade policy or public production to vary producer prices independently of taxes. The main reason for the introduction of production distortions can be seen in the final term in equation (14), as the first two terms are simply ensuring that producer price changes satsify the zero profit conditions (4) and (5). The term in square brackets represents the extent to which the shadow consumer tax on good i is not optimal, and equation (13) assures us that this term would be zero if good i were the only good in its tax group. Thus production distortions are warranted by the fact that tax restrictions have prevented the government from setting the optimal consumer prices some goods and that variation of producer prices might get those prices nearer the optimum[7]. However, as Munk (1980) points out, this produces distortions on the production side of the economy. Thus equation (14) represents a balance between improving consumer prices and distorting production.

This result, that tax restrictions make it desirable to introduce a difference between private producer prices and public shadow prices, has far-reaching implications for public investment and trade policy. Dealing first with public investment, the difference between the two sets of prices implies that it is possible for socially desirable public investment in the production of private goods to make losses at market prices. This might occur if the project had a desirable effect on private producer prices and thus via the tax restrictions on consumer prices. The implications for trade policy follow from the fact that, for a small country, public shadow prices equal world prices (a result that follows from condition (11)). Thus, differences between shadow and producer prices for traded goods correspond to trade taxes and subsidies. For example, a tariff might be justified if the government wished to increase the consumer prices of the good, or of factors which produced the good, but could not do so through the tax system. The detailed implications for trade are examined in Heady and Mitra (1984a).

A further implication for public investment and trade policy follows from the fact that producer prices affect consumer prices when taxes are restricted. Looking back at the government's maximization problem, we see that producer prices are constrained by equation (5), which requires private activities in use to break even. This raises the possibility that government production or trade could replace some private activities and thus relax the constraint imposed by equation (5) on some prices. This would give the government more latitude in setting producer prices, and thus consumer prices, and could result in improvements in social welfare. Our paper on trade policy (Heady and Mitra (1984a)) gives some numerical examples of this possibility.

In extending these results to the dual economy (Heady and Mitra (1984b and 1985)) we have avoided issues of income distribution by assuming that all households are equally endowed. This assumption was made in order to concentrate on the special features of the model: the non-taxability of trades within agriculture and the migration from rural to urban areas. The non-taxability issue can be dealt with by regarding each farm as a consumer that purchases goods from the rest of the economy and finances these purchases by sales of agricultural products. The fact that the agricultural products are produced by labour and land is irrelevant to the government as the supplies of the factors cannot be taxed. Thus it is only the urban sector that needs its production to be modelled explicitly.

The introduction of migration means that the government must take account of the effect of its policies on inter-sectoral labour mobility. However, this does not cause any difficulties as we specify the migration equilibrium condition in terms of utility. Thus, any policy that increases the utility of urban residents will promote rural-urban migration, while any policy that increases the utility of rural residents will reduce such migration. This means that if, for example, the government wishes to promote rural-urban migration the tax policies would be the same as if it put a higher weight on urban utility and a lower weight on rual utility. Thus we can still represent the government as maximizing a function of individual utilities and equation (13) must still describe optimal taxes, although the values of b^h will be altered by the migration consideration. However, it should be noted that in the absence of commodity specific tax restrictions there will be two sets of taxes, each of which satisfy (13). Thus taxes on urban consumers and rural farms will separately satisfy the tax rule described above, and even if all households are equally endowed the proportionate reductions will generally be different in the two sectors. If commodity-specific tax restrictions are in operation, the proportionate reductions would have to alter for those goods subject to the restrictions.

One aspect of tax policy that arises in this model is the question of how the tax burden is divided between agriculture and non-agriculture. The answer to this question depends on whether migrants retain the rights to their land income. If they do then the tax burden per cpaita should be the same in each sector. The reason for this is that marginal migrants do not gain from migrating and, if they keep their land rights, no other households gain either. However, if the per capita tax burdens were unequal the government could gain revenue by altering the number of urban jobs. Such possibilities of gain mean that government policy is not optimal. Therefore optimal policy must be characterised by equal per capita tax burdens.

This result has to be modified if migrants lose some of their land rights because non-migrants will benefit from the migration of others. In this case the per capita tax burden in agriculture should be higher than in non-agriculture so that, at the optimum, the gain to non-migrants of further migration is balanced by the loss to government revenue.

Another way of looking at this result is that, when migrants lose land rights, the act of migration has a beneficial externality which is rewarded by lower taxation of urban residents. However, when migrants keep all their land rights no such externalities arise and there is no reason for differential taxation.

Turning to production and trade policy, we have already argued that agricultural prices should be different from shadow prices. As these prices cover inter alia agricultural inputs such as fertilizer and agricultural output, this implies that farmers are not facing shadow prices when making their production decisions. Thus is will generally be optimal to tax international trade in agricultural inputs and outputs. Also, government projects in rural areas should use shadow prices that differ from local market prices.

In contrast, the inability to tax trades within agriculture does not consititute a reason for introducing production inefficiency into urban production. This is true even if urban taxes on some goods are constrained to be the same as rural taxes (the commodity specific tax restrictions) because, as long as consumer prices can be set independently of urban producer prices, there is no advantage to be gained from manipulating private urban production. Thus the issue of whether shadow prices should equal urban producer prices, with all that implies for production and trade policy, depends only on whether there are tax restrictions within the urban sector itself.

Finally, this summary of theoretical results confirms what was said in the Introduction. The theory provides us with useful insights into optimal government but the results are not in a form which makes it easy to draw direct conclusions about the likely values of optimal taxes, tariffs or shadow prices. It is for this reason that we have supplemented this theoretical analysis with the numerical analysis that is described in the next two sections.

V. COMPUTATIONAL TECHNIQUES

This section, which may be omitted without loss of continuity, outlines the computational techniques we have used in our work. It assumes that the reader is familiar with the basic ideas of the Scarf (1973) algorithm: an excellent brief exposition is given in Scarf (1982). As stated above, our first work in this area (Heady and Mitra, 1980) was concerned with obtaining numerical solutions to the optimal tax formula derived by Diamond and Mirrlees (1971). This work involved adapting Scarf's algorithm to the special requirements of the problem. We have continued to use Scarf's algorithm and have extended it to deal with restricted taxes (Heady and Mitra, 1984c). However, in our recent work on dual economies we have used a dynamic nonlinear programming algorithm called CONOPT (Drud, 1984). The main reason for this was that we also wanted to analyze the dynamic properties of the dual economy model, work that is still in progress.

The rest of this Section will be concerned with the use of Scarf's algorithm in our work. As the precise details and necessary proofs are published elsewhere, we will confine ourselves to an informal sketch of our procedures, concentrating on the simpler case of computing unrestricted taxes.

In setting up the model of unrestricted taxation we could follow Section III in specifying a choice of taxes and producer prices. However, that approach was only really required because of the fact that, with restricted taxes, producer prices have a real effect on consumer prices. When taxes are unrestricted we can regard the government as directly controlling consumer prices so that the problem becomes:

$$\text{Maximize} \qquad V(q) \tag{15}$$

$$\text{subject to:} \qquad Gz - X(q) \geqq 0 \tag{16}$$

where we have disregarded any government net revenue raising requirement and have made use of the fact that no distinction between private and public production need be made.

The first-order conditions for maximization are:

$$V_q - \lambda[X_q]s \leqq 0 \qquad (q \geqq 0) \tag{17}$$

$$s^T G \leqq 0 \qquad (z \geqq 0) \tag{18}$$

where the notation is the same as in Section III.

This problem is similar to the type of non-linear programme which has been solved by Hansen (1969), using the Scarf algorithm. However, Hansen's procedure dealt with concave programmes and used a standard constraint qualification to prove convergence to the optimum. In contrast, this problem is not concave and so Hansen's argument cannot be used directly.

A second difficulty with Hansen's algorithm is that it searches over a simplex of all the control variables, which in our case would be the elements of q and z. Now z can be a vector of very high dimension, especially if there are wide substitution possibilities. Thus the algorithm might have to search over a simplex with a large number of dimensions and this would make it very slow.

Our procedure solves the second problem by using a parametric linear programme to find a z that corresponds to each q. Thus, the algorithm need only search over the simplex of consumer prices, q.

We then showed that our modified version of Hansen's algorithm would converge to a solution of the first-order conditions of our problem provided that a new constraint qualification was satisfied. This constraint qualification required that when the government budget is in deficit there is always a small tax change that will reduce the deficit. This is equivalent to ruling out Edgeworth's tax paradox, but only when the budget is in deficit. Unfortunately, the lack of concavity means that a solution to the first-order conditions might not be a maximum. However, the algorithm can be started at different points in an attempt to find all the solutions to the first-order conditions[8], and the value of social welfare at the different solutions can be compared to find the maximum.

Thus our algorithm searches over a grid of vectors $q^1,\ldots,q^k$ on a unit simplex and it gives a vector label to

each vector in the grid. For vectors on the sides of the simplex, the standard Scarf-Hansen labels are used. However for each vector, q, in the interior of the simplex, the following linear programme is solved:
choose z and r to minimize r

$$\text{subject to} \qquad Gz + re_n \geqq X(q) \qquad (19)$$

where e_n is an n-dimensional vector with unit entries.

This programme is choosing production levels, z, which minimize the largest difference between demand and supply. Note that when r = 0 the feasibility condition (16) is satisfied and so this programme provides a test for the feasibility of X(q). Also, corresponding to (19) there will be a set of shadow prices, s, which by duality will satisfy condition (18):

$$s^T G \leqq 0 \qquad (z \geqq 0) \qquad (18)$$

If the minimal value of r is negative or zero, X(q) is feasible and we give q the label:

$$[e_n + V_q]$$

If the minimal value of r is positive, X(q) is infeasible and we give q the label:

$$[e_n - [X_q]^T s]$$

where s was derived from the linear programme.
Scarf's algorithm can then be applied to the labelled simplex and it will terminate at a primitive set which we

show provides an approximation to a vector $\hat{q}$ that satisfies feasibility (16) and the first-order condition (17), provided that the regularity condition is satisfied. Furthermore, the labelling was constructed so that (18) is satisfied and so we have an approximate solution to the first-order conditions. This approximation is typically more accurate if the grid is finer and we use Merrill's (1972) refinement technique to obtain solutions that are as accurate as we require.

The extension of this technique to restricted taxes requires us to search over a grid of tax rates and private producer prices, while shadow prices are generated by a linear programme which incorporates private sector activities satisfy the no-positive profit and zero profit constraints (4) and (5). This is technically difficult because of the complementary slackness involved in these constraints and interested readers are referred to our paper on computing restricted taxes (Heady and Mitra, 1984c).

The exact time taken by these algorithms depends on the precise nature of the problem and on the computer used. However, in the models we have investigated, which usually have two factors and three consumer goods, it has usually taken well under a minute to obtain a solution with a final grid size of 10,000.

IV. NUMERICAL EXAMPLES

The purpose of this Section is to give some idea of the sort of results that numerical analysis of optimal public policy can provide. We will give two rather brief examples here and the reader is referred to our other papers for more detailed and extensive analysis. The first example comes from our paper on trade policy (1984a) and deals with the distributional case for tariffs, while the second example looks at optimal taxes for revenue raising in the dual economy model (1984b). As stated in the introduction, one of the main reasons for interest in numerical analysis of optimal public policy is the ability to conduct sensitivity analysis, and we will concentrate on that aspect here.

(a) Redistributive Tariffs

In this model there are two types of labour, skilled and unskilled, which the government must tax at the same rate. This tax restriction raises the possibility of using tariffs because the imposition of a tariff would raise the producer price, and thus the consumer price, of the type of labour that is used intensively in producing the protected good. The effect of a tariff on the relative wages of the two types of labour will depend on the production technology. In particular one would expect the effect to be greater if there are greater differences in the skill mix between industries and if the elasticity of substitution is low. Our example will concentrate on the significance of the elasticity of substitution, although an earlier paper (1982) presents results on skill mix differences.

For these examples there is assumed to be no substitution between intermediate inputs or between any intermediate input and either type of labour. However, there is substitution between the two types of labour. Table 1 presents the input requirements for activities producing one unit of each output. The labour inputs reported represent the least cost combinations when the factor prices are equal. The elasticity of substitution is assumed to be the same for each industry but is varied parametrically for the sensitivity analysis.

It is assumed that households supply their labour inelasticially but that their demands for consumer goods can be represented by the linear expenditure system. The utility function which generates these demands is:

$$\log (u_h) = \sum_{i=1}^{3} b_i \log (x_i^h - c_i), \qquad \sum_{i=1}^{3} b_i = 1$$

The parameter values used in our examples are reported in Table 2.

Inequality in the model is generated by the fact that households differ in both the type (skilled or unskilled) and efficiency of the labour they supply. The distribution between four classes is given in Table 3.

The government has no net revenue raising requirement and there is no public production. Its objective is to reduce the degree of inequality, but is is also concerned about the average utility level. These concerns are represented by a social welfare function of the type discussed in Section III, above.

$$W = \frac{1}{\rho} \sum_h (u_h)^{\rho} \quad , \quad \text{when } \rho \neq 0$$

$$W = \sum_h \log(u_h) \quad , \quad \text{when } \rho = 0$$

Clearly, the value of ρ will affect the choice of optimal tariff and sensitivity to this parameter is analyzed below.

In the calculations reported in Table 4 it is assumed that the only tax restriction is the one on the two types of labour. This means that taxes on consumer goods can be manipulated to offset some of the effects of tariffs on

TABLE 1 Input requirements for Unit Activity Levels

Inputs	Unit Good 1	Activities Good 2	Producing Good 3
Good 1	0	0.01	0.10
Good 2	0.04	0	0.12
Good 3	0.10	0.19	0
Unskilled Labour	0.77	0.38	0.43
Skilled Labour	0.09	0.66	0.35

TABLE 2 Consumption Parameters

	Good 1	Good 2	Good 3
b	0.35	0.25	0.40
c	11.0	2.5	0.0

TABLE 3 Labour Endowments in Efficiency Units

	Class I	Class II	Class III	Class IV
Proportion of Population	0.54	0.38	0.06	0.02
Unskilled Labour	20.48	35.95	0.0	0.0
Skilled Labour	0.0	0.0	108.5	289.0

consumer prices. It is also assumed that the country is small and thus faces given terms of trade, whose value (0.87) is such that the country imports Good 1 and exports Good 3. Good 2 is assumed to be non-traded. For simplicity, the producer prices are scaled so that the world price of Good 3 equals its domestic producer price. Thus the choice of tariff for Good 1 is the only element of trade policy. The optimal choice for this tariff is given in Table 4, for different values of ρ and σ (the elasticity of substitution between the two types of labour).

TABLE 4 Effect of ρ and σ on Optimal Redistribution Tariff

ρ	0.0	0.0	0.0	0.25	-1.0	-5.0
σ	2.5	3.2	3.0	3.0	3.0	3.0
optimal tariff	18.6%	11.7%	14.2%	10.9%	18.0%	26.9%

The first three columns fo Table 4 show that the tariff becomes considerably larger when the elasticity of substitution is reduced by a small amount. Indeed, the effect of the elasticity of substitution is so strong that the optimal tariff becomes prohibitive for elasticities slightly less than 2.5 and domestic production of Good 1 is completely abandoned for elasticities slightly greater than 3.2. The fact that smaller elasticities of substitution increase the tariff is strongly suggested by the theory: small elasticities imply a greater effect on relative prices and smaller distortionary cost. However, the theory could not indicate just how sensitive the optimal tariff is to this parameter.

The last four columns show how sensitive the optimal tariff is to variations in ρ, the degree of concern for inequality. As one would expect, the tariff becomes larger when the government is more egalitarian. The effect is significant, but this example shows that this subjective parameter is no more important than the (objective) elasticity of substitution, a characteristic that is common to many of our numerical examples.

(b) Revenue-rasing Taxes

In this example, we look at the effect of changing the government's revenue raising requirement on taxes in the dual economy model. In this particular version of the model all households are equally endowed, so no issues of equity arise. Also, the government owns all of the capital stock in the manufacturing sector and so receives significant capital income. This means that when the government's revenue requirement is small it has money to distribute, but we assume that this must be distributed through subsidies (negative taxes) rather than direct payments to households.

The government can set taxes on all urban goods and factors, as well as trades between the urban and rural sectors. However, the government cannot tax trades within the rural sector and is subject to the commodity specific tax restriction that food and clothing must have the same relative prices in the two sectors. However, the other consumer good, services, can have different prices in the two sectors.

In addition to the distortion caused by taxes, we assume that rural-urban migrants lose their rights to land and thus generate a beneficial externality.

The agricultural sector produces food using inputs of land, labour and imported fertilizer. We assume a nested CES technology with land and fertilizer forming a subaggregate (with $\sigma = 1.5$) which is then combined with labour to produce food (with $\sigma = 1.1$).

The urban sector produces clothing and services, again with a nested CES technology. However they use capital and imported energy to produce the subaggregate (with $\sigma = 0.5$ for both industries) which is then combined with labour to produce output (with $\sigma = 1.1$ for clothing, $\sigma = 0.9$ for services).

Households in both sectors have identical linear expenditure system utility functions, as in example (a). However, labour is not inelastically supplied and must therefore be included in the utility function (thus extending it to four goods). The consumption parameters are given in Table 5.

TABLE 5 Consumption Parameters

	Food	Clothing	Services	Labour*
b	0.06	0.15	0.3	0.49
c	1.7	1.0	0.4	-9.53

*Note that labour supply is a negative number so that a reduction in labour supplied will _ceteris paribus_ increase utility.

As all households have the same utility level, the government's objective is simply to maximise that level subject to raising the necessary revenue. The optimal taxes for this purpose are given in Table 6 for a range of revenue requirements, expressed as a percentage of national income[9]. These results are presented graphically in Figure 1.

The revenue requirement of 36.6% corresponds to a situation where the government's capital income just covers its revenue requirement. Thus the taxes raised on clothing, services and fertilizers are simply financing the payments to urban labour (represented as a positive tax because it produces a consumer price that is greater than the corresponding producer price). These payments are made to urban workers in order to encourage rural-urban migration, which generates a beneficial externality. The pattern of taxation on clothing, services and fertilizer is determined by the equal proportionate reductions rule derived in Section IV, modified so that clothing is taxed equally in the two sectors. The most striking feature of the tax pattern is the low tax on fertilizer. Thus, although, as predicted in Section IV, production inefficiency is caused by what is in effect a tariff on fertilizer imports, the extent of the distortion is not very great[10].

When we compare the pattern of taxes when the revenue requirement is increased, we see that all of the taxes increase (except that on urban labour) but that their relative positions remain generally unchanged[11]. Also, when the revenue requirement is zero the goods which were previously highly taxed are now highly subsidised. This pattern is unsurprising as one would expect that the relative distortionary costs of taxes on different goods would be approximately the same at different rates of taxation, including negative rates. However, a different functional form for the demand system might yield a less consistent pattern, and the fact that the sign of the taxes on different goods change at different levels of revenue requirement shows that the determination of optimal taxes is not quite as simple as the remarks above might suggest.

TABLE 6 Optimal Taxes with Varying Revenue Requirement

Revenue Requirement

	0%	5%	10%	20%	30%	36.6%	50%	60%
Urban								
Clothing	-22.2%	-16.8%	-10.7%	4.6%	25.4%	42.9%	103.7%	247.1%
Services	-7.7%	-3.1%	-1.7%	12.5%	24.8%	33.5%	53.3%	76.8%
Labour	77.9%	76.1%	73.8%	68.3%	61.3%	56.8%	45.1%	46.5%
Rural								
Clothing	-22.2%	-16.8%	-10.7%	4.6%	25.4%	42.9%	103.7%	247.1%
Services	-31.2%	-25.3%	-18.5%	-0.3%	26.1%	49.7%	128.3%	188.5%
Fertilizer	-6.0%	-4.7%	-3.4%	-0.8%	1.6%	3.0%	4.9%	4.9%

VII. CONCLUSIONS

This paper has outlined our work on public policy and has shown the sort of contribution that our methodology can make. We believe that our work to date makes a substantial contribution to the understanding of what determines optimal public policy. We have extended the theory to include such institutional features as tax restrictions and the dualistic nature of many underdeveloped economies. Our numerical work has illustrated the significance of these institutional features as well as demonstrating the sensitivity of optimal policy to changes in key parameters.

However, we are also aware of several shortcomings in our models. The most important shortcomings, the ones we will discuss here, are concerned with the way in which we model the markets for factors. This is most obvious in the

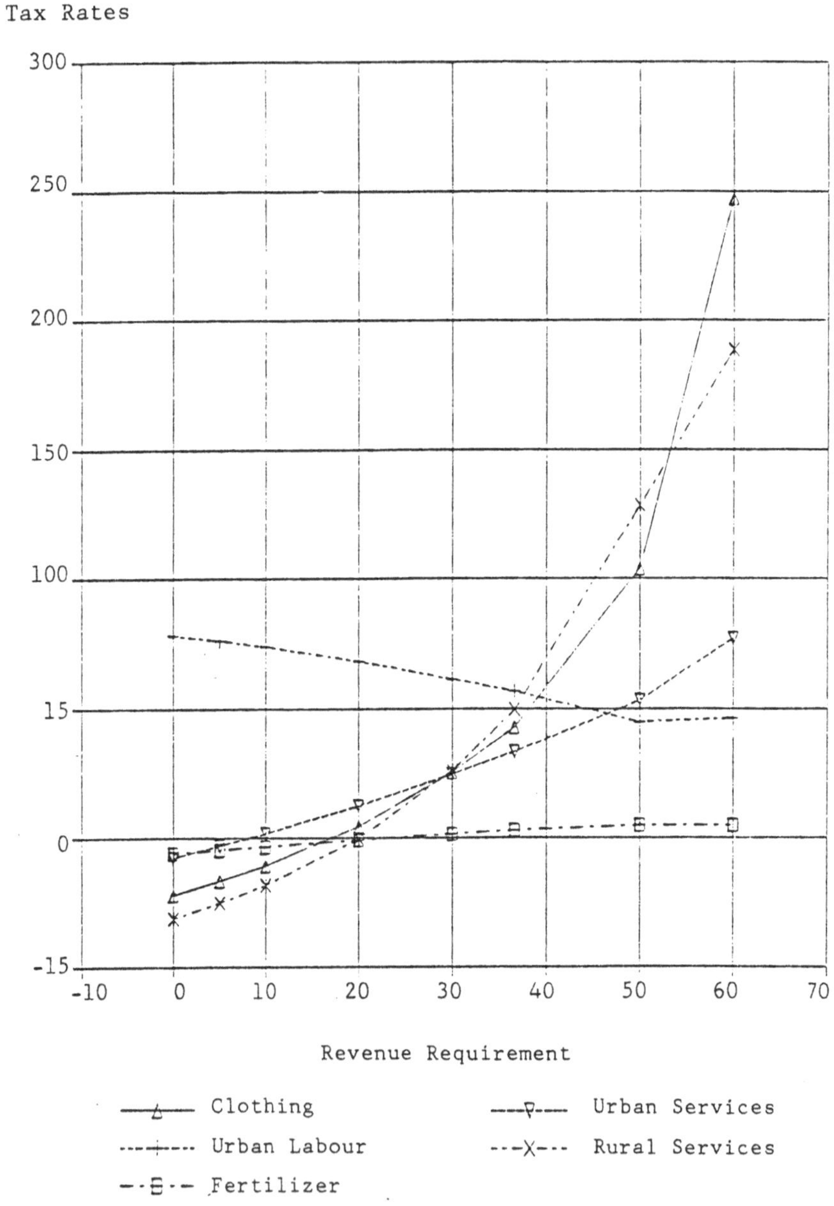

FIGURE 1 Sensitivity of Tax Structure to Revenue Requirement

case of capital because the models reviewed here are static while the supply of savings (which augment the capital stock) must depend on expectations about the future. Thus those of our models which include capital (supplied either elastically or inelastically with respect to the current rate of return) are omitting important influences on its supply.

We have made some progress in making the dual economy model dynamic, using CONOPT to solve the numerical examples, but that work is still incomplete. However, even in the dynamic model it is only the government that is undertaking savings. What is really required is a model of private sector savings, which will require the modelling of household expectations.

Turning to the labour market, all of our models assume that the labour market clears and that the total number of workers of each type is fixed. It would clearly be desirable to include the possibility of unemployment, especially for underdeveloped countries. Also, it would be interesting to introduce training explicitly so that the number of each type of worker could vary in response to policy changes.

We plan to extend our dual economy model to include urban unemployment by introducing a rigid urban wage and induced migration, as in Harris and Todaro (1970), but have not yet addressed the problems of modelling training.

FOOTNOTES

1. The World Bank does not accept responsibility for the views expressed herein which are those of the author(s)

and should not be attributed to the World Bank or to its affiliated organizations. The findings, interpretations, and conclusions are the results of research supported by the Bank; they do not necessarily represent official policy of the Bank. The designations employed, the presentation of material, and any maps used in this document are solely for the convenience of the reader and do not imply the expression of any opinion whatsoever on the part of the World Bank or its affiliates concerning the legal status of any country, territory, city, area, or of its authorities, or concerning the delimitation of its boundaries, or national affiliation.

2. There would still, of course, be an argument for trade intervention if the country was not "small".
3. Harris and Mackinnon (1979) also developed a technique for computing optimal commodity taxes which permitted flexible producer prices and arbitrary income distributions and demand systems. Unfortunately, they have not extended their techniques to the analysis of restricted taxes.
4. Two of the exceptions are Stiglitz and Dasgupta (1971) and Munk (1978).
5. We have generally used the linear expenditure system and cardinalized the indirect utility function so that for any set of consumer prices utility is proportional to the value of endowments minus the value of the minimum consumption levels.
6. If there are multiple equilibria we must assume that the government can get the economy to its preferred equilibrium.
7. This does not mean that there will be no shadow producer taxes on goods whose taxes are unrestricted. The need for producer prices to satisfy (4) and (5) will mean that a change in one producer price will necessarily involve the change of at least one other.
8. We cannot guarantee that we can find them all.
9. Consumer prices have been scaled so that food is untaxed.
10. A different form of production function or utility function of agricultural householdsmight imply a higher tariff.
11. The exception is that the tax on rural services falls below that on clothing for very high revenue requirements.

REFERENCES

S.E. Ahmad and N.H. Stern, The theory of reform and Indian indirect taxes, Journal of Public Economics, 25, 259-289, (1984).

S.E. Ahmad and N.H. Stern, The evaluation of sources of additional government revenue in India. In D. Newbery and N. Stern (eds.), The Theory of Taxation for Developing Countries, forthcoming, (1985).

A.B. Atkinson and J.E. Stiglitz, The structure of indirect taxation and economic efficiency, Journal of Public Economics, I, 97-119, (1972).

A.B. Atkinson and J.E. Stiglitz, Lectures on Public Economics, New York: McGraw-Hill, (1976).

P.S. Dasgupta, S. Marglin and A.K. Sen, Guidelines for Project Evaluation, New York: United Nations Industrial Development Organisation, (1972).

A.S. Deaton, Equity, efficiency and the structure of indirect taxation, Journal of Public Economics, 8, 299-312, (1977).

P.A. Diamond and J.A. Mirrlees, Optimal taxation and public production: I and II, American Economic Review, 61, 8-27 and 261-278, (1971).

P.A. Diamond and J.A. Mirrlees, Private constant returns and public shadow prices, Review of Economic Studies, 43, 41-47, (1976).

A. Drud, CONOPT: A GRG code for large sparse dynamic nonlinear optimization problems, Mathematical Programming, forthcoming, (1984).

T. Hansen, A fixed point algorithm for approximating the optimal solution of a concave programming problem, Cowles Foundation Discussion Paper No. 277, Yale University, (1969).

J.R. Harris and M.P. Todaro, Migration, unemployment and development: a two-sector analysis, American Economic Review, 60, 126-142, (1970).

R.G. Harris and J.G. MacKinnon, Computing optimal tax equilibria, Journal of Public Economics, 11, 197-212, (1979).

C.J. Heady and P.K. Mitra, The computation of optimum linear taxation, Review of Economic Studies, 47, 567-585, (1980).

C.J. Heady and P.K. Mitra, Restricted redistributive taxation, shadow prices and trade policy, Journal of Public Economics, 17, 1-22, (1982).

C.J. Heady and P.K. Mitra, Distributional and revenue raising arguments for tariffs, Mimeo, (1984a).

C.J. Heady and P.K. Mitra, Optimum taxation and shadow pricing in a developing economy. In D. Newbery and N. Stern (eds.), The Theory of Taxation for Developing Countries, forthcoming, (1984b).

C.J. Heady and P.K. Mitra, A computational approach to optimum public policies. In R. Cottle and A. Manne (eds.), The Solution and Application of Economic Equilibrium Models, forthcoming, (1984c).

C.J. Heady and P.K. Mitra, Optimal taxation in a dual economy, Mimeo, (1985).

W.A. Lewis, Economic Development with unlimited supplies of labour, The Manchester School, 22, 139-191, (1954).

I.M.D. Little and J.A. Mirrlees, Project Appraisal and Planning in Developing Countries, London: Heinemann, (1974).

O.H. Merrill, Applications and Extensions of an Algorithm that Computes Fixed Points of Certain Upper Semi-Continuous Point to Set Mappings, University of Michigan, Ph.D. Thesis, (1972).

J.A. Mirrlees, An exploration in the theory of optimum income taxation, Review of Economic Studies, 38, 175-208, (1971).

J.A. Mirrlees, The theory of optimal taxation. In K.J. Arrow and M.D. Intriligator (eds.), Handbook of Mathematical Economics, Volume III, New York: North Holland, (1985).

K.J. Munk, Optimal taxation and pure profit, Scandinavian Journal of Economics, 80, 1-19, (1978).

K.J. Munk, Optimal taxation with some non-taxable commodities, Review of Economic Studies, 47, 755-765, (1980).

H.E. Scarf, The Computation of Economic Equilibria, New Haven: Yale University Press, (1973).

H.E. Scarf, The computation of equilbrium prices: an exposition. In K.J. Arrow and M.D. Intriligator (eds), Handbook of Mathematical Economics, Volume II, New York: North Holland, (1982).

J.B. Shoven and J. Whalley, Applied general-equilibrium models of taxation and international trade: an introduction and survey, Journal of Economic Literature, 22, 1007-1051, (1984).

N.H. Stern, On the specification of models of optimum income taxation, Journal of Public Economics, 6, 123-162, (1976).

J.E. Stiglitz and P.S. Dasgupta, Differential taxation, public goods and economic efficiency, Review of Economic Studies, 38, 151-174, (1971).

ECONOMIC ESTIMATION OF MICROECONOMIC RECREATION PARTICIPATION MODELS

JOHN MULLAHY
Resources for the Future

I. INTRODUCTION

In the last decade or so, estimation of microeconomic models of consumer behaviour using large individual or household level data sets has flourished and proved an important advance in applied economics. Details typically masked in aggregate time-series data analysis are often available in individual cross-sectional data, thus enabling the testing of hypotheses about responses of individual or household demand-supply bundle choices to changes in constraints.

It is in such micro data sets that one is prone to find measures of demands and supplies that economists would characterize either as corner solution realizations of instantaneous optimizing decisions or as discrete representations of such decisions. An example of the former case would be where one has data on the number of hours an individual worked in the market over a given year, and for some subset of individuals no market hours were worked. An instance of the latter case is where data are available only on whether or not an individual had purchased some consumer durable over the previous twelve months, but not on the amount of the expenditure. Assuming the statistical models determining labour supply and durables demand to be the objectives of estimation, then the former is an example of what have come to be known as limited dependent variable (LDV) models, while the latter is a member of the class of qualitative dependent variable (QDV) models. Tobin's pioneering 1957 paper on durables demand is the forerunner of LDV estimation in economics. Using data on 735 micro spending units, Tobin modelled the ratio of durables expenditure to disposable income; for 183 of these spending units, no durables were purchased during the time period of interest and a "corner solution" had to be treated. As is well known, the solution to this problem was the genesis of the Tobit estimator, which will be discussed below. Note that had Tobin only data on whether or not there was some durable puchased rather than on the actual amount, a QDV model (such as binary probit or logit) would have been the appropriate approach.

In this article we discuss the theory and practice of econometric estimation of recreational participation models. It is seen that, owing to the nature of the available micro data, standard econometric techniques such as ordinary least squares (OLS) will typically be inappropriate tools for the analysis of recreation participation. The available data on participation decisions, rather, are of a nature best described as qualitative or limited dependent variables. This being the case, more complicated estimation techniques are in general required in order to obtain consistent estimates of the parameters governing the participation outcomes. Maximum likelihood is the estimation method most commonly used in such analysis.

In previous empirical analysis of recreation participation (Vaughan and Russell (1982)), efforts were focused less on the subtleties of the statistical and econometric methods used than on the development of a unified framework for assessing empirically the effects of water quality changes on participation. As such, the analysis was restricted to utilizing those econometric methods that were less resource-consuming than is true of many of the more sophisticated iterative maximum likelihood techniques to be described below[1]. This strategy was followed in awareness, yet at the expense, of the possible inconsistencies resulting from ignoring such subtleties. In the present endeavour, emphasis is shifted to an evaluation of the implications of certain characteristics of the participation measures (e.g., non-negativity of some measures, discrete or grouped measures) for estimation strategy and, as a consequence, for benefit estimation.

The treatment here is necessarily brief. However, several high quality surveys are available for the reader who wishes more detailed treatments of the topics to be discussed below. The 1981 and 1984 surveys by Amemiya are excellent overviews of qualitative and limited dependent variable models, respectively, and the 1983 monograph by Maddala provides broad coverage in both these areas. The often-cited 1981 volume edited by Manski and McFadden is also an excellent survey of topics in qualitative and limited dependent variable estimation.

Some definitional preliminaries are appropriate here. First, standard practice is followed and random variables are represented in upper-case notation, their realizations in lower-case. Second, the terms "censored distribution" and "truncated distribution" will be used with considerable frequency in the sequel. The introduction to chapter 6 of Maddala (1983) provides a good heuristic explanation of censoring and truncation as they pertain to the normal econometric model. For completeness, we present two more formal explanations of these two phenomena as found in the statistical literature.

First, Kendall and Stuart (1973) describes truncation and censoring as follows, using their now-classical "target" example:

'Suppose first that the underlying variate x simply cannot be observed in part or parts of its range. For example, if x is the distance from the centre of a vertical circular target of fixed radius R on a shooting range, we can only observe x for shots actually hitting the target. If we have no knowledge of how many shots were fired at the target (say, n) we simply have to accept the m values of x observed on the target as coming from a distribution ranging from 0 to R. We then say that the distribution of x is truncated on the right at R. Similarly, if we define y in this example as the distance of a shot from the vertical line through the centre of the target, y may range from -R to +R and its distribution is doubly truncated. Similarly, we may have a variate truncated on the left (e.g. if observations below a certain value are not recorded). Generally, a variate may be multiply truncated in several parts of its range simultaneously. A truncated variate differs in no essential way from any other but it is treated separately because its distribution is generated by an underlying untruncated variable, which may be of familiar form.'

'On the other hand... suppose that we know how many shots were fired at the target. We still only observe m values of x, all between 0 and R inclusive, but we know that n-m = r further values of x exists, and that these will exceed R. In other words, we have observed the first m order-statistics $x_{(1)},\ldots,x_{(m)}$ in a sample of size n.

The sample of x is now said to be censored on the right at R. (Censoring is a property of the sample whereas truncation is a property of the distribution.) Similarly, we may have censoring on the left (e.g. in measuring the response to a certain stimulus, a certain minimum response may be necessary in order that measurement is possible at all) and double censoring, where the lowest r_1 and the highest r_2 of a sample of size n are not observed, only the $m=n-(r_1+r_2)$ being available for estimation purposes.' (Kendall and Stuart (1973), p.541).

A second explanation is that of Johnson and Kotz (1969), who note that:

'There is clearly a close analogy between censoring and truncation, but the differences are evident. Censoring modifies the selection of the random variables; truncation directly modifies the distribution. In other words, censoring is an agreement to ignore observed values because they are larger (or samller) than a certain number of other observed values, while truncation is omission of values outside predetermined, fixed, limits.' (Johnson and Kotz (1969), p.27).

It should also be noted at the outset that the following discussion of estimation techniques for quantitative dependent variables (e.g. measures like time, days, number of trips, etc.) does not deal with the system or multi-activity structure of recreation participation models. That is, one can easily conceive of a system of recreation participation models (fishing, boating, swimming) analogous to more familiar systems of demand equations (food, drink, shelter, and clothing, for example) discussed in the econometrics literature and estimated by techniques such as seemingly unrelated regressions. However, although there exist systems estimation techniques for limited dependent variable models of the nature assessed below (see, e.g., Wales and Woodland (1983)), such techniques are expensive and not easily implemented. Estimation techniques for the single-equation or single-activity models discussed in this chapter are far more easily and relatively less expensively implemented, and, as such, the discussion to follow is confined to those models that can be estimated at reasonable cost.

We also elect to set aside for future research consideration of models of the sort discussed by Dubin and McFadden (1984) and Hanemann (1984), these concerned in part with situations wherein individuals select one good or activity from a set of k possible goods or activities. Although such research has potentially fruitful applications in the analysis of recreation participation decisions, full treatment is beyond the scope of this article.

The plan for the remainder of the paper is as follows. First, we briefly assess problems associated with least squares estimation of participation models. Then we turn to a discussion of some techniques that might be considered more or less appropriate for the estimation problems attendant to recreation participation analysis. Following this we turn to a discussion of prediction based on the estimation of the various models. A summary concludes the article.

II. SOME PROBLEMS WITH LEAST-SQUARES ESTIMATION OF PARTICIPATION MODELS

As we mentioned above, our object is to survey various econometric techniques for estimating recreation participation models. As will be seen throughout, these techniques are generally such that iterative (and sometimes costly) maximum likelihood methods are required in order to obtain consistent and efficient estimates of the models' parameters. Since sound econometric policy analysis depends at least in part on obtaining consistent, if not efficient, parameter estimates, the question is then begged: why is it necessary to utilize such complicated and expensive methods when simple and inexpensive least-squares algorithms abound? In a nutshell, the answer is that least-squares estimates of models of the genre we are considering will generally be biased and inconsistent. The purpose of this section is to briefly demonstrate why this is so. To this end, a brief exposition of the fundamentals of the basic linear econometric model is presented, the requirements for consistent estimation of the parameters thereof are explained, and why at least some of these requirements are unlikely to be met in the participation models to be considered is discussed. The exposition of the linear model and its properties follows that of Schmidt (1976), which is among the most lucid in published texts.

Of fundamental concern is consistent and, if possible, efficient estimation of the parameter vector β in the case where random varibles Y_i are distributed in some manner with finite mean μ_i and finite variance σ^2. Specifying $\mu_i=X_i\beta$ makes the problem nontrivial, with X_i a 1xk vector of independent variables and β a kx1 vector of unknown parameters to be estimated. Given these assumptions, we can write

$$Y_i = X_i\beta + \varepsilon_i, \tag{1}$$

where, because $E(Y_i) = X_i\beta$ and $Var(Y_i) = \sigma^2$, ε_i has mean zero and variance σ^2. The unobserved realizations of ε_i correspond to the observed realizations of Y_i, y_i. It is assumed that there exist T independent observations on (Y_i, X_i).

The model described satisfies full ideal conditions (Schmidt, p.2) when

i) X is a nonstochastic matrix of rank $k<T$, and has the property that $Q = \lim_{T\to\infty} X'X/T$ is finite and nonsingular;

ii) $\varepsilon=[\varepsilon_i]$ is distributed multivatiate $N(0,\sigma^2 I_T)$. Here X is the Txk matrix of independent variables. y will henceforth denote the Tx1 vector of the realizations y_i.

It can be demonstrated that, with or without the assumption of normality for ε, the OLS estimator of β, $\hat{\beta} = (X'X)^{-1}X'y$, is consistent:

i) $\hat{\beta} = (X'X)^{-1}X'y$

$= (X'X)^{-1}X'(X\beta+\varepsilon)$

$= \beta + (X'X)^{-1}X'\varepsilon$

$E(\hat{\beta}) = \beta + (X'X)^{-1}X'E(\varepsilon)$

$= \beta + 0$

$= \beta$, so that $\hat{\beta}$ is unbiased for β;

ii) The covariance matrix of $\hat{\beta}$ is $\sigma^2(X'X)^{-1}$ so that, with all limits taken for $T\to\infty$,

$$\begin{aligned} \lim \sigma^2 (X'X)^{-1} &= \sigma^2 \lim (X'X/T)^{-1} T^{-1} \\ &= \sigma^2 \lim (Q^{-1} T^{-1}) \\ &= 0, \end{aligned}$$

because from above Q is finite nonsingular so that its inverse exists and is finite, and σ^2 is finite;

iii) Therefore, since $\hat{\beta}$ is unbiased and its covariance matrix vanishes in the limit, $\hat{\beta}$ is consistent.

Because of its computational ease, least squares is obviously an appealing tool for model estimation. The analyst must assess whether any or all of the above conditions fail to characterize the data or model under consideration to see if least squares maintains its consistency properties. Should least squares prove inconsistent, alternative, and generally more costly, methods of estimation must be utilized in order to obtain consistent estimates of β.

As discussed in detail in the sequel, a very general characterization of quantitative participation data is that it is data bounded from below by zero, i.e. it is realized only in nonnegative quantities. Of specific concern here are measures like "amount of time spent engaged in some activity." Such measures are generally modelled econometrically as the censored or truncated counterparts of normally-distributed latent random variables Y_i^* having $E(Y_i) = X_i\beta$, $Var(Y_i) = \sigma^2$. However, if the realizations of Y_i are censored from below at zero, we have

$$E(Y_i^* | y_i > 0) = X_i\beta + \sigma\phi_i/\Phi_i, \tag{2}$$

$$E(Y_i^*) = X_i\beta\Phi_i + \sigma\phi_i,$$

where ϕ_i and Φ_i are the standard normal density and distribution functions evaluated at $(X_i\beta/\sigma)$.[2] In the truncated case, where $Pr(y_i>0) = 1$,

$$E(Y_i^*) = X_i\beta + \sigma\phi_i/\Phi_i. \tag{3}$$

When defined in terms of these expectations, the problems inherent in least squares estimation become apparent. Since $E(\sigma\phi_i/\Phi_i) \neq 0$, then $E(\varepsilon_i) \neq 0$ when ε_i is defined as the difference between either $E(Y_i)$ or $E(Y_i|y_i>0)$ and $X_i\beta$ in (2). Thus least squares regression of y on X will yield inconsistent estimates of β, given that the null error expectation assumption has been violated. Heckman (1976) is a good general discussion of such problems.

Although not all measures of interest in our analysis are cast in terms of normally-distributed, partially-observed random variables, these constitute the main realm of our inquiry. In the other cases we shall investigate, however, there are yet different characteristics of the data or statistical distributions assumed that render least squares inappropriate given the objective of consistent parameter estimation. For example, least-squares estimation strategy is generally completely inappropriate when outcomes are qualitative as no objective function of interest can be cast in terms of linear expectations functions like those above. We now turn to an assessment of various approaches to the estimation of participation models.

III. MODELS OF TRUNCATION AND CENSORING

(a) Tobit Participation models

A logical starting point in any discussion of limited dependent variable model estimation is the basic Tobit model. The nature of several of the participation measures of interest in micro data sets relating to recreation is such that Tobit estimation would seem - at least at first blush - to be a sensible approach.

Tobit estimation has been utilized in a variety of areas in applied microeconomics, ranging from labour supply (see the excellent survey by Killingsworth (1983)), to health economics (Ostro, (1983)), to commodity demands or expenditures (Tobin (1957), Pitt (1983)), and many others (see Amemiya (1984) for an extensive bibliography). The basic idea underlying Tobit estimation is that one posits the existence of (latent) random variables $Y_i^* \sim NID(X_i\beta, \sigma^2)$. In many interpretations of the Tobit model, the Y_i^* are stochastic indicators of intensity of desire for undertaking some activity. Owing to the nature of the activity, however, some realizations of the Y_i^* are censored while for the others, the intensities are mapped directly into actual undertakings of the activity. Some threshold, in effect, is crossed such that the activities are actually undertaken. For example, the fundamental idea behind Tobin's seminal paper is that the Y_i^* represent intensities of desire to purchase consumer durables. When certain (assumed known) thresholds are crossed, these intensities become actual purchases. In most applied areas, the thresholds are zero, so that the mappings from intensities into undertaken activites can be looked at as occuring when the realization of the Y_i^* occur in the interior of commodity space. Otherwise, corner solutions obtain (for one discussion of estimation in the Kuhn-Tucker/corner-solution/Tobit context, see Wales and Woodland (1983)).

Assuming, then, that the thresholds are known and constant across individuals, the basic Tobit model can be described by (4):

$$y_i^* \sim NID(X_i\beta,\sigma^2)$$

$$y_i = \max(C,y_i^*). \tag{4}$$

Setting C = 0 gives the model we shall discuss in the sequel. Letting Ω_0 signify the index set for observations for which $\max(0,y_i^*) = 0$, and Ω_1 be the index set for observations for which $\max(0,y_i^*) > 0$, then the likelihood function for the Tobit model described here is

$$L = \prod_{i\varepsilon\Omega_0}(1-\Phi(\frac{X_i\beta}{\sigma})) \prod_{i\varepsilon\Omega_1} (\phi(\frac{y_i-X_i\beta}{\sigma})/\sigma), \tag{5}$$

where Φ is the standard normal distribution function and $\phi(Z) = d\Phi(Z)/dZ$. In log form (5) is

$$\ell = \sum_{i\varepsilon\Omega_0} \ln(1-\Phi_i) - |\Omega_1|\ln\sigma - \sum_{i\varepsilon\Omega_1}\ln\phi_i \tag{6}$$

where $|.|$ denotes cardinality and where terms not involving (β,σ) are dropped.

The first-order conditions for maximizing ℓ are the $(k + 1)$ equations

$$\partial\ell/\partial\beta = \sum_{i\varepsilon\Omega_0} (-\lambda_i/\sigma)X_i' + \sum_{i\varepsilon\Omega_1} (y_i-X_i\beta)X_i'/\sigma^2 = 0$$

$$\partial \ell / \partial \sigma = \sum_{i \epsilon \Omega_0} \lambda_i (X_i \beta)/\sigma^2 + \sum_{i \epsilon \Omega_1} ((y_i - X_i \beta)^2 - \sigma^2)/\sigma^3 = 0, \quad (7)$$

where $\lambda_i = \phi_i/(1-\Phi_i)$. Using terms in these equations, the method of Berndt-Hall-Hall-Hausman (1974) among others, can be used for optimization, and statistical inference is based on the asymptotic t-tests generated by utilizing $[\sum_{i=1}^{N}(\ell_i \ell_i')]^{-1}$ as the estimate of $\text{cov}(\hat{\beta})$ (ℓ_i is the i-th term of $[(\partial \ell/\partial \beta)', [\partial \ell/\partial \sigma)]')$.[3]

Several characteristics of the Tobit model are noteworthy. First, as Amemiya (1984) points out, the likelihood function (5) can be rewritten as

$$L = [\prod_{i \epsilon \Omega_0}(1-\Phi_i) \prod_{i \epsilon \Omega_1} \Phi_i] \; [\prod_{i \epsilon \Omega_1}(\phi_i/\Phi_i \sigma)] \quad (8)$$

Written in this form, the likelihood function of the Tobit model can be viewed as the product of the likelihood functions of a probit model with parameter vector $\alpha = (\beta/\sigma)$ (first brackets) and a truncated-at-zero normal distribution with parameters (β,σ) and $E(Y_i) = X_i \beta + \sigma \phi_i/\Phi_i$ (second brackets). As such, separate maximization subject to the restrictions that the probit parameter vector be a positive scalar multiple (specifically $1/\sigma$) of the parameter vector of the truncated normal model yields the Tobit model. The probit component can, of course, be viewed as the model of whether or not the threshold is crossed, while the truncated normal component models the conditional phenomenon of the magnitude of the activity given that the activity is undertaken.

It is certainly reasonable to consider the possibility that the parameter restrictions described in the preceeding paragraph are in fact invalid indicating, therefore, that the model of threshold crossing is not as intimately related to the conditional model of the magnitude of the undertaken activity as is implied by the Tobit model. In the context of recreation participation, this could mean that the decision about whether or not to engage in some form of water-based activity is governed by a set of parameters different than that determining the amount of participation undertaken given that some participation occurs. We discuss such issues in greater detail later on.

Another characteristic of the Tobit model that merits discussion is the fact that the parameters estimated under the assumptions of the Tobit model are in general nonrobust to departures from many of the underlying assumptions. That is, violation in the data of some of the properties implied when the likelihood function is written in the form (5) will lead to inconsistent estimates of the parameters (β, σ). This phenomenon, which is not uncommon in many types of models that are estimated by means of maximum likelihood, stands in contrast to more familiar formulations such as OLS and nonlinear least squares where, in spite of a variety of departures from the assumed ideal structure of the error terms, one can still obtain consistent estimates of the structural parameters.

Two of the most often discussed violations that bode dire consequences for Tobit parameter estimates are violations of the NID assumption: first, that the error variances are nonconstant across observations, and second, that the error structure, though perhaps homoscedastic, is nonnormal. Note that normal, homoscedastic errors are implied when writing the likelihood function in the form (5). The results of several studies, summarized by Amemiya (1984). indicate that under either type of departure, the maximum likelihood Tobit parameter estimates are inconsistent.

It is, of course, generally unknown ex ante whether or not the data being analyzed are characterized by the ideal properties. It then becomes essential to determine whether there exist such violations if one is to have some degree of confidence in the consistency properties of the Tobit parameter estimates. We describe briefly two tests that have been proposed to detect departures from the Tobit "ideal" conditions. The first test is for heteroscedasticity of a given form, while the second is a more general test for misspecification.

The idea behind the test for heteroscedasticity, proposed by Smith and Maddala (1983), can be motivated as follows. The (k+1)-st first order condition of the Tobit ML model, $\partial\ell/\partial\sigma=0$, can trivially be rewritten $(\partial\ell/\partial\sigma)(\partial\sigma/\partial\theta)=0$ if we assume that $\sigma=\sigma(\theta)=\theta$, where the dimensionality of θ is one, and that $\partial\sigma/\partial\theta=1$. In general, however, it is possible that $\dim(\theta)>1$ and that σ follows a perhaps complicated parametric relationship that can vary across observations. In what follows, we consider the case where $\sigma_i = Z_i\theta = \theta_0 + Z_{i1}\theta_1$, where Z_i is some proper or improper subset of X_i. Homoscedasticity implies $\theta_1 = 0$.

In this context, the nature of the inconsistency of the Tobit estimates under heteroscedasticity is easily seen. In assuming homoscedasticity, the analyst estimates the parameters (β,σ) based on the (k+1) likelihood equations (7). Given heteroscedasticity of the above form, not only do these equations depend on θ_1, as well as (β,θ_0), but the p likelihood equations $(\partial\ell/\partial\sigma)(\partial\sigma/\partial\theta_1) = 0$, where $p = \dim(\theta_1)$, are entirely omitted from estimation. Given this, the inconsistency is hardly surprising.

Smith and Maddala propose a simple test for heteroscedasticity when the $\sigma_i = Z_i\theta$ hypothesis seems a reasonable alternative to the $\sigma_i=\theta_0$ (homoscedasticity) hypothesis. The test is simply to base estimation on the (k+p+1) likelihood equations

$$(\partial \ell/\partial \beta) = 0$$

$$(\partial \ell/\partial \theta_0) = 0 \qquad (9)$$

$$(\partial \ell/\partial \theta_1) = 0$$

The test for heteroscedasticity, then, is a likelihood ratio test based on the restriction $\theta_1 = 0$. One can also examine the asymptotic t-statistics on the individual elements of θ_1 to see if any of the hypotheses $\theta_{1m} = 0$, $m = 1,\ldots,p$, can be rejected.

A second and more general test for misspecification of the Tobit model is that proposed by Nelson (1981). Because of its generality, it is both valuable and non-illustrative. It is valuable because the analyst need not specify the nature of the suspected departure from the Tobit assumptions. It is non-illustrative because, as an omnibus test, should misspecification be indicated the source thereof is not made apparent. The test in principle can detect problems such as errors in measurement on the dependent variable (Stapleton and Young (1984)), non-normality, and heteroscedasticity, but can also detect other phenomena such as omitted variables. As such, a significant Nelson statistic is important, but still leaves the researcher in somewhat of a quandary.

The Nelson test is a Hausman (1978) test based on moment estimators of functions of the model's parameters which are consistent but inefficient under general conditions. The details are fairly complicated though not difficult and the reader is referred to Nelson's work for their development. In the discussion of truncated models below, an extension of Nelson's test is proposed, and some details of the basic Nelson procedure are discussed in that development.

(b) Cragg-Class Participation Models

In a 1971 paper, Cragg proposed a set of models for situations that can be depicted as follows. An economic agent makes two (simultaneous) decisions. A dichotomous decision is made about whether or not to engage in some activity. Conditional on an affirmative for this decision, a decision is made regarding how much of the activity to pursue. The activities can be construed in the broadest of terms: expenditures, quantities demanded or supplied, or the amount of time spent in recreation participation. Such models have come to be known as hurdles models, that is, conditional on some hurdle being crossed, a decision is made about some magnitude of interest. Although these decision processes might in some cases seem logically to be ordered in a temporal manner, the statistical properties of the model abstract from any temporal considerations, the quantity decision being described in terms of conditional densities.

Cragg proposed several models. However, because of the nature of the present study, only two members of this set will concern us here, these being the formulations wherein the quantity or second-stage decisionis defined only on the positive reals. This is in obvious reference to ideas like "given that an individual participated in activity x, how much time was spent engaging in the activity." Although Cragg's other formulations are not uninteresting, their discussion is omitted for economy of space.

For notational ease, we will assume that the same vector of independent variables, X_i, influences both the first-and second-stage decisions. This is a completely innocuous assumption, however, as elements of parameter vectors can be restricted equal to zero to accommodate more general cases. Regardless of the specification of the second-stage or conditional decision, the first-stage is described by a binary probit model, i.e. the existence of latent random variables $Y^*_{i1} \sim N(X_i\beta_1, \sigma_1^2)$ is posited. Only the signs of the realizations are recorded, however, and are codified according to

$$y_{i1} = 1, \; y^*_{i1} \geq 0 \qquad (10)$$
$$= 0, \; y^*_{i1} < 0$$

Because of this codification scheme, there is no information about the scale of the random variables Y^*_{i1} (i.e. the mappings of y^*_{i1} into y_{i1} are unaffected by transformations of Y^*_{i1} of the form θY^*_{i1} for $\theta > 0$). Therefore, some normalization is required, the most common being $\sigma_1 = 1$. This formulation gives rise to Cragg's equation (7), where, with obvious change from Cragg's notation, we specify

$$\Pr(y_{i1} = 1) = \Phi(X_i\beta_1)$$
$$\Pr(y_{i1} = 0) = \Phi(-X_i\beta_1), \qquad (11)$$

where Φ is the standard normal distribution function.

For strictly positve second-stage quantity realizations, Cragg proposes two alternative formulations. Both are based on the specification of the conditional densities for random variables Y_{i2} given that the activity is in fact undertaken.

The first formulation, described by Cragg's equation (9), is one where the conditional density for the realizations of the Y_{i2} is truncated-normal, with the truncation point at zero. Thus we have

$$g(y_{i2}|y_{i1}=1) = \phi(\frac{y_{i2}-X_i\beta_2}{\sigma})/\sigma\Phi(\frac{X_i\beta_2}{\sigma}), \qquad y_{i2} > 0 \qquad (12)$$

$$= 0 , \qquad \text{otherwise}$$

where ϕ and Φ are the standard normal density and distribution functions. With obvious notational change, Cragg's equation (9), the (unconditional) likelihood of the positive realizations, can be written as

$$f(y_{i2}) = g(y_{i2}|y_{i1}=1)Pr(y_{i1}=1) =$$

$$\phi(\frac{y_{i2} - X_i\beta_2}{\sigma})\Phi(X_i\beta_1)/\sigma\Phi(\frac{X_i\beta_2}{\sigma}) \qquad (13)$$

for $y_{i2} > 0$. Therefore, the likelihood function of the Cragg equations (7)-(9) model is

$$L = \prod_{i\varepsilon\Omega_0}\Phi(-X_i\beta)\prod_{i\varepsilon\Omega_1}\phi(\frac{y_{i2}-X_i\beta}{\sigma})\ \Phi(X_i\beta_1)/\sigma\Phi(\frac{X_i\beta_2}{\sigma}) \qquad (14)$$

where Ω_0 is the index set for i such that $y_{i1} = 0$ and Ω_1 is the index set for $y_{i1} = 1$. Written in log form,

$$\ell = \sum_{i\varepsilon\Omega_0} \ln(1-\Phi(X_i\beta_1)) + \sum_{i\varepsilon\Omega_1}(\ln\phi(\frac{y_{i2}-X_i\beta_2}{\sigma}) + \ln\Phi(X_i\beta_1)$$

$$- \ln\sigma - \ln\Phi(\frac{X_i\beta_2}{\sigma})). \tag{15}$$

In the form (15), it is straightforward to see that maximization of ℓ is fully equivalent to the two-stage maximization problem:

1) Probit estimation of the parameter vector β_1 via maximization of

$$\ell_1 = \sum_{i\varepsilon\Omega_0} (\ln(1-\Phi(X_i\beta_i)) + \sum_{i\varepsilon\Omega_1} \ln\Phi(X_i\beta_1); \tag{16}$$

2) Truncated-normal estimation of the parameters (β_2, σ) via maximization of

$$\ell_2 = \sum_{i\varepsilon\Omega_1}(\ln\phi(\frac{y_{i2}-X_i\beta_2}{\sigma}) - \ln\sigma - \ln\Phi(\frac{X_i\beta_2}{\sigma})). \tag{17}$$

Techniques for probit estimation are well known. Methods for estimating the truncated-normal model are straightforward, though not so well known, and are discussed in depth in the next subsection. Because of the complexity of the log likelihood (15), estimation in this two-stage fashion is likely to be somewhat easier than attempting to maximize (15) with respect to the (2k+1) parameters $(\beta_1, \beta_2, \sigma)$.

Cragg's second formulation again depends on the probit first-stage model, but the conditional density of the positive realization is respecified. Instead of assuming that the conditional density of the positive realizations of Y_{i2} is truncated-normal, the model is now formulated such that the logarithms of the y_{i2} are normal, i.e. conditional on $y_{i1}=0$, $\log(y_{i2}) \sim N(X_{i2},\beta_2\sigma^2)$. This is Cragg's equation (10). The conditional density for the $i\varepsilon\Omega_1$ is

$$h(y_{i2}|y_{i1}=1) = (y_{i2}\sigma)^{-1}\phi(\frac{\log(y_{i2})-X_i\beta_2}{\sigma}) \tag{18}$$

where the term $(y_{i2})^{-1}$ is the Jacobian of the transformation from y_{i2} to $\log(y_{i2})$. Therefore, the likelihood for the $i\varepsilon\Omega_1$, which is Cragg's equation (11), is

$$f(y_{i2}) = h(y_{i2}|y_{i1}=1)\Pr(y_{i1}=1)$$

$$= (y_{i2}\sigma)^{-1}\phi(\frac{\log(y_{i2})-X_i\beta_2}{\sigma})\Phi(X_i\beta_1) \tag{19}$$

The likelihood function for the entire sample is

$$L = \prod_{i\varepsilon\Omega_0} \Phi(-X_i\beta_1) \prod_{i\varepsilon\Omega_1} (y_{i2}\sigma)^{-1}\phi(\frac{\log(y_{i2})-X_i\beta_2}{\sigma})\Phi(X_i\beta_1) \tag{20}$$

In log form,

$$\ell = \sum_{i\varepsilon\Omega_0} \ln(1-\Phi(X_i\beta_1)) + \sum_{i\varepsilon\Omega_1}(\ln\phi(\frac{\log(y_{i2}-X_i\beta_2}{\sigma})$$

$$+ \ln\Phi(X_i\beta_1) - \ln y_{i2} - \ln\sigma) \tag{21}$$

As in the equations (7)-(9) model, the equations (7) - (11) model can be estimated in two stages:

1) Probit estimation of β_1 as above;
2) OLS estimation of (β_2,σ) using the log transform of the y_{i2} as dependent variables and X_i as the independent variables. This is perhaps surprising, but results because the terms in (21) involving (β_2,σ)

are identical to those of the likelihood function of the familiar normal linear model.

Because of the simplicity of this two-stage approach, estimation in such a framework is obviously appealing. Duan, et.al. (1983) have proposed the Cragg (7) - (11) model to estimate medical expenditures: individuals either have or do not have medical expenses, and given that they have medical expenses, the conditional density of the expenditures is lognormal, $\log(Y_{i2}) \sim N(X_i\beta_2, \sigma^2)$. However, the Duan, et.al. model likelihood function (their equation 3.7) is incorrect. They omit the multiplicative term $(1/y_{i2})$ in the density for the positive terms, this as mentioned above being the Jacobian of the transformation from y_{i2} to $\log(y_{i2})$. Cragg correctly incorporates this in his equation (11). The values of the parameters that maximize the log-likelihood function do not depend on this transform, although the value of the log-likelihood function itself does, of course, depend on the transform.

(c) Truncated-normal Estimation

As described above, estimation of the truncated-normal model is the relevant second step in estimating the Cragg (7) - (9) model where the positive observations are assumed to follow a truncated-from-below normal distribution. Although there are several variants of the truncated normal - truncated-from-below, truncated-from-above, doubly-truncated; constant or nonconstant point(s) of truncation - the discussion here will concentrate on the case of the truncated-from-below distribution where the point of truncation is constant across observations and is assumed to be zero. The results easily generalize, however, and for a discussion of the statistical properties of the truncated normal distribution in the most general case, the reader is referred to Johnson and Kotz (1970, pp.81-87).

It should be noted that interest in the truncated normal should not be confined to the role it plays in the Cragg model. The distribution is indeed useful in many empirical situations. Hurd (1979) notes that

'(e)stimation based on only positive y's comes about very naturally in a number of kinds of studies. For example, in many labour supply studies one of the right-hand variables, the wage rate, is only observed when the left-hand variable, labour supply, is positive. Imputing the unobserved wage rates causes a number of complications that can be avoided by discarding those observations for which labour supply is zero. Another example is a demand study where the price is not known unless a purchase is made.' (Hurd, 1979, p.248).

Furthermore, as we will see below, estimation of the truncated normal model on the nonlimit observations of a data set in which data on both limit and nonlimit observations available, in conjunction with an informal test suggested by Olsen (1980), can give some indication as to whether a Tobit model estimated on all observations is an appropriate specification.

For our purposes, the likelihood function of the truncated normal can be constructed as follows. We assume the existence of $T_1 + T_2$ realizations of random variables Y_i~NID $(X_i\beta,\sigma^2)$. However, for whatever reasons, only the positive realization of the Y_i are used in the analysis, these assumed to number T_1. Given these assumptions, the likelihood function is

$$L = \prod_{i=1}^{T_1}(\phi_i/\sigma\Phi_i) \tag{22}$$

where ϕ_i is the standard normal density evaluated at $((y_i - X_i\beta)/\sigma)$, and Φ_i is the standard normal distribution function evaluated at $(X_i\beta/\sigma)$ which serves as the normalizing factor of the truncated density. The log-likelihood function (suppressing terms not depending on (β,σ)) is

$$\ell = \sum_{i=1}^{T_1} -.5((y_i - X_i\beta)/\sigma)^2 - \log\sigma - \log\Phi(\frac{X_i}{\sigma}) \qquad (23)$$

Estimation is by means of maximum likelihood. The first-order conditions for a maximum of ℓ are

$$\partial\ell/\partial\beta = \sum_{i=1}^{T_1}[\frac{-\phi_i}{\sigma\Phi_i} + (\frac{y_i - X_i\beta}{\sigma^2})]\ X_i' = 0$$

$$\partial\ell/\partial\sigma = \sum_{i=1}^{T_1}(\frac{\phi_i}{\Phi_1})(\frac{X_i\beta}{\sigma^2}) - \frac{1}{\sigma} + \frac{(y_i - X_i\beta)^2}{\sigma^3} \qquad (24)$$

The second derivatives are complicated and will not be presented here. Experience has demonstrated that the Berndt-Hall-Hall-Hausman first derivative approach for optimization works rather well.

In the case of the truncated-normal, like most all other limited dependent variable models, ordinary least squares estimation of the parameters (β,σ) yields biased and inconsistent estimates. However, in the case of the truncated normal, Olsen (1980) has shown how the OLS estimates can be used fruitfully to generate estimates of (β,σ) that, while inconsistent, can provide remarkably good approximations to the maximum likelihood estimates (our experience in other areas is consistent with Olsen's finding) and, as such, serve as excellent starting values for maximum likelihood estimation algorithms.

Olsen's method relies on a method of moments technique

whereby the moments (specifically the mean and variance) of the empirical incomplete distribution that of the positive y_i, are related to the moments of the complete distribution via formulae developed by Pearson and Lee (1908). Extending the Pearson-Lee methodology to the multiple regression case, Olsen demonstrates that the least squares slope coefficients differ from the true slope coefficients by a common factor, and he presents in tabular form the multiplicative correction factors needed to transform the OLS estimates of the slope, intercept, and standard error parameters (based on data from the incomplete distribution) to the corresponding complete distribution estimates. In practice, we have fitted polynomial functions of the third degree to Olsen's tabled data so that the transformations are facilitated.

Olsen also presents the multipliers for transforming (mean/standard error) ratio estimated by OLS on the incomplete distribution to the corresponding ratio of the complete distribution, (μ/σ). Olsen notes that $\Phi(\mu/\sigma)$, where Φ is the standard normal cumulative distribution, should give an idea of the expected ratio of nontruncated to total observations. Therefore, if one is considering Tobit estimation of the parameters of a censored distribution, it should hold that the $\Phi(\mu/\sigma)$ based on the (μ/σ) estimated using Olsen's method and treating the nonlimit observations as truncated normal should accord approximately with the ratio of noncensored to total observations. There is no formal test to assess how closely these should accord however. Olsen suggests that a disagreement here could well indicate that the Tobit is an inappropriate specification.

As in the case in the censored normal model discussed

earlier, misspecification of the truncated-normal model has serious consequences for the consistency of maximum likelihood estimates. We describe briefly a general test for such misspecification.

Use of the Hausman (1978) specification test has become increasingly popular. Nelson (1981) has proposed a version of the test for misspecification of the censored-normal (Tobit) model. We here follow closely Nelson's development and adapt his test to the case where the model of interest is truncated-normal.

For the complete distribution where random variables $Y_i \sim N(X_i\beta, \sigma^2)$, the truncated-from-below normal density is defined by

$$f(y_i|y_i>0) = f(y_i) = \phi((y_i - X_i\beta)/\sigma)/\sigma\Phi(X_i\beta/\sigma), \quad y_i>0$$
$$= 0 \ , \quad \text{otherwise} \tag{25}$$

where ϕ and Φ are the standard normal density and distribution functions, and the point of truncation is assumed to be zero. As in the case of the censored-normal model, if the maintained hypotheses (e.g. correctly measured dependent variables, homoscedasticity normality) are violated, inconsistent estimates of the parameters (β, σ) will generally result if estimation is by maximum likelihood based on (25). This is, of course, analogous to the problems inherent when the censored-normal is misspecfied.

The basic idea underlying the Nelson test is that there exist functions of the parameters of the model that under a large variety of circumstances are robust against misspecification of the underlying density. Such functions serve as the "consistent-inefficient" component of the Hausman test. The "inconsistent-efficient" component is the MLE of the model's parameters or (because of ML invariance properties (see Cox and Hinkley (1974, p.287)), functions thereof estimated under the null hypothesis of no misspecification.

Because the censored- and truncated-normal densities are intimately related, we, like Nelson, use estimates of $E(T^{-1}X'Y)$ as the basis for the test. Here, X is the Txk matrix of independent variables, and Y is the Tx1 vector having typical element Y_i. Our development follows that of Nelson on pages 1327 and 1328 of his paper.

For the truncated-normal model as defined by (25) (see Johnson and Kotz (1970), pp.81-87) we have:

$$E(Y_i) = X_i\beta + \sigma\phi(X_i\beta/\sigma)/\Phi(X_i\beta/\sigma) \tag{26}$$

$$E(Y_i^2) = (X_i\beta)^2 + \sigma^2 + (X_i\beta)\sigma\phi(X_i\beta/\sigma)/\Phi(X_i\beta/\sigma) \tag{27}$$

$$E_{XY} = E(T^{-1}X'Y) = T^{-1}(X'X\beta + \sigma X'\lambda) \tag{28}$$

where λ is the Tx1 vector with typical element (ϕ_i/Φ_i). The method of moments estimator of $E(T^{-1}X'Y)$ is $T^{-1}X'y$. Clearly, the limiting variance of $T^{.5}(T^{-1}X'y)$ is

$$V_1 = T^{-1}X'V_YX, \tag{29}$$

where V_Y is the TxT diagonal matrix with typical element $(E(Y_i^2)-E^2(Y_i))$ as defined in (26) and (27).

The efficient estimator of $E(T^{-1}X'Y)$, denoted $\hat{E}_{XY}$, is obtained by evaluating (28) at $(\hat{\beta},\hat{\sigma})$ ("^" signifies a MLE). the limiting variance of $\hat{E}_{XY}$ is obtained via the analog to the approximation of Nelson's equation (3.9) and is

$$V_0 = T^{-2}[X'X|X'\lambda]C(\hat{\beta},\hat{\sigma})[\frac{X'X}{\lambda'X}] \tag{30}$$

evaluated at $(\hat{\beta},\hat{\sigma})$. It is estimated as $\hat{V}_0$ by evaluating λ at $(\hat{\beta},\hat{\sigma})$. $C(.) = TI(.)^{-1}$ where I is the estimated information matrix.

The test statistic is

$$m = T[T^{-1}X'y - \hat{E}_{XY}]'[\hat{V}_1 - \hat{V}_0]^{-1}[T^{-1}X'y - \hat{E}_{XY}], \tag{31}$$

where $\hat{V}_1$ is (29) evaluated at $(\hat{\beta},\hat{\sigma})$. Under the null hypothesis of no misspecification, $m \sim \chi^2_{(k)}$.

(d) Heckman's Approach: Sample Selection Bias

Currently, the most prevalent limited dependent variable estimation technique is the sample selection bias model, attributable largely to Heckman (1976, 1979). The model has a number of applications (see Heckman's 1976 article in particular), and is quite easy to estimate. Because it is so well-known, we will only provide a sketch of the details. The following sub-section, which contrasts and compares the Tobit, Cragg and Heckman models, sheds some more light on subtleties of Heckman's formulation.

Heckman considers the following two-equation model:

$$y_{i1} = X_i\beta_1 + \varepsilon_{i1} \tag{32}$$

$$y^*_{i2} = X_i\beta_2 + \varepsilon_{i2} \tag{33}$$

It is assumed that ε_{i1} and ε_{i2} are distributed joint normal, with marginal densities $N(0, \sigma_1^2)$ and $N(0, \sigma_2^2)$ respectively, and covariance σ_{12}. It can be further assumed that the realizations y_{i2}^* are unobserved. Assumed available are discrete sign indicators y_{i2} which are mapped as

$$\begin{aligned} y_{i2} &= 1, \; y_{i2}^* > 0 \\ &= 0, \; y_{i2}^* \leq 0. \end{aligned} \tag{34}$$

In Heckman's model, the realizations y_{i1} are available to the analyst only when $y_{i2}^* > 0$, i.e. when $y_{i2} = 1$.

A concrete sample is where (32) is a model determining market wage rate (or its log) by a linear function of X_i and random error and where (33) is a model determining hours of labour supplied in the market. It is assumed that either hours of labour supplied or a discrete binary indicator of whether or not any hours were supplied is available for all observations. However, because market wage rates are only observed for individuals for whom the market wage rate exceeds the reservation wage at zero hours, data on the y_{i1} are available only when $y_{i2}^* > 0$ ($y_{i2} = 1$).

Heckman then considers the expectation $E(Y_{i1}|y_{i2} = 1)$, which can be written as

$$E(Y_{i1}|y_{i2} = 1) = X_i\beta_1 + E(\varepsilon_{i1}|y_{i2} = 1). \tag{35}$$

If one considers least-squares estimation of (35), the question is: Do there obtain consistent estimates of ${}_1$ when y_{i1} is regressed on X_i for those i for whom $y_{i2}=1$? Basically the issue is whether the expectation $E(\varepsilon_{i1}|y_{i2} = 1)$ is null. In general, and thus as the core of the sample selection bias problem, the answer is "no". Based on well-known formulae, it holds that

$$E(\varepsilon_{i1}|y_{i2} = 1) = \sigma_{12}\phi_i/\sigma_2(1-\Phi_i), \tag{36}$$

where ϕ_i is the standard normal density evaluated at $(X_i\beta_2/\sigma_2)$ and Φ_i is the distribution function evaluated at the same point. Because σ_{12} is in general non zero and since ϕ_i, $(1-\Phi_i)$, and σ_2 are all positive, then least squares estimation of (35) will be based on an expectation function with nonnull disturbance expection, and will therefore yield inconsistent estimates of β_1.

Heckman's suggested procedure in this situation is as follows. Estimate on the entire sample a probit model for the discrete indicator representation of the model (33). This yields a consistent estimate of the parameter vector (β_2/σ_2) from which consistent estimates of $\lambda_i = \phi_i/(1-\Phi_i)$ are constructed. Form the Tx(k+1) matrix $Z = [X|\Lambda]$, where Λ is a Tx1 vector with typical element λ_i, and regress y_i on $[x_i, \lambda_i]$. This procedure yields consistent estimates of the parameters β_1 and (σ_{12}/σ_2), having effectively solved the omitted variables problem by using a consistent estimate of $E(\varepsilon_{i1}|y_{i2} = 1)$ as a regressor.

(e) Tobin, Cragg and Heckman: A Digression

As there are some similarities between and among the models described above and identified for expositional parsimony as the models of Tobin, Cragg and Heckman, it is probably appropriate to summarize their similarities and differences and in so doing to elucidate the circumstances in which each model is more or less appropriate. (The discussion of Cragg's model here is the Cragg (7) - (9), i.e. probit/truncated-normal, model as that version is most similar to the others discussed here.)

First to note is that the Tobit model results as a restricted version of both the Cragg and the Heckman models. The reason for this is purely mechanical, however, and should not be taken to imply that the Cragg and Heckman models are in general identical. As we shall see below, these models are structurally somewhat different.

To see that the Cragg model reduces to the Tobit, the Cragg log-likelihood function can be written (following Lin and Schmidt (LS) (1984)) as

$$\ell = \sum_{i\varepsilon\Omega_0} \ln\Phi(-X_i\beta_1) + \sum_{i\varepsilon\Omega_1}[\ln\Phi(X_i\beta_1) - \ln\Phi(\frac{X_i\beta_2}{\sigma}) - (1/2\ln(2\pi\sigma^2) - (1/2\sigma^2)(y_i - X_i\beta_2)^2] \quad (37)$$

If the restriction $\beta_1 = \beta_2/\sigma$ is imposed, then the first two terms in the square brackets cancel and (37) is easily seen to be identical to (6) with β in (6) replaced by β_2 from (37). The upshot of such parameter restrictions is hardly trivial, however. As specified, and discussed briefly earlier, the Tobit model is fairly restrictive in its behavioural implications, as the parameter vector that governs the probability of observing an above-threshold realization of the dependent variable is the same as that governing the quantity realization of the dependent variable given that it is above the threshold. Owing to the implications of such restrictions, LS have concluded that "...the Tobit model is typically used with more faith than it warrants..." and have developed a test (which we discuss below) for the appropriateness of the $\beta_1 = \beta_2/\sigma$ restriction of the Cragg model that is implied by the Tobit specification. The following excerpt from LS provides a particularly cogent summary description of the appropriateness of the restricted (Tobit) versus the unrestricted versions of the Cragg model:

(I)n the Tobit model any variable which increases the

probability of a non-zero value must also increase the mean of the positive values; a positive element of β means that an increase in the corresponding variable (element of X_i) increases both $Pr(y_1>0)$ and $E(y_1|>0)$. This is not always reasonable. As an example, consider a hypothetical sample of buildings, and suppose that we wish to analyze the dependent variables "loss due to fire", during some time period. Since this is often zero but otherwise positive, the Tobit model might be an obvious choice. However, it is not hard to imagine that newer (and more valuable) buildings might be less likely to have fires, but might have greater average losses when a fire did occur. The Tobit model can not accommodate this possibility. Another problem with the Tobit model is that it links the shape of the distribution of the positive observations and the probability of a positive observation. For rare events (like fires), the shape of the distribution of the positive observations would have to resemble the extreme upper tail of a normal, which would imply a continuous and faster than exponential decline in density as one moved away from zero. Conversely, when zero occurs less than half of the time, the Tobit model necessarily implies a non-zero mode for the non-zero obervations.

Cragg's model avoids both of the above problems with the Tobit model. A reasonably strong case can be made for it as a general alternative to the Tobit model, for analysis of data sets to which Tobit is typically applied - namely, data sets in which zero is a common (and meaningful) value of the dependent variable, and the non-zero observations are all positive. The distribution of such a dependent variable is characterized by the probability that it equals zero and by the (conditional) distribution of the positive observations, both of which Cragg's model parameterizes in a general way. (LS, pp.174-175).

Turning now the Heckman's formulation, his two-equation model is seen to reduce to the Tobit model as follows. Recall that the model can be written (with notational changes obvious) as

$$y_{i1} = X_i \beta_1 + \varepsilon_{i1}$$
$$y^*_{i2} = X_i \beta_2 + \varepsilon_{i2}. \tag{38}$$

Y^*_{i2} is a latent variable, however, and only a discrete (0,1) sign indicator of its realization y_{i2} is available. y_{i1} is observed only when $y_{i2} = 1$. Letting $\beta_1=\beta_2$ and $\varepsilon_{i1}=\varepsilon_{i2}$ (i.e. the error structure is univariate rather than bivariate), then the Heckman model is the standard Tobit model. The logic is that when these restrictions are imposed in the Heckman two-equation model, the remaining single equation plays both the censoring and the determination-of-intensity roles. Since the censoring occurs as a result of a non-positive realization of the random variable Y^*_{i2}, the Tobit requirement that the quantity or intensity realization be confined to the nonnegative orthant is automatically satisfied when the restriction $y_{i1}=y^*_{i2}$ (i.e. $\beta_1=\beta_2$, $\varepsilon_{i1}=\varepsilon_{i2}$) is imposed.

In sketching some of the differences between the Heckman two-equation formulation and the Cragg models with particular reference to data sets where the zero or corner solution outcomes are meaningful and where nonzero outcomes are strictly positive, LS observe that in such cases the Heckman model's assumptions are not particularly representative of the situation because in the Heckman formulation:

> ...the observed values of y_{i1} need not be positive, in the sense that the model implies a non-zero probability of observed $y_{i1} < 0$; and the unobserved y_{i1} are literally unobserved, rather than observed as equal to zero. The first of these problems can be circumvented, for example, by measuring y_{i1} in logarithms,...and the second problem is in any case fundamental. (LS p.175).

IV. MODELS FOR COUNT DATA

(a) Poisson-distributed Paticipation Days

In modeling event counts (non-negative integer data) over some time interval (t, t+dt), the Poisson distribution is commonly used. Here, a random variable Y_i follows the probability law

$$\Pr(Y_i = y) = \exp(-\lambda_i)\lambda_i^y/y!, \quad y\varepsilon\{0,1,2,...\} \tag{39}$$

$$= 0 \;, \quad \text{otherwise}$$

with $E(Y_i) = Var(Y_i) = \lambda_i$.

It happens that there exist recreational participation

data of interest that are recorded as nonnegative integers, most obviously as counts of days of participation. For any individual, such measures can, over a time interval (t,t+dt), say one year, assume only integer values in$\{0,1,2,...,365\}$. Because of the paucity of observations likely to be found at the upper (365 day) limit, we ignore the fact that these measures obey upper bounds and concentrate instead on the complications presented by the large number of individuals who in a typical random sample of the population report zero days of participation in the relevant categories.

Analogous to the familiar normal distribution where for econometric work one typically specifies $\mu_i = X_i\beta$, the λ_i parameter of the Poisson distribution can be reparameterized to admit the influence of covariates. Since for all i, $\lambda_i > 0$, a straightforward approach is to assume $\lambda_i = \exp(X_i\beta)$ and to estimate β by maximum likelihood (see Hausman, Hall, Griliches (1984), Hausman, Ostro, Wise (1983), Portney and Mullahy (1986)). This is the approach adopted here for modeling the participation-days outcomes.

One drawback of the Poisson model is the restriction that $E(Y_i) = Var(Y_i)$. Should this restriction not in fact characterize the data, the maximum likelihood estimates of the covariance matrix of $\hat{\beta}$ based on minus the inverse of the estimated Hessian will be inconsistent and t-tests based thereon would be misleading. Hausman, Ostro, and Wise circumvent this restriction by allowing for an overdispersion parameter. A different approach is used here, using an estimator of the covariance matrix that is robust against departures from the mean=variance restriction, this procedure described below.

Given T independent observations, the log-likelihood

function of the Poisson participation model can be written as

$$\ell = \sum_i -\exp(X_i\beta) + y_i X_i\beta + C, \tag{40}$$

where $\exp(X_i\beta) = \lambda_i$, y_i is the observed participation day count, and C does not depend on β. It is obvious that ℓ is concave in β. The first-order conditions of the maximization of ℓ are

$$\partial\ell/\partial\beta = \sum_i -\exp(X_i\beta)X_i' + y_i X_i' = 0 \tag{41}$$

with the maximum guaranteed by the condition

$$\partial^2\ell/\partial\beta\partial\beta' = \sum_i -(X_i'X_i)\exp(X_i\beta) \tag{42}$$

negative definite.

The maximum likelihood estimates of β obtained by maximizing (40) are consistent, but the estimate of the covariance matrix of $\hat{\beta}_{ML}$ using $[-\partial^2\ell/\partial\beta\partial\beta']^{-1}$ evaluated at $\hat{\beta}_{ML}$ will be inconsistent if the data are not in fact generated by the specified Poisson distribution.

This is most easily seen as follows. Note that the model can be equivalently cast as a nonlinear least squares regression, the i-th observation being

$$y_i = E(Y_i) + \varepsilon_i \qquad = \exp(X_i\beta) + \varepsilon_i \tag{43}$$

with $E(\varepsilon_i) = 0$. Clearly, $var(\varepsilon_i) = var(Y_i) = \exp(X_i\beta)$, so that the ε_i are heteroscedastic. If nonlinear weighted least squares is used with the weights $\exp(-X_i\beta)$ formed using consistent estimates of β, and if the data are in fact Poisson as specified, the maximum likelihood consistent estimates of β and $\mathrm{cov}(\hat{\beta})$ will obtain. (The consistency of $\hat{\beta}ML$ for β does not depend on the weighting scheme.) However, if the data are not Poisson-distributed, the estimate of $\mathrm{cov}(\hat{\beta})$ obtained in this manner will be inconsistent and asymptotic t-tests based thereon will be misleading. The case is fully analogous to the estimation of the heteroscedastic linear model which yields inconsistent covariance estimates (and, therefore, t-statistics) if the heteroscedastic nature of the error structure is either ignored or incorrectly specified.

Royall (1984) has demonstrated a method whereby estimates of $\mathrm{cov}(\hat{\beta})$ robust against misspecification of the underlying distribution of the data can be obtained for various distributions, including the Poisson, when $[-\partial^2\ell/\partial\beta\partial\beta']^{-1}$ evaluated at $\hat{\beta}_{ML}$ fails to yield a consistent estimate of $\mathrm{cov}(\hat{\beta})$. Denoting $I(\beta)$ as $[-\partial^2\ell/\partial\beta\partial\beta']$, Royall's suggestion is to estimate $\mathrm{cov}(\hat{\beta})$ as

$$I(\beta)^{-1}[\sum_i(\partial\ell_i/\partial\beta)(\partial\ell_i/\partial\beta)']I(\beta)^{-1} \tag{44}$$

where ℓ_i is the i-th observation's contribution to the log-likelihood function and where all relevant evaluations in (44) are at $\hat{\beta}_{ML}$.

(b) Geometric-distributed Participation Days

One alternative to the Poisson model for the modeling of count data is the geometric distribution. Though seemingly not as often used by econometricians as the Poisson, the geometric is a logical choice should an alternative to the Poisson be desired. Furthermore, the basic geometric specification does not suffer from the mean=variance restriction that is implied in the basic Poisson model. As will be seen below, the variance of a geometric-distributed discrete random variable is greater than its mean, although the fact that the variance depends on the mean limits somewhat the flexibility of the distribution.

Our description of the properties of the geometric distribution follows that of Johnson and Kotz (1969). First, it should be noted that the geometric is a special case of the negative binomial. Discussion is confined here to the geometric because it is computationally far more straightforward than is the general negative binomial. The geometric distribution is defined as follows:

$$\Pr(X=k) = P^k(1+P)^{-(k+1)}, \quad k = 0,1,2\ldots \tag{45}$$

$$= 0, \quad \text{otherwise}$$

with $P>0$. It holds that $E(X) = P$ and $Var(X) = P(1+P)$. As in the econometric specification of the Poisson model considered earlier, one allows the P to vary across observations as P_i, and again $P_i = \exp(X_i\beta)$ is a sensible parameterization due to the required positivity of the P_i.

Given this, the likelihood function for T independent observations can be written as

$$L = \prod_{i=1}^{T} \exp(k_i X_i \beta)(1 + \exp(X_i\beta))^{-(k_i+1)} \tag{46}$$

with loglikelihood

$$\ell = \sum_{i=1}^{T} k_i x_i \beta - (k_i+1) \log (1 + \exp(x_i \beta)) \tag{47}$$

where k_i is the observed count for the i-th observation. The ML estimate $\hat{\beta}$ satisfies

$$\partial\ell/\partial\beta = \sum_{i=1}^{T} [k_i - (k_i + 1) \exp(X_i\beta)/(1 + \exp(X_i\beta))]X_i' = 0 \tag{48}$$

The Hessian is

$$H = \partial^2\ell/\partial\beta\partial\beta' = \sum_{i=1}^{T} -(k_i + 1)[\exp(X_i\beta)/(1 + \exp(X_i\beta))^2]X_i'X_i, \tag{49}$$

which is seen by inspection to be negative definite. Because it is a fairly uncluttered expression, estimation and inference can proceed using -H as an estimate of the information matrix and $(-H)^{-1}$ as an estimate of the covariance matrix. (It might also be noted that (49) bears a strong resemblance to the Hessian of the well-known binary logit model, a point of no particular relevance insofar as the present development is concerned.)[5] Unfortunately, much like the Poisson specification, the covariance estimate thus obtained is not robust to departure from the data being in fact geometric. However, the methods proposed by Royall (1984) and described for the Poisson model can be used for the geometric distribution also. As the development is identical, the details are omitted for economy of space.

(c) Multinomial-distributed Participation Days

One type of micro data of particular interest in recreation economics is of the following nature. We observe over the course of some fixed time period (say one year) the number of times (say days) that an individual participates in (k-1) mutually exclusive recreation activities and, therefore, the number of days on which no recreational activity was undertaken which can be viewed as the k-th activity. To be concrete, the annual recreation profile for some individual who has in his/her recreation possibility set three activities (fishing day (=F), boating day (=B), swimming day (=S)) and nonparticipation (=N) days (=365-F-B-S) might look like

$$F = 12$$
$$B = 17$$
$$S = 0$$
$$N = 336$$

We also presume that the profiles of N individuals are observed.

In the analysis of such data, it is helpful to make two (fairly strong) assumptions:

(1) the data characterizing the individuals, i.e., the independent variables, are invariant over the fixed time period. That is, the characteristics of individual i, X_i, are representative of i for the entire year;

and

(2) the decision to participate in any one activity - including nonparticipation - on any given day depends neither on what activities have been undertaken on the previous days nor on expectations of recreational participation in future days. That is, the daily decisions are (statistically, at least) independent.

Note that both these assumptions are more or less questionable, with (2) perhaps being the more restrictive assumption. However, we proceed under the constraints that these assumptions impose.

Given observations on the type of recreational profiles described above, and the assumptions there set forth, it is appropriate to view the data characterizing the recreation participation of individuals as realizations of multinominal random variables (see Morey (1981) for a related discussion). Recall from discrete statistical theory that the multinominal distribution of a random variable $\underset{\sim}{Y}$ with parameters $(T; P_1, \ldots, P_k)$ can be written

$$\Pr(\underset{\sim}{Y} = \underset{\sim}{y}) = T! \prod_{j=1}^{k} (P_j^{t_j}/t_j!), \tag{50}$$

where T is the number of trials (here days), the t_j are the number of occurrences of the j-th outcome, and P_j are the probabilities that the j-th outcome will occur on a single trial. To extend the statistical model to the recreation participation measure, we consider each daily participation decision (where "participation" now refers to participation in nonrecreational activities also) as one trial from a multinominal distribution with individual-specific parameter vector for the m-th individual $(T_m; P_{1_m}, \ldots, P_{k_m})$. Assuming $T_m = T'_m = T$ for all m, m', we henceforth drop the subscripts on the T parameters. The yearly profile, then, is the 356 (by assumption independent) daily trials for each individual. The econometric objective is the estimation of the P_{j_m}, i.e. estimation of the probabilities of engaging in the k possible activities on a given day.

For computational simplicity, we proceed as follows. A logistic distribution for the daily outcome probabilities is assumed. Thus, the probability that the outcome is Z on any trial is

$$P_{Z_m} = \exp(X_m\beta_Z)/ \sum_{j\varepsilon\Omega} \exp(X_m\beta_j) \tag{51}$$

for $Z\varepsilon\Omega=\{F, B, S, N\}$. The logistic distribution assures that for all m the multinomial requirement ($\sum_{j\varepsilon\Omega} P_{j_m}=1$) is met.

Since the probabilities (51) are unique only up to a difference in parameter vectors ($\beta_j-\beta_{j'}$), some normalization is required. The normalization most convenient and easily interpreted is $\beta_N = 0$, so that β_F, β_B, and β_S are interpreted as differences between the respective activity parameter vectors and the nonparticipation parameter vector.

The objective, then, is estimation of the parameter vectors β_F, β_B, and β_S. This is, of course, fully analogous to the widely-used multinomial logit model where a single outcome from a set of mutually exclusive outcomes is considered. In fact, that case is merely a special case of the present exposition for which $T_m = 1$ for all m.

Estimation is by means of maximum likelihood. Assuming the existence of N independent profile draws from the population, the likelihood of the data as a function of the parameters is

$$L(\beta) = \prod_{m=1}^{N} \Pr(\underset{\sim}{y}_m = \underset{\sim}{y}) = \prod_{m=1}^{N} T! \prod_{j\varepsilon\Omega} (P_{j_m}^{t_{j_m}}/t_{j_m}!) \tag{52}$$

where the P_{j_m} are as defined in (51) and where Ω is the choice index set. In log form,

$$\ell(\beta) = \sum_{m=1}^{N} \sum_{j\varepsilon\Omega} t_{j_m} \log P_{j_m} + C, \tag{53}$$

where C is a constant not depending on β. Given the assumed logistic probabilities, we have

$$\ell(\beta) = \sum_{m=1}^{N} \sum_{j\varepsilon\Omega} t_{j_m} [X_m \beta_j - \log (\sum_{k\varepsilon\Omega} \exp(X_m \beta_k))] + C. \quad (54)$$

Maximization of the log-likelihood can be accomplished with only a slight modification of most existing (single-trial) multinomial logit programs[6].

V. GROUPED OR INTERVAL DATA

Estimation under the Normality Assumption

There are often institutional or other constraints in the sampling or data-recording processes that have the effect of generating inexact data for research purposes. A common case is the situation where continuous measures of interest, such as the amount of time spend participating in some recreational activity, are cast in the recorded micro data as grouped or interval data. We discussed above strategies that might be considered when the outcomes are recorded as "number of days" or "number of times", i.e. where the data can be viewed as realizations of discrete statistical processes rather than as discrete/integer codings of fundamentally continuous processes. In this section we concern ourselves with the situations where the underlying processes are best viewed as continuous phenomena but where the vagaries of either the sampling or data-coding procedures are such that only a finite number of intervals in which the continuous measure is defined are determined and the only data available to the analyst are indicators of the interval bounds in which the (unknown) continuous measure is realized. For example, the latent continuous measure might be "time spent participating in activity x over time period y (say t)," but owing to whatever reasons, all one knows is whether t=0, $t\varepsilon(0,4$ days], $t\varepsilon(4$ days, 8 days], or $t\varepsilon(8$ days, 365 days)(for y=one year). The purpose of this section is to present an estimation technique designed to handle such situations.

The method is based on the work of Rosett and Nelson (RN) (1975), who developed what is known as the two-limit probit estimation technique, and of Stewart (1983), who gneralized the RN method to account for multi-interval data. We will, therefore, refer to the model expounded here as the RNS method. Here is posited the existence of normally distributed random variables $Y_i^* \sim NID(X_i\beta,\sigma^2)$. The realizations y_i^* are unobserved, however. Available is the knowledge that the realization y_i^* is an element of some proper subset of R. More formally, partition R into $P(\geq 2)$ subsets J_k, such that $\bigcup_{k=1}^{P} J_k=R$, $J_k \cap J_j = \phi$, $\forall k,j$. The data available to the analyst are: k (such that $y_i^* \varepsilon J_k$), $\inf(J_k)$, and $\sup(J_k)$. Note that when P=2 this reduces to the binary probit model while for P=3, the RN two-limit probit model emerges.

Following Stewart, we define the p-th interval by (A_{p-1}, A_p), and set $A_0=-\infty$, $A_P=+\infty$. Given T independent observations, the log-likelihood function of this model can be written.

$$\ell = \sum_{i=1}^{T} \log(\Phi_{p(i)} - \Phi_{(p-1)(i)}) \tag{55}$$

where $\Phi_{p(i)} = \Phi(A_p - X_i\beta/\sigma)$,$\Phi$ being the cumulative distribution of the standard normal. Estimation is by maximum likelihood. The first-order conditions for maximizing ℓ are

$$\partial \ell/\partial \beta = \sum_{i=1}^{T} (\phi_{(p-1)(i)} - \phi_{p(i)})/\sigma(\Phi_{p(i)} - \Phi_{(p-1)(i)})X_i' = 0$$

and (56)

$$\partial \ell/\partial \sigma = \sum_{i=1}^{T} (\theta_{(p-1)(i)} - \theta_{p(i)})/\sigma(\Phi_{p(i)} - \Phi_{(p-1)(i)}) = 0,$$

where $\theta_{p(i)} = (A_p - X_i\beta/\sigma)(\phi(A_p - X_i\beta/\sigma))$, and $\phi(c)$ is the standard normal density $(2\pi)^{-1} \exp(-.5c^2)$. Because the matrix of second derivatives of ℓ is fairly complicated, it seems best to use for optimization purposes the method of Berndt, Hall, Hall, and Hausman (1974), which utilizes only the first derivative vector $((\partial\ell/\partial\beta)', (\partial\ell/\partial\sigma))'$. (Note that when P = 2, i.e. when the model is binary probit, a parameter normalization is required. Typically $\sigma = 1$ is used. This, of course, reduces the number of first order conditions from (M+1) to m, where m is the dimensionality of β.) Stewart has shown how iterative least squares can be used to obtain the ML estimate. The reader is referred to his work for the details.

VI. PREDICTION IN ESTIMATED PARTICIPATION MODELS

The preceding sections have surveyed some econometric methods for estimating recreational participation models. Because there exist a variety of structural or behavioural assumptions about the mechanisms that give rise to the statistical formulations, as well as a variety of data collection methods and coding configurations, it has been necessary to consider a set of possible approaches to estimation strategy. As the models considered are largely of a non-nested nature (i.e. Model A cannot generally be obtained as a restricted version of Model B and vice-versa), and because the techniques for non-nested model evaluation are largely undeveloped in situations where the model error structures are nonnormal, it is necessary that comparisons be made in terms of alternative predictions across specifications if policy is to be guided sensibly. The goal, of course, is that - depending on the exigencies of the behavioural assumptions made or data available - appropriate techniques might be used to obtain consistent parameter estimates of participation models, however specified.

In and of themselves, consistently estimated models are nothing more than aesthetically-pleasing curiosa. Their raison d'être insofar as the present analysis is concerned is of course to serve as tools for predicting impacts of changes, for example in water quality on recreation participation.

We think it appropriate to close this survey with a discussion of prediction in the context of the econometric models discussed earlier because the relevant prediction formulae and methods vary considerably across the model specifications. Though the results presented below are hardly profound, their presentation merits the space used basically because there exists to our knowledge no unifed treatment of prediction across the elements of the set of proposed econometric models. Such a unified treatment should be of interest to the policy analyst interested in juxtaposing the estimated policy outcomes from the various econometric specifications, which are, as noted above, largely nonnested.

Prediction in the context of the econometric participation models discussed above is the process whereby one assesses the change in the estimated response with respect to a change in some control variable, specifically water quality. The statistical models estimated are typically of a nature wherein it is possible to describe one or more of the following:

(a) the expection of the dependent variable, $E(Y_i) = f(X_i\beta)$;

(b) the conditional expectation of the dependent variable, e.g., $E(Y_i | y_i > 0) = g(X_i\beta)$;

(c) the probability that the dependent variable equals some value, e.g., $Pr(Y_i = y_i) = h(X_i\beta)$ (this description pertains mainly to qualitative dependent variable models such as the multinominal described earlier).

For example, the objective of the econometric estimation of some model might be to obtain an estimate of $E(Y_i)$ as $\hat{Y}_i = f(X_i\hat{\beta})$. Prediction, then, would be the process whereby one estimates $\partial E(Y_i)/\partial x_{ik}$ by $\partial\hat{Y}_i/\partial x_{ik}$, with x_{ik} some control variable specific to i. Frequently, the estimated changes are couched in terms of elasticities in order to abstract from magnitudinal considerations; here one might use estimates of $\partial \log E(Y_i)/\partial \log x_{ik}$. We turn now to an analysis of how prediction of the above nature would apply to the econometric models discussed in this article.

The ordinary least squares (OLS) specification is an obvious starting point. Although we have seen how OLS will generally be an inappropriate analytical tool given the nature of most participation data likely to be encountered, the analytics of prediction in the OLS model are quite simple and serve to motivate the remainder of the discussion.

Recall that the basic linear model can be written as

$$Y_i = X_i\beta + \varepsilon_i \tag{57}$$

If we have $E(\varepsilon_i)=0$, then $E(Y_i)=X_i\beta$. OLS estimates β by $\hat{\beta} = (X'X)^{-1}X'y$ and estimates $E(Y_i)$ by $\hat{Y}_i = X_i\hat{\beta}$. Note that $E(\hat{Y}_i) = E(X_i\hat{\beta}) = X_i(X'X)^{-1}X'(X\beta+E(\varepsilon)) = X_i\beta = E(Y_i)$ so that $\hat{Y}_i$ in the OLS model is an unbiased estimator of $E(Y_i)$ given the ideal conditions described earlier in this chapter. Prediction in this case is simply $\partial Y_i/\partial x_{ik} = \hat{\beta}_k$, or the k-th slope estimate. In the linear model, it is fairly standard practice t use the elasticity $\partial \log\hat{Y}_i/\partial \log x_{ik}$ and evaluate the elasticity at the means of the observed y_i and x_{ik}, viz. $\hat{\beta}_k\bar{X}_k/\bar{Y}$, where the overbar denotes a sample mean.

The Tobit model lends itself to description by either its expectation function or its conditional expectation function. Respectively, these are

$$E(Y_i) = X_i\beta\Phi_i + \sigma\phi_i \tag{58}$$

and

$$E(Y_i|y_i>0) = X_i\beta + \sigma\phi_2/\Phi_i, \tag{59}$$

where ϕ_i and Φ_i are evaluated at $X_i\beta/\sigma$. Following Maddala

(1983), the respective predictions are

$$\partial E(Y_i)/\partial x_{ik} = \Phi_i \beta_k \tag{60}$$

and

$$\partial E(Y_i|y_i>0)/\partial x_{ik} = \beta_k(1-(X_i\beta\phi_i/\Phi_i\sigma)-(\phi_i/\Phi_i)^2). \tag{61}$$

In elasticity form, these partial derivatives are multiplied by $x_{ik}/E(Y_i)$ and $x_{ik}/E(Y_i|y_i>0)$, respectively. Evaluation, again, might be at the sample means of the y_i and X_i. However, note that in this specification, as in other nonlinear-in-parameters specifications, the evaluated predictions will typically depend not only on the selected y and x_k evaluation points, but also on the other (non-control) elements of the X-vectors. In the general non-linear case, evaluation at the means of the X_i does not generate the same prediction as is yielded by calculating the mean of the estimated individual predictions. This is merely a corrollary of a general property of nonlinear functions where $E(f(Z)) \neq f(E(Z))$. Thus, another obvious method of evaluation would be to calculate the prediction of each individual in the sample and average the individual predictions. Such a strategy might be valuable when contemplated policy measures take the form of, say, an x-percent change in the control variable of each individual from that individual's prevailing or pre-policy level.

In the probit/truncated-normal version of the Cragg estimator (the Cragg equations (7) and (9)), the expectation function can be written as

$$E(Y_i) = E(Y_i|y_i>0)\Pr(y_i>0) \tag{62}$$

$$= [X_i\beta_2 + \sigma_2\phi_{i2}/\Phi_{i2}]\Phi_{i1} \tag{63}$$

and

$$E(Y_i|y_i>0) = X_i\beta_2 + \sigma_2\phi_{i2}/\Phi_{i2},$$

where ϕ_{ip} and Φ_{ip} are the standard normal density and distribution functions evaluated at $X_i\beta_p/\sigma_p$ (p=1,2). (Recall that σ_1 is normalized = 1). In this specification the formula for $\partial E(Y_i|y_i>0)/\partial x_{ik}$ is identical to that for the Tobit specification, equation (59) above. The formula for the unconditional version is

$$\partial E(Y_i)/\partial x_{ik} = \beta_{2k}\Phi_{i1} + X_i\beta_2\phi_{i1}\beta_{ik} + \sigma_2\lambda_{i2}[\phi_{i1}\beta_{1k} -$$

$$(\Phi_{i1}Z_{i2}\beta_{2k}/\sigma_2) - (\lambda_{i2}\Phi_{i1}\beta_{2k}/\sigma_2)], \tag{64}$$

where $\lambda_{i2} = \phi_{i2}/\Phi_{i2}$ and $Z_{i2} = (X_i\beta_2/\sigma_2)$. Note that when $\beta_1 = \beta_2$ and $\sigma_1 = \sigma_2$, i.e. when the Tobit restrictions are imposed on this version of the Cragg model, (64) reduces to the far less-complicated expression (60).

The second version of the Cragg model considered earlier is that where the second-stage conditional density is lognormal, with $\log Y_i \sim N(X_i\beta_2,\sigma_2^2)$ conditional on $y_i>0$. Again defining the appropriate expectation functions yields

$$E(Y_i) = E(Y_i|y_i>0)Pr(y_i>0) = \exp(X_i\beta_2 + .5\sigma_2^2)\Phi_{i1} \quad (65)$$

and

$$E(Y_i|y_i>0) = \exp(X_i\beta_2 + .5\sigma_2^2), \quad (66)$$

where we have used the well-known property of lognormal densities that where the log of a lognormally-distributed random variable has mean μ and variance θ^2, then the expected value of the random variable is $\exp(\mu + .5\theta^2)$ (See Johnson and Kotz (1970, Chapter 14) for further details on the properties of the lognormal). The relevant partial derivatives are

$$\partial E(Y_i)/\partial x_{ik} = \exp(X_i\beta_2 + .5\sigma_2^2)\ [\phi_{i1}\beta_{1k} + \Phi_{i1}\beta_{2k}] \quad (67)$$

and

$$\partial E(Y_i|y_i>0)/\partial x_{ik} = \exp(X_i\beta_2 + .5\sigma_2^2)\beta_{2k}. \quad (68)$$

In all cases, elasticity forms are calculated by the appropriate multiplication by either $x_{ik}(E(Y_i))^{-1}$ or $x_{ik}(E(Y_i|y_i>0))^{-1}$ of the partial derivative formulae derived above.

The Heckman two-equation model, recall, is cast in terms of unconditional densities of the random variables Y_{i1} and Y_{i2}^*. Thus, the unconditional expectation of Y_{i1} is merely a linear function of parameters,

$$E(Y_{i1}) = X_i\beta_1, \quad (69)$$

with

$$\partial E(Y_{i1})/\partial x_{ik} = \beta_{1k} \tag{68}$$

If the moment of interest is the conditional expectation of Y_{i1} given $y_{i2}=1$ (in the notation of equation (34)), then we have from equations (35) and (36)

$$E(Y_{i1}|y_{i2}=1) = X_i\beta_1 + \sigma_{12}\phi_{i2}/\sigma_2(1-\Phi_{i2}), \tag{69}$$

where ϕ_{i2} and Φ_{i2} are the standard normal density and distribution functions evaluated at $(X_i\beta_2/\sigma_2)$. Here,

$$\partial E(Y_{i1}|y_{i2}=1)/\partial x_{ik} = \beta_{1k} + (\sigma_{12}\lambda_{i2}\beta_{2k}/\sigma_2^2)[\lambda_{i2}-Z_{i2}], \tag{70}$$

where now we define $\lambda_{i2} = \phi_{i2}/(1-\Phi_{i2})$ and $Z_{i2} = X_i\beta_2/\sigma_2$.

The derivations of the prediction formulae for the Poisson model are straightforward. Recall from equation (49) that the expectation function for the Poisson specification is

$$E(Y_i) = \exp(X_i\beta). \tag{71}$$

(Note that the Poisson specification differs from the others discussed above in that the conditional expectation function has not been considered.[8])
Thus we have

$$\partial E(Y_i)/\partial x_{ik} = \beta_k \exp(X_i\beta) \tag{72}$$

or, in elasticity form

$$\partial E(Y_i)x_{ik}/\partial x_{ik}E(Y_i) = \beta_k x_{ik}, \tag{73}$$

The formulae for the geometric specification, with $E(Y_i) = \exp(X_i\beta)$, are also (72) and (73).

Recall for the Stewart or grouped-dependent variable model that in any interval (a_{p-1}, a_p) one has for a conditional expection

$$E(Y_i|y_i\varepsilon(a_{p-1},a_p))=X_i\beta+\sigma[\phi(Z_{p-1})-\phi(Z_p)]/[\Phi(Z_p)-\Phi(Z_{p-1})], \tag{74}$$

where $Z_p=(a_p-X_i\beta)/\sigma$. The probability that the random variable Y_i is realized in (a_{p-1},a_p) is of course $(\Phi(Z_p)-\Phi(Z_{p-1}))$. Therefore, the unconditional expectation function is

$$E(Y_i) = \sum_{p=1}^{P} E(Y_i|y_i\varepsilon(a_{p-1},a_p))\Pr(y_i\varepsilon(a_{p-1},a_p))$$

$$= \sum_{p=1}^{P} X_i\beta(\Phi(Z_p)-\Phi(Z_{p-1})) + \sigma(\phi(Z_{p-1})-\phi(Z_p)). \tag{75}$$

$$= X_i\beta$$

The strong resemblance between (75) and (58) is clearly more than coincidence, such of course owing to the foundations of both the Tobit and the GDV estimators in normally-distributed latent variables.

In all the above formulations, the dependent variables

or their latent bases were of a quantitative nature, thus allowing direct quantitative representation of the moments or conditional moments of interest. The prediction strategy when the dependent variable is qualitative rather than quantitative is somewhat different. However, in the one qualitative dependent variable model discussed in this paper - the multinominal - the nature of the dependent variable is such that a fairly direct translation from the qualitative outcome to a quantitative prediction is possible. The strategy is as follows. Recall that the qualitative outcome measures of interest in the multinominal model are the probabilities of engaging in any of a set of activities on a given day. To translate these probabilities into quantitative participation measures for some time interval (a year, e.g.,), one simply sums the activity-specific day probabilities over the year. If the day participation probabilities are

Fish	.02
Boat	.01
Swim	.05
Nonrecreation	.92

Then the annual quantitative participation measures are

Fish	.02(365) = 7.12 days
Boat	.01(365) = 3.56 days
Swim	.05(365) = 17.80 days
Nonrecreation	.92(365) = 327.52 days

The prediction strategy, therefore, is to assess the responsiveness of the daily activity-specific probabilities to changes in the control variable, assess the ex post magnitude of annual participation in the various activities, and compare these post-policy magnitudes to those that were estimated to prevail in the pre-policy period.

The prediction equations are based on the probabilities defined in (51). For individual i and choice Z, one has

$$P_{Z_i} = \exp(X_i\beta_Z)/\sum_{j\varepsilon\Omega}\exp(X_i\beta_j), \tag{76}$$

where Ω is the choice index set.

Therefore,

$$\partial P_{Z_i}/\partial x_{ik} = P_{Z_i}(\beta_{Z_k}-[\sum_{j\varepsilon\Omega}\exp(X_i\beta_j)\beta_{jk}/\sum_{j\varepsilon\Omega}\exp(X_i\beta_j)]). \tag{77}$$

The elasticity formulation is

$$(\partial P_{Z_i}/\partial x_{ik})(x_{ik}/P_{Z_i})=x_{ik}(\beta_{Zk}-[\sum_{j\varepsilon\Omega}\exp(X_i\beta_j)\beta_{jk}/\sum_{j\varepsilon\Omega}\exp(X_i\beta_j)]). \tag{78}$$

FOOTNOTES

1. The Vaughan-Russell (1982) logit-OLS models are in fact in the class of models described by Cragg (1971) equations (7) and (8). Here, the participation decision is a discrete (0,1) outcome (which Cragg assumes to be governed by a normally-distributed latent variable and, therefore, to be a probit model), while the conditional participation decision is a standard linear model to which OLS can be applied. The main subtlety ignored in the Vaughan-Russell analysis is that the nonnegativity of the participation measures is not dealt with by using OLS on the observation for which participation is positive. Measuring conditional participation in logs would circumvent this.
2. The derivation of (2) is straightforward. Given $X \sim N(\mu,\sigma^2)$, then we wish to show:

$$E(X|x>0) = \mu+\sigma[f(\mu/\sigma)/F(\mu/\sigma)]$$

$$E(X|x>0) = \frac{1}{F} \cdot \frac{1}{\sqrt{2\pi}\sigma} \int_0^\infty xe^{-(x-\mu)^2/2\sigma^2} dx$$

$(F=F(\mu/\sigma); f=f(\mu/\sigma))$

$$= \frac{1}{K} \int_0^\infty xe^{-(x-\mu)^2/2\sigma^2} dx \qquad (K = \sigma F\sqrt{2\pi})$$

Let $z=x-\mu$; thus

$$E(X|x>0) = \frac{1}{K} \{ \int_{-\mu}^{\infty} (z+\mu)e^{-z^2/2\sigma^2} dz \}$$

$$= \frac{1}{K} \{ \int_{-\mu}^{\infty} ze^{-z^2/2\sigma^2} dz + \mu \int_{-\mu}^{\infty} e^{-z^2/2\sigma^2} dz \}$$

$$= \frac{1}{K} \{ -\sigma^2 e^{-z^2/2\sigma^2} \Big|_{-\mu}^{\infty} + (\sqrt{2\pi}\sigma F)\mu \}$$

$$= \frac{\sigma^2}{K} e^{-\mu^2/2\sigma^2} + \mu$$

$$=\sigma f/F + \mu.$$

Setting $x = y_i^*$ and $\mu=X_i\beta$ yields the promised result.

3. Maddala (1977) is a good reference on maximum likelihood estimation, in general, and estimation methods for limited dependent variables, in particular.
4. In the Lagrange-multiplier hypothesis testing approach, one formulates the problem by considering the maximization of the log-likelihood function $\ell(\theta)$ subject to a set of (perhaps nonlinear) restrictions on θ of the form $h_j(\theta)=0$. Thus, one can consider the Lagrangean function.

$$Q(\theta) = \ell(\theta) + \sum_j h_j(\theta),$$

and maximize $Q(\theta)$ w.r.t. θ. The test relies on the idea that when the restricted estimate $\tilde{\theta}$ is "near" the unrestricted ML estimate $\hat{\theta}$, the vector $\ell(\tilde{\theta})$ will approach the zero vector. Further discussion is found in the excellent piece by Breusch and Pagan (1980).

5. The resemblance is due to the fact that, given the $P_i = \exp(X_i\beta)$ parameterization, if the geometric specification is reduced to the binary outcomes $Pr(k_i=0)$ versus $Pr(k_i=1$ or $k_i=2$ or...), then the binary logit model results. This result is interesting in that consistent estimates of β in the goemetric model as specified can be obtained via a binary logit model. Such estimates are inefficient, however, as information on the magnitudes of the $k_i \geq 1$ is discarded.

6. The only difference, as is obvious from inspection of (53), is that in the one-trial case, $\Sigma t_{j_m} = 1$ for all m while in the multiple-trial case considered here $\Sigma t_{j_m} = T$. Existing programs then are modified as to the number of times the $\log P_{j_m}$ terms are summed in computing the log-likelihood.

7. Inf and sup are the abbreviations for infimum and supremum, respectively the greatest lower bound and least upper bound of a set S if these bounds exist. If S has a minimum (resp. maximum) element, then inf (S) = min(S) (resp. sup(S) = max(S)).

8. It would certainly be possible to define a truncated version of the Poisson model where only strictly positive integer realizations were admitted. Here one would have

$$Pr(Y_i = y) = \frac{\exp(-\lambda_i)\lambda_i^y}{y!(1-\exp(-\lambda_i))}, \quad y = 1,2,3,...$$
$$= 0, \quad \text{otherwise}$$

where $(1-\exp(-\lambda_i))$ is the truncation normalizing constant equal to $(1-Pr(Y_i=0))$. This could, then, be considered a conditional distribution for the $y_i \neq 0$. Some of the same questions as arise in the Lin-Schmidt critique of the Tobit model are present in the discussion of the truncated Poisson formulation. Specifically, one might question whether the Poisson binary probabilities $Pr(Y_i=0)$ and $Pr(Y_i=1$ or $Y_i=2$ or $Y_i=3$ or...) $(=1-Pr(Y_i=0))$ are governed by the same statistical process as are the conditional probabilities $Pr(Y_i=y|y=1$ or $y=2$ or...). Because such considerations require considerable further development, we postpone their discussion for future research.

REFERENCES

T. Amemiya, Qualitative Response Models: A Survey, Journal of Economic Literature, Vol.19, pp.1483-1536, (1981).

T. Amemiya, Nonlinear Regression Models, in Z. Griliches and M.D. Intriligator, eds., Handbook of Econometrics, Vol.1, (Amsterdam:North-Holland), (1983).

T. Amemiya, Tobit Models: A Survey, Journal of Econometrics, Vol.24, pp.3-61, (1984).

E.R. Berndt, B.H.Hall, R.E. Hall and J.A.Hausman, Estimation and inference in Nonlinear Structural Models, Annals of Economic and Social Measurement, Vol.3, pp.653-665, (1974).

T. Breusch, and A.R. Pagan, The Lagrange Multiplier Test and its Application to Model Specification in Econometrics, Review of Economic Studies, Vol.47, pp.239-253, (1980).

D.R. Cox and D.V. Hinkley, Theoretical Statistics (London: Chapman and Hall), (1974).

J.G. Cragg, Some Statistical Models for Limited Dependent Variables with Application to the Demand for Durable Goods, Econometrica, Vol.39, pp.829-844, (1971).

N. Duan, W.G. Manning, C.N. Morris and J.P. Newhouse, A Comparison of Alternative Models for the Demand for Medical Care, Journal of Business and Economic Statistics, Vol.1, pp.115-126, (1983).

______, ______, ______, and ______, Choosing Between the Sample-Selection Model and the Multi-part Model, Journal of Business and Economic Statistics, Vol.2, pp.283-289, (1984).

L. Dudley and C. Montmarquette, A Model of the Supply of Bilateral Foreign Aid, American Economic Review, Vol. 66, pp.132-142, (1976).

J.A. Hausman, Specification Tests in Econometrics, Econometrica, Vol.46, pp.1251-1271, (1978).

J.A. Hausman, B. Hall and Z. Griliches, Econometric Methods for Count Data with an Application to the Patents-R&D Relationship, Econometrica, Vol.52, pp.909-938, (1984).

J.A. Hausman, B. Ostro and D. Wise, Air Pollution and Lost Work, NBER Working Paper 1263, January, (1984).

J.W. Hay, and R.J. Olsen, Let Them Eat Cake: A Note on Comparing Alternative Methods of the Demand for Medical Care, Journal of Business and Economic Statistics, Vol.2, pp.279-282, (1984).

J. Heckman, The Common Structure of Statistical Models of Truncation, Sample Selection and Limited Dependent Variables and a Simple Estimator for Such Models, Annals of Economic and Social Measurement, Vol.5, pp.475-492, (1976).

J. Heckman, Sample selection bias as a specification error, Econometrica, 47, p.153-162, (1979).

M. Hurd, Estimation in truncated samples when there is heteroscedasticity, Journal of Econometrics, 11, p.247-258, (1979).

M.D. Intriligator, Economic and econometric models, in Griliches and Intriligator, op.cit., (1983).

N.L. Johnson and S. Kotz, Discrete Distributions, Boston: Houghton Mifflin, (1969).

N.L. Johnson and S. Kotz, Continuous Univariate Distributions, Boston: Houghton Mifflin, (1970).

M.G. Kendall and A. Stuart, The Advanced Theory of Statistics, Volume 3, London: Griffin, (1973).

M. Killingsworth, Labour Supply, Cambridge University Press, (1983).

T.F. Lin and P. Schmidt, A test of the Tobit specification against an alternative suggested by Cragg, Review of Economics and Statistics, 66, p.174-177, (1984).

G.S. Maddala, Econometrics, New York: MacGraw Hill, (1977).

G.S. Maddala, Limited Dependent and Qualitative Variables in Econometrics, Cambridge University Press, (1983).

C. Manski and D.L. McFadden, eds., Structural Analysis of Discrete Data, MIT Press, (1979).

E.R. Morey, The demand for site-specific recreational activities: a characteristics approach, Journal of Environmental Economics and Management, 8, p.345-371, (1981).

F.D. Nelson, A test for misspecification in the censored normal model, Econometrica, 49, p.1317-1329, (1981).

R. Olsen, A least squares correction for selectivity bias, Econometrica, 48, p.1815-1820, (1980).

B.D. Ostro, The effects of air pollution on work loss and morbidity, Journal of Environmental Economics and Management, 10, p.371-382, (1983).

K. Pearson and A. Lee, On the Generalized probable error in multiple normal correlations, Biometrika, 6, p.59 68, (1908).

M.M. Pitt, Food preferences and nutrition in rural Bangladesh, Review of Economics and Statistics, 65, p.105-114, (1983).

P.R. Portney and J. Mullahy, Urban Air Quality and Acute Respiratory Illness, Journal of Urban Economics, Forthcoming, (1986).

C.R. Rao, Linear Statistical Inference and its Applications, New York: John Wiley, (1965).

R.N. Rosett and F.D. Nelson, Estimation of the two-limit probit regression, Econometrica, 43, p.141-146.

R. Royall, Robust Inference Using Maximum Likelihood Estimators, Johns Hopkins University, Depart.of Biostatistics Working Paper 1984.

P. Schmidt, Econometrics, New York: Marcel Dekker, (1976).

M.A. Smith and G.S. Maddala, Multiple model testing for non-nested heteroskedastic censored regression, Journal of Econometrics, 21, p.71-81, (1983).

D.C. Stapleton and D.J. Young, Censored normal regression with measurement error on the dependent variable, Econometrica, 52, p.737-760, (1984).

M. Stewart, On least squares estimation when the dependent variable is grouped, Review of Economic Studies, 50, p.737-753, (1983).

J. Tobin, Estimation of relationships for limited dependent variables, Econometrica, 26, p.24-36, (1958).

W.J. Vaughan and C.S. Russell, Freshwater Recreational Fishing, The National Benefits of Water Pollution Control, Resources for the Future, Washington D.C.(1982).

T.J. Wales and A.D. Woodland, Estimation of consumer demand systems with binding non-negativity constraints, Journal of Econometrics, 21, p.263-285, (1983).

H. White, Maximum likelihood estimation of misspecified models, Econometrica, 50, p.1-26, (1982).

H. White, Corrigendum, Econometrica, 51, p.513, (1983).

A. Zellner, Statistical theory and econometrics, in Griliches and Intriligator, op.cit., (1983).

ECONOMETRIC DISEQUILIBRIUM MODELS : A SIMPLIFIED SURVEY

MALCOLM PEMBERTON
University College London

I. INTRODUCTION

The pioneering contribution of Fair and Jaffee (1972) provided the first serious econometric attempt to escape from the market-clearing paradigm. Since then there has been a considerable theoretical output on econometric disequilibrium models, an excellent survey of which is contained in Quandt (1982). Empirical applications are, however, rather thinner on the ground especially for the UK.

The purpose of the present paper is to provide a simplified pathway through the theory of econometric disequilibrium models, less technical than the survey by Quandt (1982), and to outline some new applications to the housing and labour markets in the UK.

In Section II we describe some basic disequilibrium models and their estimation. Section III is concerned with how the equilibrium hypothesis may be tested. In Section IV we consider some criticisms and possible modifications and extensions of the basic models. Finally in Section V we describe briefly some new applications of econometric disequilibrium models to the housing and labour markets in the UK and in Section VI we give some conclusions.

II. SOME BASIC DISEQUILIBRIUM MODELS AND THEIR ESTIMATION

In this section we consider the most frequently encountered disequilibrium models for a single market. Common features of such models are a demand function and a supply function:

$$D_t = \alpha_1 p_t + \beta_1' x_{1t} + u_{1t} \qquad (1)$$

$$S_t = \alpha_2 p_t + \beta_1' x_{2t} + u_{2t} \qquad (2)$$

where D_t, S_t and p_t denote respectively the quantity demanded, the quantity supplied and the price of the good, x_{1t}, x_{2t} are vectors of exogenous variables and u_{1t}, u_{2t} are error terms usually assumed to be jointly normal with mean vector zero, constant covariance matrix and serially uncorrelated.

The main problem of estimation is that, in the absence of an equilibrium condition, D_t and S_t are unobservables. It is impossible to proceed from here without a further assumption and the first candidate put forward by Fair and Jaffee (1972) was that the observed quantity traded, Q_t, satisfies either (1) or (2). For T observations, there are 2^T different ways of assigning the Q_t to either (1) or (2) i.e. there are 2^T different <u>sample separations</u>. For a given sample separation, the likelihood function of the model can be obtained and maximum likelihood (or, equivalently, least squares) estimates of the parameters α_1, α_2, β_1 and β_2 may be found. In general, the sample separation is unknown and the estimation method proposed is first to find the maximum of the likelihood function for each sample separation and then to search over the 2^T maxima thus obtained to find the overall maximum.

It is clear that the above approach is feasible only when T is small. A stronger assumption than that Q_t satisfies either (1) or (2) is thus required and the one most commonly used is the "min condition":

$$Q_t = \min (D_t, S_t) \tag{3}$$

The usual justification for this is that exchange is voluntary: no potential purchaser can be made to buy more than he wishes, nor can a supplier be made to sell more than he wishes.

Equations (1) - (3) constitute the simplest disequilibrium model which can be made operational. The price p_t is taken to be exogenous and the only observable random variable in the model is Q_t. In the absence of prior information, the sample separation is unknown and, since this is the case which is likely to occur in practice, we concentrate on it here. The likelihood function for this model was first obtained by Maddala and Nelson (1974) and is also given in Goldfeld and Quandt (1975). We sketch the derivation here.

The problem is to derive the probability density function, $h(Q_t)$, of the observable Q_t from the joint density function, $g(D_t, S_t)$, of the unobservables D_t and S_t. For any interval I,

$$P(Q_t \varepsilon I) = P(Q_t \varepsilon I \text{ and } D_t < S_t) + P(Q_t \varepsilon I \text{ and } D_t \geq S_t) \tag{4}$$

Appealing to (3) we see that the first term on the right hand side of (4) may be written $P(D_t \varepsilon I \text{ and } D_t < S_t)$, while the second is $P(S_t \varepsilon I \text{ and } D_t \geq S_t)$. We may therefore write (4) as

$$P(Q_t \varepsilon I) = \int_{D_t \varepsilon I} \left(\int_{D_t}^{\infty} g(D_t, S_t) dS_t \right) dD_t + \int_{S_t \varepsilon I} \left(\int_{S_t}^{\infty} g(D_t, S_t)\, dD_t \right) dS_t \qquad (5)$$

Differentiating (5) with respect to the right hand endpoint of I we obtain the desired density function

$$h(Q_t) = \int_{Q_t}^{\infty} g(Q_t, S_t) dS_t + \int_{Q_t}^{\infty} g(D_t, Q_t) dD_t \qquad (6)$$

If u_{1t}, u_{2t} are jointly normally distributed with mean vector zero and covariance matrix Σ, then

$$g(D_t, S_t) = \frac{1}{2\pi(\det\Sigma)^{\frac{1}{2}}} \exp\left\{ -\frac{1}{2}(u_{1t}\ u_{2t})\ \Sigma^{-1} \begin{pmatrix} u_{1t} \\ u_{2t} \end{pmatrix} \right\} \qquad (7)$$

Substitution for u_{1t} and u_{2t} from (1) and (2) respectively followed by substitution of the resulting expression for $g(D_t, S_t)$ into (6) yields $h(Q_t)$ in terms of the cumulative normal function

$$\Phi(z) = \frac{1}{(\sqrt{2\pi})} \int_{-\infty}^{z} \exp\left(\frac{-x^2}{2} \right) dx.$$

Finally assuming that the errors are serially uncorrelated, the likelihood function is obtained in the form

$$L = \prod_{t=1}^{T} h(Q_t) \qquad (8)$$

Fair and Jaffee (1972) supplement the model (1) - (3) with the assumption that the price increases when there is excess demand, which they allow to take the form of either a directional relation

$$p_t - p_{t-1} \gtreqless 0 \quad \text{as } D_t - S_t \gtreqless 0 \tag{9}$$

or an equation

$$p_t - p_{t-1} = \gamma (D_t - S_t) \tag{10}$$

where γ is a non-negative constant. In either case the sample can be separated on the basis of the observed price changes and thus the sample separation is known. It is now tempting to estimate (1) by OLS on the sub-sample in which $Q_t = D_t$ and (2) by OLS on the sub-sample in which $Q_t = S_t$. However, as Fair and Jaffee (1972) point out, this method is inconsistent since the expectations of the errors, given the sample separation, are not zero. This source of inconsistency is discussed further by Monfort in his comments after Quandt's survey (1982). In fact, for the case where the model consists of (1) - (3) and (10), Fair and Jaffee (1972) describe a two-stage least squares procedure which they wrongly claim is consistent. Amemiya (1974) pointed out the error and gave a consistent estimation method.

Of greater practical interest is the case where the price adjustment equation is stochastic and hence, in the absence of prior information, the sample separation is unknown. The simplest form is

$$p_t - p_{t-1} = \gamma (D_t - S_t) + u_{3t} \tag{11}$$

where γ may be specified to have different values γ_1, γ_2 according to whether $D_t > S_t$ or $D_t < S_t$ and u_{3t} is an error term. We may also consider the more general specification

$$p_t - p_{t-1} = \gamma(D_t - S_t) + \beta_3' x_{3t} + u_{3t} \tag{12}$$

where x_{3t} is a vector of exogenous variables. Another possible formulation is to have lagged rather than current excess demand on the right hand side.

The derivation of the likelihood function for the models given by (1) - (3) and either (11) or (12) is similar to that for the model without a price adjustment equation. The price p_t is now endogenous and the first step is to obtain the joint probability density function, $h(Q_t, p_t)$, of the observables Q_t and p_t in terms of the joint density function, $g(D_t, S_t, p_t)$. A similar argument to before gives

$$h(Q_t, p_t) = \int_{Q_t}^{\infty} g(Q_t, S_t, p_t)dS_t + \int_{Q_t}^{\infty} g(D_t, Q_t, p_t)dD_t \tag{13}$$

where, because of the presence of p_{t-1} in the adjustment equation, this density function is conditional on p_{t-1}. If now u_{1t}, u_{2t}, u_{3t} are assumed to be jointly ormally distributed with mean vector zero and covariance matrix Σ, then

$$g(D_t, S_t p_t) = \frac{|1+\gamma(\alpha_2-\alpha_1)|}{(2\pi)^{\frac{3}{2}}(\det\Sigma)^{\frac{1}{2}}} \exp\left\{ -\frac{1}{2}(u_{1t} u_{2t} u_{3t})\Sigma^{-1} \begin{bmatrix} u_{1t} \\ u_{2t} \\ u_{3t} \end{bmatrix} \right\} \tag{14}$$

Here $|1+\gamma(\alpha_2-\alpha_1)|$ is the absolute value of the Jacobian of the transformation from D_t, S_t, p_t to u_{1t}, u_{2t}, u_{3t}. Similarly to before, substitution for u_{1t}, u_{2t} and u_{3t} from (1), (2) and either (11) or (12) followed by substitution into (13) gives $h(Q_t, p_t)$ in terms of the cumulative normal function and, finally, the assumption of serially uncorrelated errors yields the likelihood function in the form

$$L = \prod_{t=1}^{T} h(Q_t, p_t) \tag{15}$$

The detailed derivation is given in Quandt (1978).

The model consisting of (1) - (3) together with either (11) or (12) and without prior information on sample separation provides the basic tool for empirical work. We now consider briefly some points to be aware of when implementing maximum likelihood estimation in this situation.

Firstly we note that Goldfeld and Quandt (1978) show that in the general case where the covariance matrix Σ is allowed to have non-zero covariance terms, the likelihood function may increase over sequences of points in parameter space which tend towards regions where the covariance matrix is singular and hence the likelihood function is undefined. This means that attempts to maximise the likelihood function may end up near regions where Σ becomes singular and hence computation will break down. Most empirical formulations, however, make the simplifying assumption that the covariance matrix is diagonal in which case the problem does not arise.

Even with the assumption of a diagonal covariance matrix, there are sequences of points in parameter space over which the likelihood function is unbounded. These sequences have one of the variances σ_1^2, σ_2^2 of u_{1t}, u_{2t}, respectively, tending to zero and the unboundedness arises essentially from the fact that, when the sample separation is unknown, the density function of the observables given in equation (13) (and in equation (6) for the model without a price adjustment equation) consists of a sum of two parts. Parameter values can be found so that the first part of the density function for a particular observation tends to infinity as σ_1^2(say)$\to 0$ while the second parts of the density function tend to non-zero limits for all observations. Hence the likelihood function is unbounded along certain sequences of points tending towards either the $\sigma_1 = 0$ or $\sigma_2 = 0$ boundary of the parameter space. Fortunately, if an interior maximum exists then it defines a consistent estimator (see Amemiya and Sen (1977), Hartley and Mallela (1977)). Thus, if the unboundedness problem is encountered in practice, it is usual to restart the optimization from a new point and continue the search for an interior maximum.

We note that when the sample separation is known, the density function of the observables is no longer the sum of two parts. Parameter values can still be found so that the density function for a particular observation tends to infinity as $\sigma_1^2 \to 0$. But this time the likelihood function will also contain a factor which tends to zero exponentially as $\sigma_1^2 \to 0$. Hence the unboundedness problem is not present in this case.

Methods of finding starting values for the maximization procedure tend to be ad hoc. On the basis of the price adjustment equation, an approximate sample separation may be found, ambiguous cases being assigned to both the demand and supply schedules. We note that in the case where the price adjustment equation takes the form (12), this procedure will involve assigning an arbitrary value to β_3. Once the approximate sample separation has been found, starting values for the parameters of the demand and supply schedules can be found by OLS on the relevant subsamples. Starting values for the parameters of the price adjustment equation can be found by OLS on the whole sample with a dummy variable, (1 for excess demand, -1 for excess supply), acting as a rough proxy for $D_t - S_t$.

We conclude this section with some brief comments on the observation that disequilibrium models which include a price adjustment equation are superficially similar to partial adjustment models. For instance substitution of (1) and (2) into (11) gives

$$p_t = \mu p_{t-1} + (1-\mu)\, p_t^* + \mu u_{3t} \tag{16}$$

where $\mu = 1/(1+\gamma(\alpha_2-\alpha_1))$ and p_t^* denotes the market clearing price.

Bowden (1978) discusses the estimation of disequilibrium models where the price equation is specified in the form (16). The parameters of the demand and supply functions are no longer necessarily identifiable in this formulation but the equilibrium counterpart of the model corresponds to $\mu = 0$ and thus is particularly conveniently nested. It is to issues of this sort that we turn our attention in the next section.

III. TESTING THE EQUILIBRIUM HYPOTHESIS

It is of considerable importance to obtain some indication of whether the underlying data generation process for the market under consideration is closer to a disequilibrium model of the sort described in Section II or to some equilibrium counterpart. Such information would suggest the directions which future attempts to refine the model should follow. It would also indicate which class of models would be more reliable for simulating the effects of exogenous changes.

The obvious candidate for the equilibrium counterpart of the various models of Section II is

$$Q_t = \alpha_1 p_t + \beta_1' x_{1t} + u_{1t} \qquad (17)$$

$$Q_t = \alpha_2 p_t + \beta_2' x_{2t} + u_{2t} \qquad (18)$$

In the case where the disequilibrium model consists simply of (1) - (3), the equilibrium model given by (17) and (18) is not nested in it and it is unknown whether generalized likelihood ratio tests, of the sort described in Cox (1961, 1962) and Pesaran and Deaton (1978), can be devised. Hwang (1980) points out that, in the equilibrium model, an equation of the form

$$Q_t = a_1' x_{1t} + a_2' x_{2t} + a_3 p_t + \varepsilon_t \qquad (19)$$

can be derived where a_1, a_2, a_3 depend only on structural parameters and ε_t is uncorrelated with p_t. In the simple disequilibrium model, given by (1) - (3), a similar equation can be derived by writing

$$Q_t = \delta_t D_t + (1-\delta_t) S_t = b_1' x_{1t} + b_2' x_{2t} + b_3 p_t + \nu_t \qquad (20)$$

where $\delta_t = 1$ if $D_t \leq S_t$ and 0 otherwise and where the right hand side of (20) is obtained by using (1) and (2). The coefficients of (20) depend on t, whereas those of (19) do not and thus Hwang argues that a test of the equilibrium hypothesis can be interpreted as a test of the stability of the parameters in a regression of Q_t on x_{1t}, x_{2t} and p_t. However, the test procedure assumes that the variables on the right hand side of (20) are exogenous; this is false since δ_t is endogenous. We conclude that, for the case where the disequilibrium model consists of (1) - (3), no satisfactory test of the equilibrium hypothesis has as yet been derived.

When the disequilibrium model has a price adjustment equation, the situtation is a little better. As in Section II, we concentrate on the model consisting of (1) - (3) together with either (11) or (12) and without prior information on sample separation. Quandt (1978) shows that, in the case where the price adjustment equation is (11), the density function of Q_t and p_t in the equilibrium model, given by (17) and (18), is the limit, as γ tends to infinity, of the density function of Q_t and p_t in the disequilibrium model. Thus the equilibrium model is nested in this asymptotic sense in the disequilibrium model.

On the basis of this result, it is argued that the hypothesis of equilibrium can be tested by testing whether $\frac{1}{\gamma}$ is significantly different from zero (in which case the equilibrium hypothesis is rejected) or by performing the analogous test in the Bowden (1978) framework of whether μ is zero. More precisely, we note that equation (11) can be written as

$$D_t - S_t = \frac{1}{\gamma}(p_t - p_{t-1}) - \frac{u_{3t}}{\gamma} \tag{21}$$

Denoting the variance of u_{3t} by σ_3^2 and writing $\tilde{\gamma} = \frac{1}{\gamma}$, $\tilde{\sigma}_3 = \frac{\sigma_3}{\gamma}$, the equilibrium hypothesis is defined by $\tilde{\gamma} = 0$,

$\tilde{\sigma}_3 = 0$. Similarly when the price adjustment equation takes the form (12), the equilibrium hypothesis is then $\tilde{\gamma} = 0$, $\tilde{\beta}_3 = 0$, $\tilde{\sigma}_3 = 0$ where $\tilde{\beta}_3 = \frac{\beta_3}{\gamma}$. The difficulties, arising from the fact that these various versions of the null hypothesis are on the boundary of the parameter space, are discussed by Monfort in his comments after Quandt's survey (1982). There are similar difficulties associated with likelihood ratio tests in which the likelihoods of a disequilibrium model and its equilibrium counterpart are compared.

For the case where the price-adjustment equation is non-stochastic, the situation is quite similar. As was shown by Gourieroux, Laffont and Monfort (1980), the density function of Q_t and p_t in the equilibrium model is still the limit, as γ tends to infinity, of the density function of Q_t and p_t in the disequilibrium model. Thus the equilibrium model is still nested asymptotically in the disequilibrium model and the suggestion by Quandt (1978) that, when the price-adjustment equation is non-stochastic, there is no asymptotic nesting, is in fact incorrect.

In this section, we have given a brief survey of the methods which have been proposed to test the equilibrium hypothesis. Our discussion has shown clearly that the problem has not been completely solved and Monfort in his comments after Quandt's survey (1982) puts the blame for this on the form of the price adjustment equation. We consider this and other criticisms of the basic models in the next section.

IV. CRITICISMS, MODIFICATIONS AND EXTENSIONS OF THE BASIC MODELS

The main targets for criticism in the basic econometric disequilibrium models have been the min condition and the price adjustment equation. Here we consider some of these criticisms and the modifications that have been suggested. We conclude the section with some remarks on possible directions in which the basic models can be extended.

The min condition is usually justified on the grounds that exchange is voluntary. As Rosen and Quandt (1978) point out, this assumption may not be fully tenable in situations in which buyers and sellers do not have equal market power. Further criticism came from Muellbauer (1978) who argued that, while the min condition may be appropriate for local markets, it is not applicable at the level of the aggregate market. He accordingly suggests that the observed quantity be modelled as an aggregate of corresponding quantities from a large number of local markets.

In the Muellbauer framework, demand, D_j, and supply, S_j, in the jth market are written as

$$D_j = D + \varepsilon_{1j} \tag{22}$$

$$S_j = S + \varepsilon_{2j} \tag{23}$$

where D and S are the average demand and supply, and ε_{1j}, ε_{2j} are random variables with zero means and joint distribution function $F(\varepsilon_{1j},\varepsilon_{2j})$. Defining z to be D - S and θ to be $\varepsilon_{1j} - \varepsilon_{2j}$, the jth market has excess demand if $z > \theta$. The assumption that the min condition applies to each individual market gives the observed quantity, Q, as the sum of demands in markets in which there is excess supply plus the sum of supplies in markets in which there is excess demand. Thus

$$Q = \iint\limits_{\theta \geq z} (D+\varepsilon_1)dF(\varepsilon_1,\varepsilon_2) + \iint\limits_{\theta < z} (S+\varepsilon_2)dF(\varepsilon_1,\varepsilon_2) \qquad (24)$$

This can be manipulated into either of the forms

$$Q = D + G(z) \qquad (25)$$

$$Q = S + H(z) \qquad (26)$$

where the functions G and H are determined by the joint distribution $F(\varepsilon_1,\varepsilon_2)$. If D (or S) and z are now modelled as functions of independent variables and if some error structure is assumed, then the parameters of (25) (or(26)) can in principle be estimated by nonlinear least squares.

Muellbauer's formulation has the advantage that its economic justification is considerably stronger than that of the simple min model. It does, however, require the explicit modelling of excess demand rather than letting this emerge from the underlying behavioural relations. The main practical problem with the approach is that the functions G and H may be intractable.

A rather ad hoc alternative to the simple min condition is due to Spencer (1975). Here Q is specified to be a convex combination of D and S as follows:

$$Q_t = \lambda_t D_t + (1-\lambda_t)S_t \qquad (27)$$

$$\lambda_t = \frac{\exp\left(\frac{S_t - D_t}{\sigma}\right)}{1 + \exp\left(\frac{S_t - D_t}{\sigma}\right)} \tag{28}$$

where σ is a parameter to be estimated. Thus when excess demand is large, the value of Q_t is close to supply and when excess supply is large, Q_t is close to demand. Also the limit as σ tends to zero of the probability density function of Q_t is that of the standard disequilibrium model, and in this sense, the Spencer model is a generalization of the standard disequilibrium model.

An obvious way of generalizing the min condition is to make it stochastic by writing it as

$$Q_t = \min\,(D_t, S_t) + \nu_t \tag{29}$$

where ν_t is an error term. For the sake of simplicity ignoring the price equation for the moment, the model is formally equivalent to the following:

$$\tilde{D}_t = \alpha_1 p_t + \beta_1' x_{1t} + u_{1t} + \nu_t \tag{30}$$

$$\tilde{S}_t = \alpha_2 p_t + \beta_2' x_{2t} + u_{2t} + \nu_t \tag{31}$$

$$Q_t = \min\,(\tilde{D}_t, \tilde{S}_t) \tag{32}$$

This is a standard min problem in which the error terms of the demand and supply functions have positive covariance.

A different way of arriving at a stochastic min problem is provided by the switching regression model

$$Q_t = \begin{cases} \alpha_1 p_t + \beta_1' x_{1t} + u_{1t} & \text{if } \Pi' x_{3t} \leq 0 \\ \alpha_2 p_t + \beta_2' x_{2t} + u_{2t} & \text{if } \Pi' x_{3t} > 0 \end{cases} \quad (33)$$

where Π is a vector of unknown coefficients and x_{3t} a vector of exogenous variables. Models of this type have been considered by Goldfeld and Quandt (1972) and Tishler and Zang (1979). Here we are interested in the special case where $\Pi' x_{3t}$ is defined by

$$\Pi' x_{3t} = \alpha_1 p_t + \beta_1' x_{1t} - \alpha_2 p_t - \beta_2' x_{2t} \quad (34)$$

If we also now let $u_{1t} = u_{2t} = \nu_t$ in the switching regression model (33), the result is equivalent to the following stochastic min model:

$$D_t = \alpha_1 p_t + \beta_1' x_{1t} \quad (35)$$

$$S_t = \alpha_2 p_t + \beta_2' x_{2t} \quad (36)$$

$$Q_t = \min (D_t, S_t) + \nu_t \quad (37)$$

This formulation has been used by Sneessens (1979, 1981) for disequilibrium modelling and is discussed further by Richard in his comments after Quandt's survey (1982). Richard reinterprets it by replacing D_t, S_t in (35) - (37) by D_t^e, S_t^e, the agents' contingent plans. The stochastic min condition now says that agents adjust their plans ex ante by agreeing on a planned quantity to be transacted which is then perturbed in the usual way by uncontrolled factors affecting the market. As well as possessing this attractive economic interpretation, the model also has statistical advantages arising from the fact that (37) postulates à univarate distribution as distinct from the bivariate distribution arising from the non-stochastic min condition but with stochastic terms in the demand and supply functions.

At the end of Section III, we pointed out that Monfort in his comments after Quandt's survey (1982) puts the blame for the difficulties encountered, when testing the equilibrium hypothesis, on the form of the price adjustment equation. Indeed, price adjustment equations of the form (11) or (12) provide only a partial answer to the whole question of specifying the dynamic structure of disequilibrium models. Barro (1972) has suggested that price adjustment equations may be derived from the assumption that the system acts so as to minimize certain adjustment costs. The problem with this is that it will generally lead to the presence of lagged values of D_t and S_t in the model and this complicates considerably the evaluation of the likelihood function.

Improvement of the dynamic specification is one of the directions in which the basic disequilibrium models have been extended. The difficulties caused by lagged endogenous variables or autocorrelated errors have been considered by Laffont and Monfort (1979) and Quandt (1981). An interesting alternative is once again provided by Richard's reinterpretation of the model (35) - (37) since it can be shown that including lagged values of D_t^e and S_t^e in this raises no major computational problems.

Another possible direction of extension of the basic models is the inclusion of expectational variables, especially price expectations. The form of the likelihood function and the method of estimation will depend on the expectations mechanism assumed to be in operation. The issues involved are largely unresolved but an application in which expectations are assumed to be formed with perfect foresight is contained in the paper by Markandya and Pemberton (1984) which is outlined in Section V.

Finally, it is natural to wish to extend the basic models to the case where more than one market may simultaneously be in disequilibrium. This is discussed in Gourieroux, Laffont and Monfort (1980a, 1980b) and Ito (1980).

V. APPLICATION TO THE HOUSING AND LABOUR MARKETS IN THE UK

The original application of disequilibrium econometrics given by Fair and Jaffee (1972) was to a monthly model of housing starts for the U S. The mortgage rate was used as the price variable and, in addition to this, a variable measuring the stock of houses in existence or under construction the previous month and a time trend were included in the demand equation while two flow of funds variables and a time trend were included in the supply equation.

Since Fair and Jaffee's paper, one of the important areas of development of work on the housing market has been the proper measurement of the user cost of housing services, this being the appropriate price varible on the demand side. Markandya and Pemberton (1984) specify the user cost of housing services to be

$$(1-\tau_t)\, r_t P_t + D_t + M_t + T_t - (P^e_{t+1} - P_t) \qquad (38)$$

where τ_t = marginal tax rate of the user

r_t = opportunity cost of capital or borrowing rate on home loans

p_t = asset price of housing

D_t = depreciation costs

M_t = maintenance costs

T_t = local property tax

$p^e_{t+1} - p_t$ = expected capital gain

all in period t.

This user cost variable is incorporated into a model of housing starts which is essentially of the form (1) - (3) together with (11). The stock demand for private housing is specified as a function of the user cost variable, an index of real household disposable income, the stock of public housing and a time trend. From this an equation for the gross change in the stock demand is derived. The gross change in the supply of private housing is specified to be a function of the asset price, the mortgage rate, public housing starts, an index of the real costs of construction and the real increase in deposits to Building Societies.

The model is estimated, using quarterly UK data from the first quarter of 1956 to the last of 1981, under the assumption that the price expectations in the user cost variable (38) are formed with perfect foresight. In the results, the estimate of $\frac{1}{\gamma}$, where γ is the adjustment coefficient,is significantly different from zero and, as explained in Section III of the present paper, this constitutes evidence of disequilibrium.

The first application of disequilibrium econometrics to the labour market was by Rosenand Quandt (1978) who used a model of the form (1) - (3) together with (12). The labour demand equation specified the log of labour demand to be a function of the log of the real wage, the log of output and a time trend. Labour supply was specified to be a function of the log of the net wage, the log of net unearned income and the log of a variable designed to capture changes in the size of the potential labour force. The adjustment equation included either a constant, allowing for an autonomous drift in real wages, or a variable designed to measure the effect of the degree of unionisation on real wages.

The model was estimated on annual US data from 1930 to 1973. The resulting supply and demand elasticities were generally sensible and both a test of $\frac{1}{\gamma}$, where γ is the adjustment coefficient, for significant departure from zero and a likelihood ratio test gave support for the disequilibrium hypothesis. However the estimated model failed to predict the excess supply of labour in the 1930s and this has led some authors to cast doubt on the value of the approach. In particular, Stenius and Virén (1984) show that Rosen and Quandt's results are not robust with respect to differencing the data, estimation on subsamples and respecifying the min condition as stochastic.

We would argue that the value of Rosenand Quandt's paper lies in the fact that it provided a first step in making operational the theoretical literature on disequilibrium models rather than in its numerical results, and that, while the findings in the paper by Stenius and Virén are interesting, they are certainly not enough to cast doubt on the whole approach.

A serious attempt to bring together recent work on the UK labour market in a disequilibrium framework is contained in Hall, Henry, Markandya and Pemberton (1985). The basic model is, as in Rosen and Quandt (1978), of the form (1) - (3) together with (12) and the variables are measured in logs.

The demand equation contains the real wage and a time trend as in Rosen and Quandt (1978) but it is now allowed also to contain

(i) one or two lagged values of employment, as suggested by inter-temporal profit maximization subject to quadratic costs of adjustment;

(ii) expected output, interpreted as a sales constraint operating in the goods market and proxied by either lagged output or by an instrumental variable estimate based on the cyclically adjusted budget deficit and a measure of international price competitiveness;

(iii)the real price of raw materials and energy.

The supply equation includes the supply price of labour, the real level of unemployment benefit, the working population and a measure of union strength. It is also allowed to include the real interest rate. The adjustment equation contains a constant, the measure of union strength used in the supply equation and an incomes policy variables as well as the usual excess demand term.

The model was estimated on quarterly UK data, from the last quarter of 1964 to the last quarter of 1982, using the two proxies for expected output mentioned in (ii), with one or two lagged employment terms in the demand equation, excluding and including the real price of raw materials and energy in the demand equation and excluding and including the real interest rate in the supply equation. Overall there is considerable uniformity among the results from the various specifications and many of the important parameters are well determined and plausibly signed, indicating that the disequilibrium approach can produce meaningful estimates, a conclusion somewhat at odds with that of Stenius and Virén (1984). Most of the specifications tried suggest that a labour demand constraint is in operation over the latter part of the 1970s and early 1980s. Indeed the framework and results produce an important insight into the role of demand and supply effects in the UK labour market. Starting from a new classical equilibrium approach based on optimal inter-temporal behaviour by firms and households, extended to allow for non-market clearing, there is considerable evidence that the sharp falls in employment after 1979 were due to a rapid fall in labour demand.

VI. CONCLUSION

In this paper we have described the basic econometric disequilibrium models and methods of estimation for them. In Section IV we considered various criticisms of the min condition and the price adjustment equation and summarized some possible modifications and extensions. The basic models emerge from the criticisms as interesting polar cases for which estimation is feasible. In addition, the various possible modifications and extensions enhance the framework for empirical work. The applications outlined in Section V provide the first steps in this direction for the UK housing and labour markets.

REFERENCES

T. Amemiya, A note on a Fair and Jaffee model, Econometrica, 42, p.759-762, (1974).

T. Amemiya and G. Sen, The consistency of the maximum likelihood estimator in a disequilibrium model, Technical Report No.238, Institute for Mathematical Studies in the Social Sciences, Stanford University, (1977).

R.J. Barro, A theory of monopolistic price adjustment, Review of Economic Studies, 39, p.17-26, (1972).

R.J. Bowden, Specification, estimation and inference for models of markets in disequilibrium, International Economic Review, 19, p.711-726, (1978).

D.R. Cox, Tests of separate families of hypotheses, Proceedings of the Fourth Berkeley Symposium on Mathematical Statistics and Probability, Vol.1, Berkeley: University of California Press, (1961).

D.R. Cox, Further results on tests of separate families of hypotheses, Journal of the Royal Statistical Society, Series B, 24, p.406-424, (1962).

R.C. Fair and D.M. Jaffee, Methods of estimation for markets in disequilibrium, Econometrica, 40, p.497-514, (1972).

S.M. Goldfeld and R.E. Quandt, Nonlinear methods in econometrics, Amsterdam: North Holland, (1972).

S.M. Goldfeld and R.E. Quandt, Estimation of a disequilibrium model and the value of information, Journal of Econometrics, 3, p.325-348, (1975).

S.M. Goldfeld and R.E. Quandt, Some properties of the simple disequilibrium model with covariance, Economics Letters, 1, p.343-346, (1978).

C. Gourieroux, J.J. Laffont and A. Monfort, Disequilibrium econometrics in simultaneous equations systems, Econometrica, 48, p.75-96, (1980a).

C. Gourieroux, J.J. Laffont and A. Monfort, Coherency conditions in simultaneous linear equations models with endogenous switching regimes, Econometrica, 48, p.675-696, (1980b).

C. Gourieroux, J.J. Laffont and A. Monfont, Tests of the equilibrium vs. disequilibrium hypothesis: a comment, International Economic Review, 21, p.245-247, (1980c).

S.G. Hall, S.G.B. Henry, A. Markandya and M. Pemberton, The labour market in the UK : a disequilibrium model, National Institute of Economic and Social Research, mimeographed, (1985).

M.J. Hartley and P. Mallela, The asymptotic properties of a

maximum likelihood estimator for a model in disequilibrium, Econometrica, 45, p.1205-1220, (1977).
H.S. Hwang, A test of a disequilibrium model, Journal of Econometrics, 12, p.319-334, (1980).
T. Ito, Methods of estimation for multi-market disequilibrium models, Econometrica, 48, p.97-126, (1980).
J.J. Laffont and A. Monfort, Disequilibrium econometrics in dynamic models, Journal of Econometrics, 11, p.353-363, (1979).
G.S. Maddala and F.D. Nelson, Maximum likelihood methods for models of markets in disequilibrium, Econometrica, 42, p.1013-1030, (1974).
A. Markandya and M. Pemberton, The estimation of a disequilibrium model of the housing market - an application to the United Kingdom, Discussion Paper 84-15, University College London, (1984).
J. Muellbauer, Macrotheory vs. macroeconometrics : the treatment of disequilibrium in macromodels, Discussion Paper 29, Birkbeck College, (1978).
M.H. Pesaran and A. Deaton, Testing non-rested nonlinear regression models, Econometrica, 46, p.677-694, (1978).
R.E. Quandt, Tests of the equilibrium vs. disequilibrium hypothesis, International Economic Review, 19, p.435-452, (1978).
R.E. Quandt, Autocorrelated errors in simple disequilibrium models, Economics Letters, 7, p.55-62, (1981).
R.E. Quandt with comments by D.F. Hendry, A. Monfort and J.F. Richard, Econometric disequilibrium models, Econometric Reviews, 1, p.1-96, (1982).
H.S. Rosen and R.E Quandt, Estimation of a disequilibrium aggregate labour market, Review of Economics and Statistics, 60, p.371-379, (1978).
H. Sneessens, On the econometrics of quantity rationing models, Econometric Research Program, Research Memo, 250, Princeton University, (1979).
H. Sneessens, Alternative stochastic specifications and estimation methods for quantity rationing models: a Monte Carlo study, London School of Economics, mimeographed, (1981).
P.D. Spencer, A disequilibrium model of personal sector bank advances 1964-1974: Some preliminary results, Working Paper, H.M. Treasury, (1975).
M. Stenius and M. Virén, Some further results on Rosen and Quandt's labour market model, European Economic Review, 26, p.369-377, (1984).
A. Tishler and I. Zang, A switching regression method using inequality conditions, Journal of Econometrics, 11, p.259-274, (1979).

EMPIRICAL MODELS OF THE UK AGGREGATE LABOUR MARKET: A SURVEY

MARTYN J. ANDREWS
ESRC Macroeconomic Modelling Bureau, University of Warwick

I. INTRODUCTION

This paper attempts to evaluate and compare the current state of the art of econometric models of the UK labour market.[1] In order to be selective we restrict our attention to time-series models, and moreover to those models that address themselves to the joint determination of the real wage and employment/unemployment. This is particularly important from a policy perspective. It is clearly misleading to analyse the effect of the replacement ratio, for example, on unemployment whilst holding the real wage constant. This is because the potential influcence of real wages on employment (via costs borne by the firm), and therefore unemployment, is completely ignored. The studies examined are those made up of at least two equations. Typically these can be thought of as a demand/employment equation and a supply/wage equation, with possibly an equation or identity for unemployment thrown in for good measure.

Within this simultaneous equations context we identify the endogenous variables to be explained as aggregate employment[2], aggregate unemployment and the aggregate real wage. The underlying assumptions as to how these variables are determined varies from model to model. The resulting different labour market configurations are emphasised in some detail as are some of the more interesting (relating to policy) reduced-form elasticities which can be derived. Although the analysis refers to the long-run we stress that this may be quite tangential if dynamic adjustment towards the long-run is very slow, or even impossible.

Two particular sources of policy intervention in the labour market are of some topical interest, and are common to most of the models. The first relates to the effect of benefits on employment, unemployment and the real wage, particularly as the evidence for such effects differs widely across the models. (The evidence is drawn together in the conclusion.) The second relates to an increase in the real price of raw materials and fuel. Whilst the implications of changing such a variable would appear to be uncontroversial - we assume throughout that the government may manipulate this relative price via changes in the nominal price level - the effect on the market should be to move real wages and employment in the same direction. It is also well accepted that a change in the replacement ratio will move these two variables in the opposite direction, and so it follows that the Government may manipulate the degree of association between real pay and jobs to an infinite degree. This simple point is worth stressing because it seems to have moved completely from view in the recent debate on the magnitude of the trade off between more jobs and lower real wages. (See Hansard, 30 October 1984 for the well-publicised policy prescription proposed on the basis of this unique association, and critiques thereof in Andrews et al., 1985, and Metcalf and Nickell,

1985). The simple long-run configurations of the models reported demonstrate this point quite adequately.

The underlying theoretical underpinnings of the four models chosen differ along a well defined spectrum. Nonetheless we choose not to emphasise these differences to a degree that might imply that they are directly responsible for the different elasticities, multipliers, and the like, observed across the models. Rather we demonstrate that a more pragmatic view represents the true state of affairs. This holds that such differences in fact relate to sample size, omitted variables, and other details of econometric specification. This point is emphasised in Section II where a framework of analysis is presented. Nonetheless the spectrum along which the models are classified provides a useful methodology of analysis. At this point it is appropriate to acknowledge the quite transparent debt this paper owes to Nickell (1984a), which also provides the reader with a more suitable reference for the underlying theoretical structures of the models discussed. Like Nickell we start with the competitive paradigm, and so Section IIIA presents the two equation market-clearing model of Andrews (1984). Section IIIB discusses a more realistic paradigm which recognises the existence of a unionised sector, an example of which is presented in Minford (1983) and forms the basis of the Liverpool model. Nonetheless such a model is only an extension of the competitive paradigm. Section IIIC is quite different and treats the determination of wages and employment in a bargaining framework, which assumes that the labour market is, for all intents and purposes, fully unionised. Finally Section IIID discusses the background to the estimation of disequilibrium models, and discusses the salient features of the Beenstock et al. (1985) model which suggests that non-market-clearing is an appropriate classification.

The four models discussed all use similar data sets, being annual and covering the first three complete decades of the post-war period. The exception is Minford (1983), who uses quarterly data from 1964, but as he is able to reproduce similar results using a data set compatible with the other three, comparisons are valid. Finally the discussion does not emphasis econometric criteria to evaluate competing claims on the data, and so the standard range diagnostic reporting is left to one side. The reader is referred to the original sources if interested.

II. A FRAMEWORK FOR ANALYSIS

This section sets up a structure by which all the models under discussion can be examined. Consider the following representative labour demand schedule,

$$n_t^d = -\alpha_1 W_t^p + \alpha_2' Z_t^d. \tag{1}$$

n_t^d is the logarithm of labour demand, W_t^p the logarithm of the real product wage, and Z_t^d is a vector of exogenous variables. If we also define w as nominal wages or earnings and p as the nominal price level, the real product wage may be written as $w(1+t_1)/p$, where t_1 is the employer's tax rate. Typically equation (1) will be dynamic. Although n_t^d is defined as labour demand, it is only in the disequilibrium models of Section IIID where this does not coincide with employment, n_t. Equation (1) encompasses two classes of estimated models. The first is the standard Brechling (1965) and Ball and St. Cyr (1966) version, where Z_t^d consists of output and its lags, and a trend, and possibly α_1 is set to zero. The second derives from the work of James Symons, where Z_t^d now contains the real price of raw materials and fuel, and the capital stock, and α_1 (in the long-run) is definitely not equal to zero. One particular feature of the latter class of models is that (1) is an unconditional demand schedule, rather than one which captures only substitution effects.

In three of the models to be examined we may identify an aggregate labour supply schedule,

$$n_t^s = \delta_1 W_t^c + \delta_3 \ell_t + \delta_2' Z_t^s \tag{2}$$

Here n_t^s is the logarithm of labour supply, W_t^c the logarithm of the real consumption wage, and Z_t^s is a vector of exogenous variables on the supply side. The real consumption wage may be written as $w(1-t_2)/p(1+t_3)$, where t_2 is employee's taxes and t_3 is the indirect tax rate. Notice that W_t^p may be written as $W_t^c + (t_1+t_2+t_3)_t$, the latter term defining the "tax wedge", T_t. Equation (2) is sufficiently general to encompass the intertemporal labour supply model of Lucas and Rapping (1969), where Z_t^s contains the real rate of interest and some index of long-run real wages, as well as other simpler models of labour supply. Models tested on aggregate data are few and far between, see for example Altonji (1982) and Alogoskoufis (1985).

One particular exogenous determinant of labour supply is singled out, the logarithm of the labour force (ℓ_t), because if its coefficient is unity (2) may be rewritten as

$$W_t^c = -\delta_1^{-1}(\ell_t - n_t^s) - \delta_1^{-1}\delta_2' Z_t^s \tag{3}$$

If it is also true that labour supply coincides with employment we can replace $\ell_t - n_t$ by the unemployment rate, u_t. Now (3) takes on the appearance of a wage equation, containing unemployment and exogenous labour supply variables. Notice that this particular wage equation can be derived under a market-clearing assumption, and so those members of the labour force not working are doing so voluntarily. This reparameterisation of labour supply is how Patrick Minford derives his wage equation, (see Section IIIB). It may be described as "structural" as it contains a right-hand endogenous variable, and therefore is not to be confused with the reduced-form wage equation of any given labour market structure.

A second type of wage equation arises naturally in the type of labour market model where the real wage cannot move instantaneously to clear the market. The speed of adjustment towards market-clearing is often postulated to be proportional to excess demand, which we may write as

$$\gamma(W_t - W_{t-1}) = (n_t^d - n_t^s) + \gamma\beta_2' Z_t^w, \qquad \gamma>0 \tag{4}$$

W_t is the logarithm of the pre-tax real wage, $(w/p)_t$. Also the variables contained in Z_t^w represent any institutional features (e.g. unions) or administered features (e.g. incomes policy) that tend to keep the real wage away from its market-clearing level. In contrast to the previous model this presupposes that some of the unemployment is involuntary and refers to those who are willing to work (at the going wage) but cannot get jobs. When $\gamma=0$ we have market-clearing, $n_t^d = n_t^s$.

Again this particular wage equation is structural, containing right-handed endogenous variables. If labour supply and labour demand are substituted out using equations (1) and (2), we obtain the reduced-form equation

$$\gamma(W_t - W_{t-1}) = -(\alpha_1 + \delta_1)W_t + \alpha_2' Z_t^d - \delta_2' Z_t^s + \gamma\beta_2' Z_t^w$$
$$+ \text{ tax terms} \qquad (5)$$

This dynamic equation, whose speed of adjustment is determined by α_1, δ_1, and γ, depends on all three types of exogenous variable. Similar reduced forms are obtained from models containing either a union sector (see Section IIIB), or models of a unionised economy (see Section IIIC). It is this problem of observational equivalence that suggests that differences between the models estimated will arise because of pragmatic considerations relating to specification, sample size, and the like, rather then arising out of different theoretical underpinnings. This point is demonstrated when comparing two quite extreme models. Consider the reduced-form wage equation (5) above, which is non-market clearing. We generate the market-clearing equivalent by setting $\gamma=0$,

$$W_t = (\alpha_1 + \delta_1)^{-1}[\alpha_2' Z_t^d - \delta_2' Z_t^s] \qquad (6)$$

In this particular formulation the distinction between the two models rests on the lack of lagged real wages in the latter. However it is readily demonstrated that when lagged real wages are included in labour demand or supply, equation (5) represents the same regression model, whether or not

$\gamma=0$. This lack of identification of a clear market structure is because it is impossible to disentangle wage dynamics arising from the actions of agents (via expectations formation, for example) from dynamics arising from imbalance between supply and demand.

We conclude this section by noting that we have identified four different types of wage adjustment equation, as given by equations (3), (4), (5) and (6). As noted earlier, employment is determined on the demand side of the market in all but one of the models under discussion. Then unemployment is determined by the familiar identity.

$$U_t \equiv L_t - N_t$$

where the upper case variables N_t and L_t are defined naturally, not in logarithms. This identity is similar to the one for the unemployment rate defined under equation (3). U_t is therefore measured in heads. This may also be rewritten as

$$U_t = (N_t^s - N_t^d) + (L_t - N_t^s)$$

Providing $N_t^d = N_t$ we may loosely refer to the first bracket as involuntary unemployment and the second as voluntary unemployment. In all of these models considered the labour force is treated exogenously, an assumption which ignores the reasons why there has been an increase in the participation of married women, for example. Until more is known about this and related issues, the best way to justify an exogeneous labour force assumption is to proxy the unemployment rate for men and women by the male unemployment rate (see Section IIIC). There we have the male unemployment rate given by $\rho(\ell_t - n_t)$, where ρ is the appropriate conversion factor.

The appendix lists a set of notation consistently used throughout the paper. Precise definitions are not provided unless important: readers are referred to original sources.

III. THE MODELS

(A) A Market-Clearing Model

In order to set the scene we start with a competitive labour market model. The neoclassical paradigm is well known; prices are parametric to agents, who are forward-looking and are endowed with rational expectations. However agents on both sides of the market are assumed to face costs of adjustment in moving to fulfilment of their optimal plans. Relative prices are assumed to respond instantaneously to ensure that all markets clear at all points in time.

Andrews (1984) presents an example of such a model. The estimated dynamic labour demand schedule explains fluctuations in employment by the relative price of raw materials and fuel, q/p, the capital stock, k, and the real product wage. Symons (1981) demonstrates that this particular model of labour demand, for the manufacturing sector, is somewhat superior at explaining such fluctuations than the previous standard model containing output. This particular class of model extends the work of Sargent (1978) in dealing with the assumed forward-looking behaviour of firms, who also face adjustment costs. For further examples and discussion see parts (C) and (D) of this Section, together with Symons (1985), Symons and Layard (1984) and Layard and Nickell (1985a: Section 2).

The labour supply equation presented is based on the Lucas and Rapping (1969) model, which allows for the possibility of inter- and intra-temporal substitution of leisure for consumption. The specification, derived from a two-period utility maximization problem (for the more general case, see Sargent 1979), includes an index of future or normal real wages, and the one period real rate of interest. In estimation these two latent variables are assumed to differ from their ex-post realised values by a ramdom forecasting error, which "goes into" the equation error (see Wickens, 1982). The equation also contains lagged dependent variables, through a standard adjustment cost argument. As far as we know this is the only model that has been fitted to UK data, although Altonji (1982) has partially succeeded using US data, again replacing the original adaptive expectations assumption by rational expectations. The two equations are estimated using 2SLS, UK annual data, 1950-1979 (for precise details see Andrews, 1984, table 1),

$$n_t(1-\underset{(.13)}{1.132}L + \underset{(.15)}{.504}L^2) = -\underset{(.05)}{.188}[w(1+t_1)/p]_{t-1}^{+} + \underset{(.05)}{.219}k_t$$

$$+ (\underset{(.020)}{.0327} - \underset{(.017)}{.0658}L)(q/p)_t + \text{constant} \tag{7}$$

$\hat{\sigma} = .0066$, $\quad$ + indicates endogenous

$$n_t(1-.713L + .208L^2) = (.245^+ + .113L)$$
$$\qquad (.23) \quad (.41) \qquad (.15) \quad (.17)$$

$$[w(1-t_2)/p(1+t_3)]_t - \underset{(.18)}{.230^+}[w(1-t_2)/p(1+t_3)]^*_t +$$

$$\underset{(.13)}{.120I_t} - \underset{(.028)}{.0139(B/w)_{t-1}} - \underset{(.0097)}{.0143D_t} + \underset{(.54)}{.795\ell_{t-1}}$$

$$+ \text{ constant} \tag{8}$$

$\hat{\sigma} = .0079$

Standard errors are in parentheses (). $[w(1-t_2)/p(1+t_3)]^*_t$ is a five year centred moving average of the real wage; I_t is a two-year backward moving average of the real interest rate, namely $R_t-p_{t+1}+p_t$, where R_t is the nominal rate of interest; D_t is a dummy whose value is unity from 1967 onwards; and $(B/w)_t$ is the replacement ratio. All variables are in logarithms except I (measured in percentage points ÷ 100), B/w (normalised on its mean), the dummy, and all the taxes (measured in percentage points ÷100).

Taken at face value these two equations appear to be perfectly satisfactory models of demand and supply, and although the latter is somewhat weaker at explaining employment fluctuations, it does provide some support for the intertemporal substitution hypothesis. We write the model in long-run "structural" form[3],

$$\begin{bmatrix} 1 & .505 \\ 1 & -.258 \end{bmatrix} \begin{bmatrix} n \\ w^c \end{bmatrix} = \begin{bmatrix} -.089(q/p) + .589k - .505(t_1+t_2+t_3) \\ .485\,I - .028(B/w) - .0288D + 1.61\ell \end{bmatrix}$$

This corresponds to a static version of equations (1) and (2). Simple application of Cramer's Rule will deliver reduced-form elasticities for employment and the real wage with respect to any variable. It is clear that all such elasticities will be signed correctly as the model conforms to the standard textbook configuration. One obvious implication is that the employment/real wage trade-off is not necessarily negative, let alone equal to the slope of the long-run demand schedule, (-.505). The scope for demand management policy in this model is as follows. First, any stimulus that changes the nominal price level and/or its rate of change will shift both schedules, and the quantitative effect on the two endogenous variables can be measured using the first-stage regressions for $(q/p)_t$, W^*_t, and I_t (not reported). This particular result presumes that the demand schedule is not prevented from moving by some purchasing-power-parity type argument that imposes $q/p = 0$. Second, an obvious direct influence on the market is via the standard tax wedge, which, because of the "irrelevance of who pays" principle, is indifferent to the choice of particular tax. Because of the relatively inelastic nature of both schedules a one percentage point cut in any tax increases employment by onle .17 of one per cent, the real product wage increases by .34 per cent and the real consumption wage falls by .66 per cent. Third, a change in the replacement ratio is a policy prescription of some interest. The elasticity for employment is -.0185, and for the real wage is .0367.

This rather cosy state of affairs does not stand up to further analysis, however. First, the dynamic properties of the system require examination. Although the paths for employment in each equation taken separately, for a given exogenous real wage shock, appear sensible (roots are $.56 \pm .34i$ for demand, $.37 \pm .28i$ for supply), this paper is particularly concerned with the joint determination of both employment and the real wage. Endogenising the real wage requires making some assumptions about $W^*_t = (W^c_{t-2} + \ldots + W^c_{t+2})/5$, and in the spirit of the equilibrium model perfect foresight is assumed. Following Blanchard and Kahn (1980) the model may be written in standard VAR(1) form, $y_t = Ay_{t-1} + b'Z_t$, where in this case $y'_t = (n_{t-1}, n_{t-2}, W_{t+2}, W_{t+1}, W_t, W_{t-1})'$. For the system to be saddlepoint stable exactly four roots are required to be inside the unit circle, and two outside (corresponding to the presence of W_{t+1} and W_{t+2}). The roots of A are -1.66, 2.20, -1.50, .42$\pm$.42i, .26 and so the long-run is unattainable. The presence of one too many unstable roots is true for the static expectations case, and also when W^*_t is assumed exogenous. Second, the estimated structural model is not an admissable transformation of the data generation process because the test for the validity of the overidentifying restrictions fails (see Sargan, 1958). One way of demonstrating this important point is to compare the solved reduced-form for the real wage and the estimated unrestricted reduced-form, which are respectively,

$$W^c_t = 1.12n_{t-1} - 2.14n_{t-2} - .35W^c_{t-1} - (.10(q/p)_{t-1} + .086D_t$$

$$-(.09 + 78L)(t_1 \div t_2 + t_3)_t + .120(B/w)_{t-1}$$

$$- .86\ell_{t-1} + .99k_t + (.10 - .20L)(q^w/p^w)_t$$

$$W^c_t = .59n_{t-1} = 1.57n_{t-2} + .45W^c_{t-1} - .10(q/p)_{t-1} + .019D_t$$

$$- (.49 + .08L)\ (t_1 + t_2 + t_3)_t = .052(B/w)_{t-1}$$

$$+ .75\ell_{t-1} + .60k_t - (-.25 -.09L)\ (q^w/p^w)_t$$

It is self-evident that the model is at odds with the data.

When added to the unstable dynamic nature of the real wage, the conclusion might be that the simple competitive model might be passed over in favour of something more realistic.

(B) A Partially Unionised Model ("The Liverpool Model")

The next model we consider is market-clearing in spirit, but takes account of the role of unionised labour. This particular paradigm has been used by Patrick Minford to estimate empirical models of the labour market, together with a model of the aggregate UK economy. The policy implications of the so-called Liverpool Model have hardly passed unnoticed (see the Guardian leading article, 5 July 1983). The model, based on annual data, is set out in Minford et al. (1984); the theoretical background to the labour market sub-sector is presented in Minford (1983), together with evidence based on quarterly data. Further evidence is given in Minford et.al. (1983). Here also is where the policy implications are spelt out in full, and suggest that a substantial fall in unemployment can be achieved by (i) setting an upper bound on the replacement ratio at 70% and (ii) de-unionising the labour market. The evidence upon which prescriptions have been made has not been received uncritically, as the recent debate in the Economic Journal illustrates (Nickell, 1984b and Minford, 1984). Further discussion is conducted in Layard and Nickell (1985a) and some of the following draws on their analysis. This section examines the two equation quarterly model; the equivalent annual version that forms part of the Liverpool macroeconometric model is discussed briefly in Wallis et al. (1985), chapter 4. Attention is paid to comparing this type of model with the previous one, where there are no unions.

The Minford paradigm is one of a labour market consisting of two sectors, one unionised (superscript u) and one non-unionised (superscript n). The real wage in the latter, $(w/p)^n$, is assumed to be able to clear this market, although the existence of unemployment benefits provides a floor below which it cannot fall. The real wage in the unionised sector, $(w/p)^u$, is determined by the outcome of bargaining between unions and firms, where it is assumed that unions choose the wage unilaterally and the firm sets employment unilaterally. The union's objective function is the expected real income of its potential membership, which is maximized against the firm's demand curve. The outcome is that the unionised real wage is set as some mark-up, m, on the competitive wage[4],

$$(w/p)^u = (1+m)(w/p)^n \tag{10}$$

If we also define μ as the proportion of firms that pay union rates ("coverage"), then the average observed real wage is simply

$$(w/p) = \mu(w/p)^u + (1-\mu)(w/p)^n \tag{11}$$

Clearly adjustments to the competitive model are required to take account of the role of the two new variables, m and μ. Nickell (1984a) demonstrates that these will only be required on the supply side, providing similar firms operate in both sectors, and so for empirical purposes suitable measures just need adding to the aggregate supply equation. The formal analysis indicates that coverage should have a positive effect on supply, and the mark-up a negative one, for a given average wage.

Equations (10) and (11) reveal that the observed average real wage is determined by the competitive real wage,

$$w/p = [\mu + (1-\mu)(1+m)](w/p)^n \tag{12}$$

which in turn is determined by the forces of supply and demand as in the type of competitive model discussed earlier. At this point Minford inverts a standard labour supply schedule, as was demonstrated in Section II (see equation (3)), which is used to substitute out the unobserved competitive wage. This yields a wage equation of the form

$$w/p = -[\mu + (1-\mu)(1+m)][U_t + \delta_2' Z_t^s]/\delta_1, \tag{13}$$

which is linearised in the usual way. He also specifies a standard labour demand model (see equation 1) except unemployment data is used in place of employment data (i.e. $n_t = -kU_t$),

$$U_t = (\alpha_1/k)W_t^p - k^{-1}\alpha_2' Z_t^d. \tag{14}$$

This two-equation system in w/p and U is then estimated.

It is worth stressing that the derivation of (13) requires a market-clearing assumption for $(w/p)^n$. Moreover the linkage from $(w/p)^n$ to w/p in (12) presumes that the mark-up is exogenous to the determination of the unionised wage. This is challenged by Nickell (1984b) who argues that as the mark-up is determined by the bargain between firms and workers, it depends on all factors affecting demand for labour in that sector as well as the alternative opportunities available to workers in the competitive sector.

Thus the mark-up might be instrumented by Z^s and Z^d, and direct exogenous measures of union power. Otherwise it must be substituted out of (13) directly. Similarly $(w/p)^n$ might be replaced by its market-clearing reduced-form (something akin to (6)), yielding an aggregate reduced-form wage equation. This differs from the "competitive" reduced-form by only coverage variables and exogenous mark-up type variables, and suggests that differences between the two should not be fundamental.

Turning to Minford's empirical results, we report the basic quarterly model (Minford 1983: table 3), which is estimated by 2SLS, 1964/II to 1979/II. t-ratios are in parenthesis (].

$$U_t(1 - \underset{(11.3]}{.744}L) = \underset{(2.7]}{1.04}(w/p+t_1)_t - \underset{(4.5]}{2.17}\overset{+}{y}_t + \underset{(2.6]}{.008}t + \text{seasonals} \qquad (15)$$

$\hat{\sigma}=.4986$

$$(w/p)_t(1 - \underset{(12.0]}{.77}L) = -\underset{(2.1]}{.024}U_t + \underset{(3.1]}{.11}(B/p+t_2)_t + \underset{(2.4]}{.45}\mu_t - \underset{(0.1]}{.016}\ell_t + \text{seasonals} \qquad (16)$$

$\hat{\sigma}=.0125$

All variables are in logarithms except t_1, t_2, and μ (all in percentage points ÷100). μ_t is defined as the "national unionisation rate", y_t is real output.

For comparisons with other models further relationships need using. First, in order to deal with the powerful endogenous presence of output[5], the following two long-run relationships are taken from Minford (1983:562),

$$y = -.65(e/p) + .46y^w \tag{17}$$

$$e/p = 1.86(w/p+t_1) - .033t. \tag{18}$$

y^w is the logarithm of an index of world trade volume and e/p is the real exchange rate. Equation (17) reflects current account equilibrium and (18) is the "long-run relationship between the real exchange rate and real wages (given by the pricing equation)". Second, we use the same relationship between (log) employment and (log) unemployment as does Minford (1983), namely $n_t = -.118U_t$. Now it is possible to <u>interpret</u> the estimated equations as a supply and demand model, at least for the long run,

$$\begin{pmatrix} 1 & .48 \\ 1 & -1.14 \end{pmatrix} \begin{pmatrix} n \\ W^c \end{pmatrix} = \begin{pmatrix} -.65(e/p) + .46y^w - .02t - 48(t_1+t_2) \\ -.55(B/p) + .08\ell - 2.22\mu + .59t_2 \end{pmatrix} \tag{19}$$

There is an obvious similarity between the demand equation here and that presented in equation (9). (The absence of t_3 in the tax wedge is because the real wage in the demand equation inappropriately normalises on the retail prices.) The supply equation is somewhat different, however, in spite of the presence of similar variables. Two clear differences are worth noting, and form the basis of the policy proposals referred to earlier. First, the reduced-form elasticity of unemployment benefits on real wages is .19, and on employment is -.33 (making use of (18) in (19)). The latter converts to an unemployment elasticity of 2.80. Second, the union density measure has powerful effects on both endogenous variables.

These "large" numbers are generated because equation (16) has a large lagged dependent variable and a small coefficient on unemployment. Nickell (1984b) suggests that this is because the model is misspecified, containing no exogenous labour demand variables (as it would if the markup were correctly substituted out). In their absence no variables are able to explain the secular increase in real wages over the sample, and so its lag picks up the omitted variables effect. The omission of lagged unemployment also may be important, and shows a lack of concern over the dynamics[6]. Minford (1984) accepts the criticism in principle, but provides evidence that the lack of demand variables makes little difference (Minford, 1984: Table 1). This rebuttal by Minford appears to be weakened when we note that in all the new regressions reported, using a larger data set of 75 observations, unemployment is never significant. This suggests some lack of robustness over the basic structure, which we now characterise as employment being a purely demand side phenomenon, whilst real wages are determined by "institutional" factors in a process that exhibits a lot of persistence. Although the policy implications remain the same, this looks remarkably similar to the model presented in (D) below and has little to do with the competitive paradigm.

(C) A Fully Unionised Model

A recent model of the UK economy, which assumes that the labour market is fully unionised, has been estimated by

Nickell and Andrews (1983). This model, for better or for worse, is often compared with the Minford model. Rather than describe in full the theoretical underpinnings we consider here why the two estimated models differ, and in particular whether this arises from the assumed lack of a competitive sector.

The justification for ignoring the competitive sector is that the evidence suggests that collective bargaining is the primary mode of wage determination in Britain. The observation that 80% of manual workers and 50% of non-manual workers are covered by collective agreements supports this view; moreover a sizeable proportion of the remainder are covered by Wage Councils and the like.

Consequently wages and employment are determined in a bargaining model of the following kind. A representative bargain involves a firm and a union, where the former is assumed to have utility over profits of $V(\pi(W,n))$, and the latter has preferences over real wages and employment given by $v(W,n)$. Both sides bargain over real wages but firms retain "the right to manage" and so set employment unilaterally. As a consequence the solution must lie on the firm's <u>competitive</u> demand schedule $n(W)$. The outcome is assumed to be the standard Nash equilibrium, which is formally written down as the solution to

$$\max_n \left[V(\pi(W,n)) - V(\bar{\pi})\right]^{\beta} \left[v(W,n)-\bar{v}\right] \quad \text{subject to } n=n(W)$$

where n is given by the solution to $\max_n \; \pi(W,n)$.

$\bar{\pi}$ and $\bar{v}$ are the "fall-back" levels of profits and utility of the firm and union respectively. In examining the solution consider the properties of $V(\pi(.))$ and $v(.)$ when constrained to the competitive demand schedule, but when neither side is constrained by the other's actions. First, as the union "moves down" n(W) from left to right utility rises and then falls; its optimum position is given by the text-book tangency solution $dv/dW = v_w + v_n n_w = 0$ (see Figure 1).

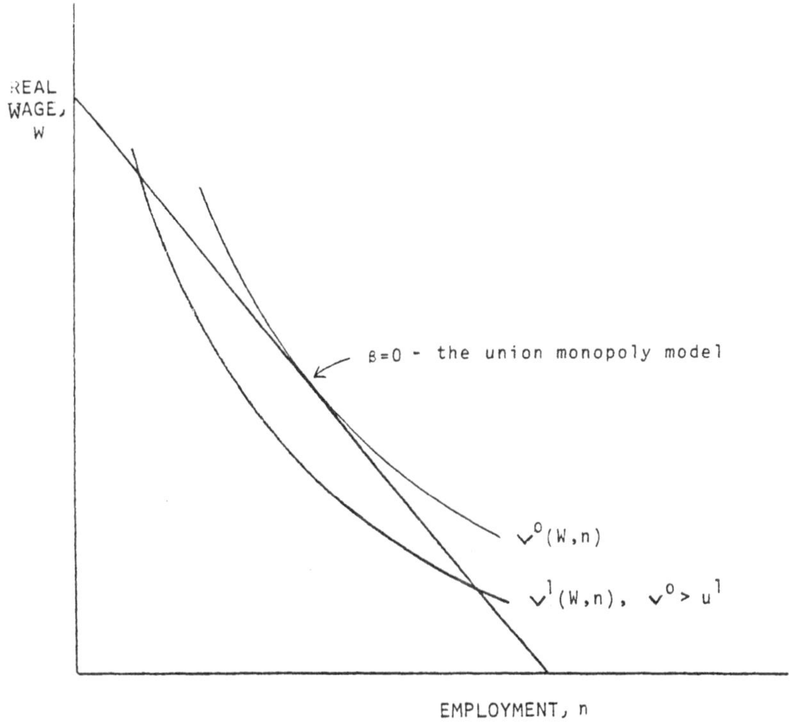

FIGURE 1 The union's preferences and labour demand

For the firm, following the same route the n(W) locus cuts the maximum of each isoprofit contour and so profits (and therefore utility) rise strictly monotonically as real wages fall, (see Figure 2). For all points on n(W) below the union's optimal position the two sides' interest conflict. The solution occurs when the union loses utility at

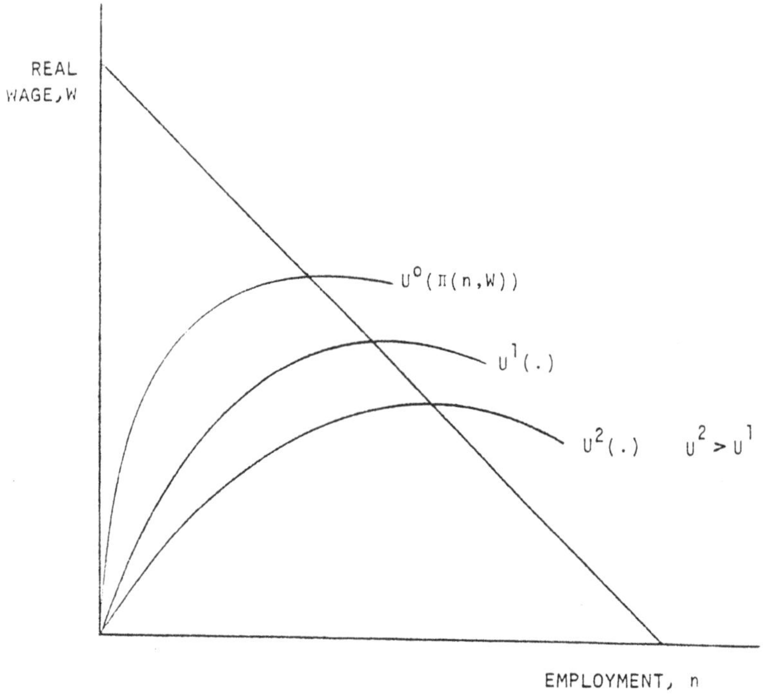

FIGURE 2 The firm's profit function and labour demand

a rate "consistent with" the firm's increase in profits, the matching-up of which depends on β, the parameter which captures the relative power of firms over unions. This is made clear in the first-order condition

$$\frac{\beta(\pi_w + \pi_n n_w)}{\pi} = \frac{-(v_w + v_n v_w)}{v}$$

The numerator of the left-hand side is negative given the standard properties of the profit function ($\pi_w<0$, $\pi_n>0$, $n_w<0$). Consequently at the optimum we observe that $v_w>v_n n_w$, which states that the union's utility curves are flatter than labour demand, and so the point is lower than the union's optimal position, (see Figure 3). This latter special case occurs when $\beta=0$, which is when the union sets wages unilaterally and the firm sets employment unilaterally.

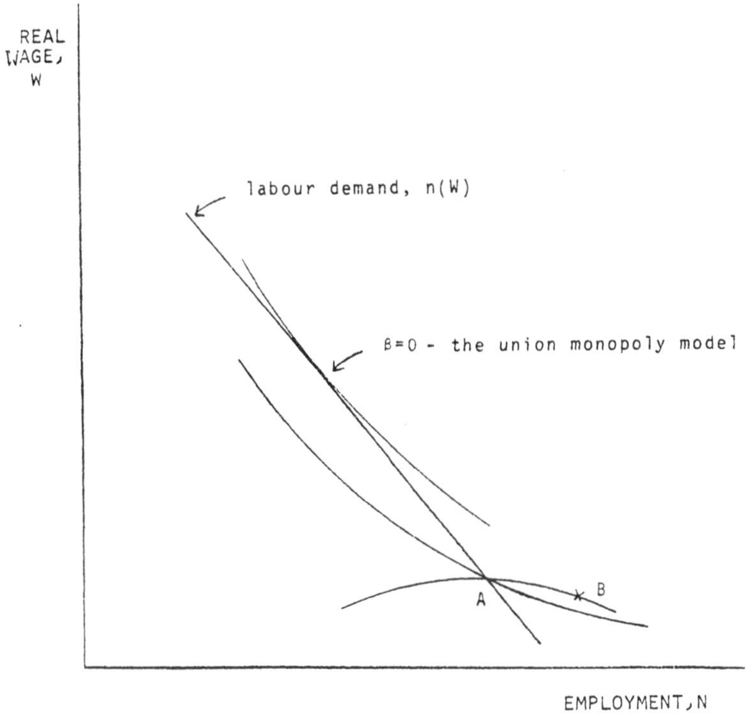

FIGURE 3 The Nash solution to the bargain between the firm and the union

It is well known (McDonald and Solow, 1981) that constraining the solution to the firm's competitive demand schedule is not Pareto efficient. An outward movement beyond n(W) along the firm's isoprofit line can make the union better off, as is illustrated by comparing point A (the Nash solution above) with point B. This reflects the underlying assumption that the union does not bargain over employment levels, one that might be supported by casual empiricism (but with some obvious counter-examples). The two models differ over their implications for employment, but not wages. For example, the more general model predicts an increase in wages and employment in response to an increase in union power, say, and there is little evidence to support this hypothesis. This model is dropped in favour of the one discussed above. For further discussion and references to the "bargaining" literature, see Nickell (1982: 2-3).

The restriction of the solution to n(W) implies that the standard competitive labour demand model of (A) above may be used as part of the structure to be estimated. Modelling the union side is more complicated and needs to take account of its "social responsibility" for those not working. This is the channel by which benefits and non-union wages may enter the model. In Nickell and Andrews (1983) a detailed account of the solution to the Nash problem is presented in a comparative statics framework, and suggests a log-linear specification for a real wage equation. A flavour of the range of possible explanatory variables is as follows. First, an increase in either lagged wages, expected wage growth or the replacement ratio should increase real wages as they all raise opportunities outside the firm and thus strengthen the bargaining power of the union. Similarly an increase in the proportion of time spent unemployed should lower the real wage outcome. An increase in the income tax rate has an ambiguous effect because of two opposing influences: (i) unions will want to compensate for lost wages, but (ii) also their preferences indicate a substitution of real wages for employment. Third, higher levels of past employment will lead to a higher real wage outcome through more bargaining power, as does a lower weight attached to "outsiders". Finally on the employer's side we have productivity variables (anything that enters Z^d), the ratio of expected producer prices to consumer's prices, and employment taxes. An increase in productivity has an income effect as firms can afford to pay more wages and employment, but a substitution effect as wage increases are more expensive at the margin than employment increases. The same argument applies for the other two variables and throughout the income effect is expected to dominate. A higher level of fall-back profits should endow the employer with more relative power, and lead to lower real wage settlements.

Many of the possibilities in the specification of the wage equation are latent variables but, once taken care of, lead to a reduced-form type equation as both sides of the "market" influence the outcome. However the variables chosen to proxy the proportion of the period spent unemployed are unemployment rate and a structural mismatch variable, which gives the wage equation the appearance of a Phillips' Curve. The specification is more general than either equations (3) or (4), containing unemployment together with Z^s,Z^w <u>and</u> Z^d type variables. Thus this example of a bargaining model provides some theoretical foundation upon which the disequilibrium wage equation (4) may be based (and wage models such as the "real wage resistance hypothesis"). Notice also that it generalises equation (3), the wage equation derived by Minford from the competitive paradigm. We stress that this is only because the latter is misspecified, containing no Z^d variables. That they should be the same illustrates that partially-unionised and fully-unionised models are observationally equivalent, in spite of their different underpinnings.

The equations estimated in Nickell and Andrews (1983) are as follows[7].

$$n_t(1 - \underset{(8.3]}{1.127L} + \underset{(3.1]}{.492L^2}) = (\underset{(0.1]}{.00678^+} - \underset{(3.0]}{.194L})[w(1+t_1)/p]_t$$

$$+ \underset{(3.3]}{.217}k_t + (\underset{(1.7]}{.0359^+} - \underset{(3.8]}{.0673L})(q/p)_t + \text{constant}$$

$\hat{\sigma} = .0068$

$$u_t \ .9(l_t - n_t) \qquad (20)$$

$$[w/p(1+t_3)]_t = \underset{(6.3]}{-4.10^+}u_t + \underset{(4.0]}{.035}M_t + \underset{(.6]}{.046^+}(1+L)(B/p)_t$$

$$- \underset{(3.1]}{.087^+}(1+L)(q/p)_t + \underset{(1.7]}{.64}(k/\ell) + \underset{(1.7]}{.705^+}\mu_t + \underset{(2.5]}{.048^+}m_t$$

$$+ \underset{(1.1]}{.785}t_{1t-1} + \underset{(2.6]}{1.25}t_{2t} - \underset{(7.3]}{1.48}t_{3t} + \text{constant} \qquad (21)$$

$\hat{\sigma}=.0112$

One variable not yet defined in this paper is M_t, the structural mismatch variable, which is proxied by the absolute annual change in the proportion of employees in the production sector. Also the measure of m_t, the union/non-union mark-up, is an updated version of a series constructed in Layard, Metcalf and Nickell (1978). Both this and the other union variable, μ, enter as proxies for the fall-back level of profits of the firm. The parameter $\rho = .9$ translates the "true" (male and female) unemployment rate into the registered male unemployment rate, as discussed at the end of Section II. All variables are in logarithms except u, M, μ and all the taxes. (The data used is published by Nickell and Andrews, 1983: 526-9).

Nothing needs to be said about equation (20) as it is

almost identical to that reported in (A) above: see equation (7). The wage equation's final specification is more restricted than is suggested by the range of possibilities outlined earlier. However it can be argued that it is a close approximation to the data-generation-process as the test of overidentifying restrictions accepts the null hypothesis, which is a big improvement on the competitive labour supply equation (8). Comparing it now to the wage equation of section (B), equation (16), we observe that Minford's version nests within equation (21) as the latter contains labour demand variables, a mismatch variable and a mark-up variable. We observe that variables common to both have markedly different roles to play, there is: no lagged dependent variable in (21), a powerful one in (16); a small unemployment effect in (16) but a large one in (21); a large coefficient on benefits in (16), an insignificant one in (21); and a powerful presence of the labour force in (21) but a completely insignificant one in (16). As we explained earlier, these differences are thought to arise because there are no demand variables in Minford's specification which might capture the secular increase in real wages if included. Therefore it is not surprising to find that the long-run reduced-form elasticities differ between the two models. This is clearly related to the size of the lags of the dependent variable, and the consequent large effect of right-hand variables on it. Thus there is a clear trade-off between having powerful effects and the time it takes for them to work.

Writing the Nickell-Andrews model in the now familiar form, replacing u_t by $.9(\ell_t-n_t)$, we have

$$\begin{bmatrix} 1 & .512 \\ -3.69 & 1 \end{bmatrix} \begin{bmatrix} n \\ W^c \end{bmatrix} =$$

$$\begin{bmatrix} -.086(q/p) + .595k - .512(t_1+t_2+t_3) \\ -4.33\ell + .035M + .092(B/p) - .174(q/p) + .64k + \\ .705 + .048m + .795t_1 + .25t_2 - 1.48t_3 \end{bmatrix} \quad (22)$$

The real benefits effect on employment is measured by an elasticity of -.0163, and on wages by an elasticity of .0296. These two numbers are remarkably close to those of the competitive model (A), where it was also concluded that such long-run values are unattainable (in the dynamic sense). The obvious implication is that the data tells the same long-run story, but the structures allow for quite different adjustment patterns. The dynamics of the Nickell and Andrews (1983) version is easy to examine. Substituting (21) into (20) gives

$$n_t(1 - 1.227L + .492L^2) = (.00678 - .194L)(3.69n_t + \ldots)$$

which yields roots of $.21 \pm .68i$. The adjustment pattern is therefore quite sensible, being reasonably fast and cyclical. Also notice that the real price of raw materials and fuel is the one channel by which demand management policy <u>may</u> influence employment and the real wage, the elasticities being .001 and -.17. However, the outcome is as if employment has a natural rate. The ratio of the effects describes a locus in employment/real wage space whose elasticity is -.006, which might be thought of as some implicit supply schedule. Such an interpretation is false as a change in the capital stock (again arising in demand) generates a locus of elasticity .09.

We conclude by restating that the models of this section and section IIIB lead to very similar specifications of the wage equation, in spite of different underlying paradigms. For example it would be incorrect to describe the bargaining model in Nickell and Andrews (1983) as neo-classical or market-clearing. As hinted at in Section II, differences in the estimated equations arise out of pragmatic considerations relating to omitted variables, sample size, and periodicity of the data. We now turn to some disequilibrium models of the labour market, which allow for some flexibility in the structures imposed upon the data.

(D) Disequilibrium Models

For many the notion that the aggregate labour market clears is untenable. For example such people find it hard to swallow the idea that the recent rapid increase in unemployment in the UK is something to do with "attacks of contagious laziness"[8]. Here we turn to models which take on board the possibility of imbalance between supply and demand, and now the idea of one aggregate market is hard to sustain. Rather the possibility of some micro-markets being in excess supply, whilst others are in excess demand, becomes appealing, particularly when we observe the co-existence of both unemployment and vacancies. We now consider what little evidence there is for the UK.

Unfortunately the added degree of complexity in modelling the multi-market pradigm has restricted the attention of investigators to aggregate disequilibrium models. Rosen and Quandt (1978) provided the pioneering attempt using U.S. data. Their model, in the notation of Section II, consists of equations (1), (2), (4) and (23) immediately below. Equation (4) deals with the problem of how to determine wages when the market does not clear[9]; equation (23) determines employment, and is given by

$$n_t = \min(n_t^s, n_t^d). \tag{23}$$

Employment is determined on the short side of the market which is based on the notion of no involuntary exchange. The model determines four endogenous variables, supply, demand, employment and the real wage, two of which are always observed. The likelihood of observing employment and the real wage can be written down once stochastic specifications for (1) and (2), and possibly for (4) and (23), have been made: see for example Pemberton (1985). Whilst estimation is feasible, as far as we know nobody has successfully applied the Rosen and Quandt model to UK data[10]. Most investigators prefer to replace (4) by the even simpler assumption that employment is always demand determined. Now estimation is simple, as the model is linear and is made up of equation (1) and by any one of the four wage equations outlined in Section II.

This particular approach forms the basis of the treatment of the labour "sector" in most large-scale macromodels of the UK. Typically the demand equation is of the Brechling (1965) or Ball and St. Cyr (1966) variety, and the wage equations are made up of a rag-bag of ad hoc specifications added on to the original Phillips' Curve specification. It is this parlous state of affairs that motivated Nickell's critique (1984a), where he implies that had Sargan's (1964) paper not been ignored by so many, the current stae of affairs need not have come to pass. Details of the treatment in the large scale macroeconometric models is set out in Wallis et al. (1984), chapter 4. There the treatment of the CUBS model is singled out because a clear market structure can be identified. Moreover it is an attempt to impose a structure that does not prejudge whether markets clear or not, and therefore is particularly noteworthy, whilst at the same time providing some estimates so the simple disequilibrium set-up. The underlying research into the CUBS labour market is presented in Beenstock et al. (1985), the estimated model corresponding to equations (1), (2) and (4).

These three equations highlight certain important characteristics of most disequilibrium models that one might expect to be observed in any empirical work. First, when $\gamma=0$ the model reduces to market-clearing. Second, at the other extreme, as γ tends to infinity equation (4) tends towards

$$W_t = W_{t-1} + \beta_2' Z_t^w \tag{24}$$

which indicates that the real wage changes only in response to institutional factors and the like. (The evidence of Altonji and Ashenfelter, 1980, supports this view). Third, in the absence of such influences ($\beta_2'=0$) the system converges to market-clearing in the long run. (Equation (4) reduces to $n_t^s=n_t^d$ and equation (5) reduces to equation (6).) Thus the unit root in equation (4) does not imply an unattainable long-run. However the long-run is <u>not</u> attained when the excess demand term is not present, as again equation (4) reduces to (24) above. Finally the speed of adjustment of this simple system is determined by the lagged dependent variable in the reduced form wage equation, and is equal to $\gamma/(\gamma+\alpha_1+\delta_1)$. The extreme values are unity when γ is infinite, and zero when γ is zero.

In the Beenstock et al. (1985) model employment is always demand determined. Labour supply is defined as employment plus unemployment, and so supply always exceeds demand. However a component of the unemployed is "equilibrium" or "natural". When the real wage is at its market clearing level, all unemployment is "equilibrium". Thus Beenstock et al.'s notion of equilibrium labour supply includes the frictionally unemployed (which is not observed), and is different from the traditional definition where equilibrium labour supply coincides with employment.

Beenstock et al. present the following labour market model, estimated by 3SLS, using UK annual data, 1953-1982:

$$n_t(1 - 1.21L + .50L^2) = \underset{(2.0]}{-.26}[w(1+t_1)/p]_t + \underset{(2.0]}{.18}\,k_t$$

$$- (\underset{(3.8]}{.21} - \underset{(2.9]}{.17}L)(q_e/p)_t + \underset{(3.2]}{.13}\,(q_m/p)_t + \text{constant}$$

$$\hat{\sigma}=.0114 \qquad (25)$$

$$n^s_t(1-L) = (\underset{(2.5]}{.056} - \underset{(2.5]}{.087}L + \underset{(3.0]}{.063}L^2)[w(1-t_2)/p(1+t_3)]_t$$

$$+ \underset{(6.3]}{1.50}(1-L)\ell_t - \underset{(6.0]}{.33}(n^s/\ell)_{t-2} - \underset{(4.9]}{.34}\ell n(1+u_{t-1}) \text{ constant}$$

$$\hat{\sigma}=.0048 \qquad (26)$$

$$(w/p)_t(1-L)(1 + \underset{(2.0)}{.23}L^2) = \underset{(5.6)}{-.34}(1-L)w_{t-1} - \underset{(2.7)}{.432}u_t$$

$$+ \underset{(3.7)}{.056}(B/p)_t + (\underset{(4.0)}{1.22} - \underset{(1.5)}{.48}L)M_t$$

$$\hat{\sigma}=.01 \qquad (27)$$

Again all variables are in logarithms (this is explicit in equation (26) to avoid confusion). q_e is the nominal price of energy and q_m is the nominal price of raw materials. n^s is defined as the sum of employment and unemployment, i.e. the working population. This is distinct from L, the population of working age. M is the structural change variable, but is defined slightly differently to the one used in (C) above.

The labour demand schedule has the same structure as those presented in parts (A) and (C) of this Section, although the long-run relative price elasticities are larger. This is because this version includes three recent observations not used by the others, although a test for structural stability is not rejected. Notice also that the coefficients on the lagged dependent variables have been constrained to ensure that labour demand does not exhibit a cyclical response to changes in exogenous variables.

The labour supply function is less general than that of model (A) above as it does not explicitly take account of intertemporal substitution possibilities. Unemployment is included to take account of participation depending on the tightness or otherwise of the market. Observe that labour supply (the working population) is constrained to be unit elastic with respect to the population of working age in the long run, implying that the participation ratio is explained mainly by unemployment (negatively) and a small, positive real wage effect.

The wage equation is necessarily dynamic and generalises an equation such as (4), whilst retaining a unit root. In the short-run we observe non-neutrality, a standard feature of the expectations augmented Phillips' Curve. This is often rationalised in the following way: workers actually bargain over nominal wages on the basis of an ex-ante forecast of the price level which may then differ from the outcome[11]. Beenstock et al. (1985) argue that this "would be consistent with the hypothesis that inflation makes risk-averse workers more cautious. They accept wage and job offers more readily than at lower and more sustainable rates of inflation". The wage equation in the long run determines equilibrium unemployment:

$$u = .13(B/p) + 1.73M \tag{28}$$

To examine the three equations as a coherent model, the two expressions for the unemployment rate are replaced by linearised functions of supply and employment[12]. The model is written in long-run structural form:

$$\begin{bmatrix} 1 & -.33 & -.05 \\ 0 & 1 & .93 \\ .77 & -.57 & 0 \end{bmatrix} \begin{bmatrix} \partial n^s \\ \partial n^d \\ \partial W^c \end{bmatrix} = \begin{bmatrix} .56\partial \ell + .12\partial n^g \\ .64\partial k - .16\partial(q_e/p) + .47\partial(q_m/p) - .93\partial(t_1+t_2+t_3) \\ .13\partial(B/P) + 1.73\partial M + .20\partial n^g \end{bmatrix} \tag{29}$$

The long-run configuration of this market is made up of an inelastic supply schedule, a unit elastic demand schedule and a horizontal schedule above the intersection of supply and demand corresponding to the wage equation. The gap between supply and demand is all "equilibrium" in the long-run. An increase in the real benefits moves the wage equation upwards and not surprisingly the effects on demand, supply and the real wage are -.357, -.096 and .39 respectively (all elasticities).

The dynamic adjustment of the model towards market-clearing can be analysed by setting it up in vector auto-regressive form (after linearisation),

$$B_0 \partial y_t = B_1 \partial y_{t-1} + \dots B_3 \partial y_{t-3} + C(L) \partial Z_t$$

where $y_t' = (n_t, n_t^s, W_t^c)'$. As the model has seven lagged endogenous variables (two, two and three respectively), there are seven roots, which are calculated as $-.18 \pm .45i$, $.37 \pm .44i$, $.63 \pm .37i$ and .91. The last root is of some interest as it measures the speed at which the real wage adjusts to a shock; its large value is a direct consequence of the small coefficient on unemployment in (27), and corresponds to a large value of $\gamma/(\gamma+\alpha_1+\delta_1)$ in our representative model discussed earlier. A simulation reveals a monotone adjustment path where the long-run is completed after 5½ years. This sluggish behaviour of real wages (and therefore employment and unemployment) may also be observed in Minford's rearrangement of the competitive supply schedule. Comparing equations (16) and (27) we see that both exhibit a large degree of persistence, although Beenstock et al's. version is closer to that of Nickell and Andrews (1983) in the size of the benefit elasticity.

We conclude this Section on disequilibrium by referring to some preliminary work on a multi-market paradigm. The model is based on Hansen (1970) and Muellbauer (1978), and is set out in Nickell (1984a). Some preliminary results are presented in Andrews and Nickell (1984). The model generalises a market-clearing paradigm exactly as represented by equation (5), for a non-zero adjustment parameter γ. The results are of some relevance here as the underlying structure is almost identical to the competitive model (A). Although the conclusions are tentative, they are (i) the null-hypothesis of market-clearing ($\gamma=0$) is rejected, (ii) the demand equation is quite robust to the more general set-up, whereas (iii) the short-run response of supply to real wages is much more elastic under non-market-clearing. Finally, the model endogenously selects regime, and suggests that the UK labour market was in equilibrium up until the late 1960's and has been in excess supply ever since.

(IV) CONCLUDING COMMENTS

This paper has examined in some detail the structure of four labour market models, all distinctly different in their underlying assumptions for the determination of the real wage, employment and unemployment. A fifth model, recently estimated by Layard and Nickell (1985b), provides another distinctly different approach to modelling the labour market. This we describe briefly before pulling together the analysis of the four models of the last Section in some final remarks.

One conclusion this paper has emphasised is that quite

similar specifications for real wage equations can be derived from quite dissimilar underpinnings. This suggests that a more pragmatic approach to modelling the labour market is possible. Layard and Nickell's model is a case in point, and thus has one distinct advantage in not imposing a particular structure upon the data. Consequently their set-up generalizes some of the models discussed earlier. The model consists of a labour demand schedule, a price equation and a wage equation. The first two are derived from the behaviour of firms assumed to be operating in imperfectly competitive product markets, where the firm sets both the price of its output and chooses its level of production (and thus its labour requirements). Moreover the position of the demand schedule for its product depends upon aggregate demand, and so the specification of the labour demand equation depends on proxies for aggregate demand in addition to the standard productivity variables that arise out of a competitive paradigm. The price equation naturally depends on the same set of variables, and allowance is made for forecasting errors in both money wages and prices.

Rather than making one particular assumption concerning real wage determination, Layard and Nickell identify four different mechanisms, all of which may operate in different areas of the economy. Real wages are either (i) determined by the equality of supply and demand, (ii) set by unions, (iii) determined by the outcome of bargaining between unions and firms, or (iv) set by firms. As all four mechanisms lead to quite similar specifications for the wage equation: the argument is that it is not hard to think of a model that encompasses them all. (Our paper has discussed the models based on (i) to (iii). The fourth possibility, where firms set wages, is discussed in Layard and Nickell (1985a, b) and Stiglitz (1984), an example of which is the efficiency wage model). In order to demonstrate this point we report, without further analysis, an example of the wage equation estimated, together with estimates of labour demand. Notice that the basic structure of the latter remains intact in spite of the addition of the extra aggregate demand variables. They are[13]

$$n_t(1 - \underset{(4.8]}{.929}L + \underset{(1.4]}{.290}L^2) = -\underset{(.46]}{.325}(w/p^f)_{t-1} + .361k_t$$

$$\underset{(3.2]}{.496}^{+}(1+L)AD_t + \underset{(2.9]}{.0891}^{+}(q/p)_t + \underset{(1.5]}{.101}y^w_t + \text{constant}$$

$$(w/p^f)_t = -\underset{(6.3]}{.0818}\log u_t + \underset{(4.5]}{.0366}M_t + \underset{(2.4)}{.277}^{+}(B/w)_t +$$

$$[\underset{(4.6]}{.432}^{+} + \underset{(3.0]}{.284}^{+}(1-L)]v(q/p)_t + \underset{(1.7]}{.0668}\, m_t$$

$$+ \underset{(1.7]}{.320}^{+}t_1 - \underset{(1.6]}{.0173}D_{1t} + 1.11(k/\ell)_t$$

In order to identify a theme throughout we have focussed on the endogenous response of employment and the real wage in response to changes in (i) the real price of raw materials and fuel and (ii) a measure of benefits. For the first case the slope of the resulting set of points traced out is measured by elasticities of .26 (Section IIIA), .006 (B), and .064 (C). The first and third are the slopes of the long-run labour supply schedule, an inappropriate concept in the second bargaining model. For all three demand management policy can induce a positive association between the two variables, which demonstrates that it is not necessary to "buy" more jobs with lower real wages. (The gain here is through a higher productivity).

The effect of a supply side shock, such as benefits, is to trace out a negative association (the labour demand schedule providing it remains fixed). The endogenous changes for the four models studied is as follows.

TABLE 1 Benefits and the aggregate labour market

	Employment		Unemplyt	Real Wage	Labour Demand
	(1)	(2)	(3)	(4)	(5)
Andrews (1983)	-.0185	-.028	.16	.0367	-.50
Minford (1983)	-.33	-.55	2.8	.19	-1.69
Nickell and Andrews (1983)	-.0163	n/a	.14	.0296	-.55
Beenstock et al. (1985)	-.357	n/a	.13	.386	-.93

Notes

Columns (1), (3) and (4) show responses (all elasticities) to a change in real benefits or the replacement ratio. All but the second model relate to the latter. Column (2) indicates the effect on employment when the real wage is held constant. Column (5) calculates the ratio of the employment change to the real wage change. Column (3) is column (1) divided by -.118, the unemployment rate used by Minford (1983), with respect to rows 1 and 2. The elasticities in rows 3 and 4 are obtained directly.

The implied unemployment elasticities are calculated by dividing by an unemployment rate of 11.8%, as used by Minford (1983). (This conversion makes the unrealistic assumption that each job separation leads to one more registered unemployed.) Various points are worth noting. First the real wage elasticity is traced out except in Minford's model, where the real exchange rate goes up in response to an increase in the real wage, shifting labour demand back in addition to the backward movement in labour supply. Nonetheless there is a consensus in the size of the long-run labour demand elasticity in the range ($-\frac{1}{2}$, -1), as indeed is assumed by the Chancellor in his policy prescription referred to earlier (HM Treasury, 1985). Second, there is a transparent disparity over the size of the benefits elasticity[14]. It is not our purpose to evaluate the validity of these estimates in any detail, mainly because the precision with which they are estimated is an order of magnitude worse than those from more reliable cross-section studies. All but one of the rows of Table 1 do fall into line with the bulk of the evidence, which suggests an upper bound of about unity. (Atkinson, (1981) provides a detailed survey of the time, to which we might add the evidence of Narendranathan, Nickell and Stern (1985), and Narendranathan and Nickell (1985), who provide <u>duration</u> elasticities of .3 and .18 to .26 respectively.) Moreover when these three elasticities are evaluated at sample mean unemployment rates (3.15%), they rise to about .6. This coincides with Maki and Spindler (1975) and is roughly consistent with Andrews and Nickell (1982) where a range of elasticities between .75 to 1.10 is estimated.

Third, our justification for examining models which jointly determine both real wages and employment was to emphasise that the implied assumption of constant real wages is misleading in a policy context. This point cannot be stressed too strongly, and is quite neatly demonstrated in column (2) of Table 1. In any model where labour demand is not completely inelastic, the total effect is always smaller than the partial. Policy analysis based on single equation estimation is misleading and should be disregarded totally. Such methodology is particularly culpable when there is, more or less a broad concensus about the shape of the "other" schedule. More importantly though, it is misleading to claim that policy analysis can be conducted on the basis of any time-series model (be it of the labour market or not) whilst such a wide divergence over the evidence is observed.

APPENDIX

Below are listed variables used throughout the paper. Some are explicitly defined in logarithmic form, given in parenthesis.

B	nominal benefits
B/w	replacement ratio
Dp	inflation
e/p	real exchange rate
e	nominal exchange rate
I	real interest rate
K	capital stock (k)
L	labour force (ℓ)
m	"union mark-up"
M	structural mismatch/change
N	employment (n)
N^d	labour demand (n^d)
N^s	labour supply (n^s)

p	nominal price level
q	nominal price of raw materials and fuel
q_e	nominal price of fuel
q_m	nominal price of raw materials
R	nominal rate of interest
t_1	employer's tax rate
t_2	employee's tax rate
t_3	indirect tax rate
U	unemployment (heads)
u	unemployment rate
V	firm's utility
v	union's utility
$\bar{v}$	"fall-back" utility
w	nominal wages of earnings
w/p	pre-tax real wage (W)
$(w/p)^c$	real consumption wage (W^c)
$(w/p)^p$	real product wage (W^p)
$(w/p)^n$	real wage in competitive sector
$(w/p)^u$	real wage in unionised sector
$(w/p)^*$	normal real (consumption) wage (W^*)
y	real output
y^w	world trade
z^d	labour demand variables
z^s	labour supply variables
μ	coverage/union density
π	real profits
$\bar{\pi}$	"fall back" real profits

FOOTNOTES

1. The views presented in this paper are those of the author alone and should not be attributed to the ESRC Macroeconomic Modelling Bureau.
2. Hours of work are not considered in any of the models discussed.
3. There is a problem interpreting the long-run of an estimated model as the agent's long-run decision rule when expectations have not been explicitly modelled. Suppose the firm's decision rule is given by

$$n_t = \lambda n_{t-1} - \alpha(\sum_{i=0}^{\infty} \delta^i W^e_{t+i})$$

where W^e_{t+i} is the expectation of the real wage for period t+i made at time t. The long-run effect of a permanent unit increase in the real wage is $-\alpha/(1-\lambda)(1-\delta)$. If wages are forecasted by the auto-regressive scheme

$$W^e_{t+1} = \rho^i W_t$$

the regression models becomes

$$n_t = \lambda n_{t-1} - \alpha(1-\delta\rho)^{-1} W_t.$$

Here a permanent increase in the real wage is calculated as $-\alpha/(1-\lambda)(1-\delta\rho)$. The difference simply arises in that expectational lags are confused with other lags, arising because of adjustment costs etc. The two coincide when $\rho=1$, that is the wage is known to be fixed apart from a random forecasting error.
4. A simple derivation, which cuts away the unnecessary dynamics of the problem, is provided in Nickell (1984b). Real income of the union's potential membership, A, is given by

$$n^u(w/p)^u + (A-n^u)(w/p)^n$$

and is maximized against demand in the unionised sector,

$$n^u = -\alpha_1(w/p)^u + \alpha_2' Z^d$$

The solution yields the following relationship between unionised and competitive real wages,

$$(w/p)^u = [\alpha_2'\alpha_1^{-1}Z^d + (w/p)^n]/2$$

which although not the same as equation (10), does explicitly show that the mark-up is a function of the position of the firm's demand schedule.

5. In Wallis et al. (1984) use is made of the rest of the Liverpool model, implicitly replacing output by its solution. The correct procedure for equation (15) is to replace y_ε by its first stage regression. This is not possible, and so we follow the example of Layard and Nickell (1985a).
6. We quote from Minford et al. (1983: 113), "Possible intensive searching would yield some insight into nuances of dynamic structure; but we doubt if much could be gained, because the major exogenous variables are ...(those)... for which the best predictor turns out to be close to the current value". This untested proposition does not justify the exclusion of lagged unemployment.
7. A second wage equation is estimated where the dependent variable normalises on expected, not actual, retail prices. This is because a price forecast error does not show up in (21), which leads to the econometric problems discussed on page 520 and this alternative specification.
8. Modigliani (1977).
9. Equation (4) may be derived by specifying partial adjustment towards the market-clearing real wage in the long-run. This can also be generalised to the so-called error correction mechanism.
10. There are exceptions. The non-market-clearing paradigm has attracted attention in the Inter-war Unemployment and Benefits debate, (see Hatton, 1985 and references therein) and in studies of Youth Unemployment (see Rice 1984, Hart 1985 and Junankar and Neale 1984). Studies which imposed sample separation upon the data are not in the spirit of Rosen and Quandt, the main problem with which is unfortunate <u>endogenous</u> classification of the sample into excess supply and demand regimes.
11. In an equilibrium world this price forecast error is of some interest and forms the basis of the so-called Lucas/Sargent/Wallace "price-surprise" function. There is an extremely rich theoretical literature on "equilibrium" Phillips' Curves, see for example Friedman (1968), Phelps (1967, 1970), Mortensen (1970) and Lucas and Rapping (1969). A rational expectations

equilibrium model, based on Friedman (1968), Lucas (1973) and Barro (1976) is applied to UK data by Alogoskoufis (1982). This particular paradigm requires an informational asymmetry across the two sides of the market. Non-neutrality also occurs in models of nominal wage rigidity, as in the literature relating to staggered contracts and implicit contracts.

12. The approximation to the unemployment rate (with lower-case variables as logarithms of upper-case ones) may be obtained by differentiating

$$u_t = (N_t - N_t^d - N_t^g)/N_t^s$$

namely

$$\partial u_t = [(N^d + N^g)/N^s]_t \partial n_t^s - (N^d/N^s)_t \partial n_t^d - (N^g/N^s)_t \partial n_t^g$$

The same expression is obtained by differentiating $\ell n(1+u)_t$. 1984 values are used for the analysis in the text.

13. All variables are in logarithms except AD, y^w, M, B/w, t_1, and D_1. p^f is value added output price, v is the ratio of imports to GDP, AD is adjusted deficit to potential GDP, y^w is deviations of world trade from trend and D_1 is an incomes policy dummy for 1976, 1977. Coefficients on k are imposed.

14. This has nothing to do with the fact that the large elasticity is derived from a study where real benefits (B/p), not the replacement ratio (B/w), is used. Indeed the effect on labour supply and employment is larger when the correction is made from real benefits to the replacement ratio, as

$$\frac{\partial n}{\partial (B/w)} = \frac{\partial n/\partial (B/p)}{1 - \partial (w/p)/\partial (B/p)} > \frac{\partial n}{\partial (B/p)} .$$

Moreover Beenstock et al. (1985) use real benefits.

REFERENCES

G.S. Alogoskoufis, Cyclical innovations in wages, prices and employment: theory and U.K. evidence, London School of Economics, Centre for Labour Economics, Discussion Paper No.136, (1982).

G.S. Alogoskoufis, Intertemporal substitution and labour supply with time separable preferences, Birkbeck College mimeo, (1985).

J.G. Altonji, The intertemporal substitution model of labour market fluctuations: an empirical analysis, Review of Economic Studies, 49, (Supplement), p.783-824,(1982).

J.G. Altonji and O. Ashenfelter, Wage movements and the labour market equilibrium hypothesis, Economica, 47, p.217-245, (1980).

M.J. Andrews, The aggregate labour market - an empirical investigation into market clearing, University of Warwick, mimeo, (1984).

M.J. Andrews, D.N.F. Bell, P.G. Fisher, K.F. Wallis and J.D. Whitley, Models of the U.K. economy and the real wage-employment debate, National Institute Economic Review, 112, p.41-52, (1985).

M.J. Andrews and S.J. Nickell, Unemployment in the U.K. since the war, Review of Economic Studies, 49, (Supplement), p.731-759, (1982).

M.J. Andrews and S.J. Nickell, A disaggregated disequilibrium model of the labour market, London School of Economics, Centre for Labour Economics, Working Paper No.669, September (1984).

A.B. Atkinson, Unemployment benefits and incentives, in The Economics of Unemployment in Britain, (ed. J. Creedy), London: Butterworths, (1981).

R.J. Ball and E.B.A. St. Cyr, Short-term employment functions in British manufacturing industry, Review of Economic Studies, 33, p.179-197, (1966).

R.J. Barro, Rational expectations and the role of monetary policy, Journal of Monetary Economics, 2, -.1-32, (1976).

M. Beenstock, P. Warburton, P. Lewington and A. Dalziel, A medium-term macroeconometric model of the UK economy,1953-82. City University Business School, Discussion Paper, April, (1985).

O.J. Blanchard and C.M. Kahn, The solution of linear difference models under rational expectations, Econometrica, 48, p.1305-1311, (1980).

F. Brechling, The relationship between output and employment in British manufacturing industries, Review of Economic Studies, 32, p.187-216, (1965).

M. Friedman, The role of monetary policy, Economic Review, 58, p.1-17, (1968).

H.M. Treasury, The relationship between wages and employment, mimeo, January, (1985).

B. Hansen, Excess demand, unemployment, vacancies and wages, Quarterly Journal of Economics, 84, p.1-23, (1970).

P.E. Hart, Youth unemployment and relative wages in the UK: a survey of recent econometric evidence, Economic Perspectives, this issue, (1985).

T.J. Hatton, The analysis of unemployment in interwar Britain: a survey of research, Economic Perspectives, this issue, (1985).

P.N. Junankar and A.J. Neale, Relative wages and the youth labour market, Institute for Employment Research, mimeo, September (1984).

P.R.G. Layard, D. Metcalf and S.J. Nickell, The effects of collective bargaining on relative and absolute wages, British Journal of Industrial Relations, 16, p.287-302, (1978).

P.R.G. Layard and S.J. Nickell, The causes of British unemployment, London School of Economics, Centre for Labour Economics, Discussion Paper No.209, (1985a).

P.R.G. Layard and S.J. Nickell, The causes of British unemployment, National Institute Economic Review, 111, p.62-85, (1985b).

R.E. Lucas, Some international evidence on output inflation tradeoffs, American Economic Review, 63, p.326-334, (1973).

R.E. Lucas and L.A. Rapping, Real wages, employment and inflation, Journal of Political Economy, 77, p.721-754, (1969).

D.R. Maki and Z.A. Spindler, The effect of unemployment compensation on the rate of unemployment in Great Britain, Oxford Economic Papers, 27, p.440-454, (1975).

I.M. McDonald and R.M. Solow, Wage bargaining and employment, American Economic Review, 71, p.896-908, (1981).

D. Metcalf and S.J. Nickell, Pay and jobs, Midland Bank Review, p.8-15, Spring, (1985).

A.P.L. Minford, Labour market equilibrium in an open economy, Oxford Economic Papers, 35, (Supplement), p.207-244, (1983).

A.P.L. Minford, Response to Nickell, Economic Journal, 94, p.954-959, (1984).

A.P.L. Minford, S. Marwaha, K. Matthews and A. Sprague, The Liverpool macroeconomic model of the U.K., Economic Modelling, 1, p.24-62, (1984).

A.P.L. Minford, with D. Davies, M. Peel, and A. Sprague, Unemployment: cause and cure, Oxford: Martin Robertson, (1983).

F. Modigliani, The monetarist controversy or, should we forsake stabilisation policies?, American Economic Review, 67, p.1-19, (1977).

D.T. Mortensen, A theory of wage and employment dynamics, in Micro-economic foundations of employment and inflation theory, (Phelps et al. eds), London: Macmillan, (1970).

J. Muellbauer, Macrotheory vs. macroeconometrics: the treatment of 'disequilibrium' in macromodels', Birkbeck College, Discussion Paper No. 29. (1978).

S.W. Narendranathan and S.J. Nickell, Modelling the process of job search, Journal of Econometrics, 28, p.29-49, (1985).

S.W. Narendranathan, S.J. Nickell and J. Stern, Unemployment benefits revisited, Economic Journal, 95, p.307-329, (1983).

S.J. Nickell, A bargaining model of the Phillips' Curve, London School of Economics, Centre for Labour Economics, Discussion Paper No.130, (1982).

S.J. Nickell, The modelling of wages and employment, in Econometrics and Quantitative Economics, (D.F. Hendry and K.F Wallis, eds.), Oxford: Basil Blackwell, (1984a).

S.J. Nickell, A review of 'Unemployment: cause and cure' by Patrick Minford, with David Davies, Michael Peel, and Alison Sprague, Economic Journal, 94, 946-953.

S.J. Nickell and M.J. Andrews, Unions, real wages and employment in Britain 1951-79, Oxford Economic Papers, 35, (Supplement), p.183-220, (1983).

M. Pemberton, Econometric disequilibrium models : a simplified survey, Economic Perspectives, this issue, (1985).

E.S. Phelps, Phillips curves, expectations of inflation and optimal unemployment over time, Economica, 34, p.254-281, (1967).

E.S. Phelps, Money wage dynamics and labour market equilibrium, in Micro-economic foundations of employment and inflation theory, (Phelps et al. eds.) London: Macmillan, (1970).

P.G. Rice, Juvenile unemployment, relative wages, and Social Security in G.B., University of Sussex, mimeo, (1984).

H.S. Rosen and R.E. Quandt, Estimation of a disequilibrium aggregate labour market, Review of Economics and Statistics, 60, p.371-379, (1978).

J.D. Sargan, The estimation of economic relationships using

instrumental variables, Econometrica, 26, p.393-415, (1958).

J.D. Sargan, Wages and prices in the U.K.: a study in econometric methodology, in Econometric Analysis for National Economic Planning, (P.E. Hart, G. Mills and J.K. Whitaker, eds.), London: Butterworths, (1964).

T.J. Sargent, Estimation of dynamic labour demand schedules under rational expectations, Journal of Political Economy, 86, p.1009-1044, (1978).

T.J. Sargent, Macroeconomic Theory, New York: Academic Press, (1979).

J.E. Stiglitz, Theories of wage rigidity, paper presented at conference on Keynes' economic legacy, Delaware, January, (1984).

J.S.V. Symons, The demand for labour in British manufacturing, London School of Economics, Centre for Labour Economics, Discussion Paper No.91, (1981).

J.S.V. Symons, Relative prices and the demand for labour in British manufacturing, Economica, 52, p.37-49, (1985).

J.S.V. Symons and P.R.G. Layard, Neoclassical demand for labour functions for six major economies, Economic Journal, 94, p.788-799, (1984).

K.F. Wallis, (ed.), M.J. Andrews, D.N.F. Bell, P.G. Fisher and J.D. Whitley, Models of the U.K. economy: A Review by the ESRC Macromodelling Bureau, Oxford University Press, (1984).

M. Wickens, The efficient estimation of econometric models with rational expectations, Review of Economic Studies, 49, p.55-67, (1982).

THE ANALYSIS OF UNEMPLOYMENT IN INTERWAR BRITAIN: A SURVEY OF RESEARCH

T.J. HATTON
University of Essex, Queen's University and Centre for Economic Policy Research

I. INTRODUCTION

It is fifty years since the British economy has experienced such a deep recession as that which is reflected in the current unemployment figures. As the labour market outlook deteriorated during the 1970s, the attention of economists and economic historians was increasingly drawn to the interwar years, the 1930s in particular. The pattern of change in the overall unemployment rate for 1920-38 is graphed in Fig. 1. Two things stand out: the major recession and recovery of the 1930s, and the persistently high level of unemployment even in the 1920s. The former feature is shared by most western countries but the latter is relatively unique to Britain. Thus, the obvious questions are: what are the proximate determinants of the observed variations in unemployment, and, why did the average level of unemployment remain so high?

In earlier historical periods, the amount and quality of data available makes it difficult to build up a full picture of the operation of the labour market to answer such questions. But, in contrast to many other countries, the labour market data for interwar Britain are relatively rich. This results directly from the operation of the

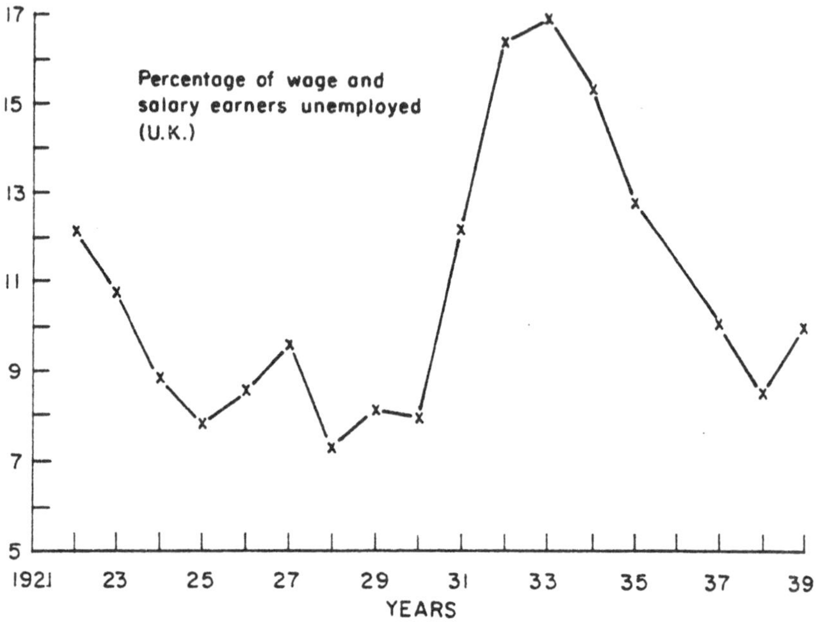

Source: Feinstein 1972, p. T128.

FIGURE 1

labour exchanges set up in 1909 and the unemployment insurance acts which, from 1920, covered nearly two thirds of the labour force[1]. In spite of such sources, applied work on the interwar period using modern techniques is a relatively recent phenomenon. Prior to this, one had to go back to the work of contemporaries to find a detailed analysis of the interwar labour market. Anyone wanting to find a discussion of the nature and causes of high interwar unemployment would be directed to Beveridge's famous book, "Full Employment in a Free Society" first published in 1944. Though Beveridge's insights into the working of the labour market were powerful and often original, the theory and methods of labour economics has moved on considerably in subsequent decades. While recent work has often been inspired by the issues salient to the 1970s and 80s, the basic questions have changed little. Thus, such issues as the relations between unemployment and the real wage, the effect of the unemployment insurance system, the role of trade unions, the mobility of labour, the concentration of unemployment, and the characteristics of the unemployed by status and demographic group were all on the agenda of contemporary debate. Though the emphasis differed somewhat, on re-reading this literature one is struck more forcibly by the parallels with current discussions that the differences.

Then as now, in an era of high unemployment, labour market issues arouse people's passions perhaps more than any other set of economic issues, even in retrospect. This was particularly so in the wake of Benjamin and Kochin's controversial paper on interwar unemployment published in 1979. Indeed this paper played an important part in directing the attention of both historians and economists back to the issue. It led to a brief and somewhat acrimonious debate which did little to reconcile differeing viewpoints on the disincentive effects of unemployment insurance benefits. Now that the dust has settled, perhaps a survey and assessment would be timely. While the role of benefits has occupied the centre stage recently, there are a variety of other issues such as those listed above which attracted the attention of contemporaries and which have also been the subject of further research. Much of the current research has only recently appeared or is as yet unpublished and other material, particularly from the contemporary literature of the interwar period, may not be as familiar to economists as to economic historians. One purpose of this survey is to given some of this work a wider airing. More importantly, it will attempt to assess and interpret the whole body of material in a coherent framework. Given the constraints of a single article, the focus is relatively narrow and issues such as the formation of economic policy, the views of policy makers, social conditions and the impact of labour market conditions on social and political trends are not treated directly.

The succeeding sections are set out in the following way. In view of the recent prominence of the issue, we turn first to the discussion of the effects of unemployment insurance. Since the putative effects of such provisions depend largely on the way the labour market is characterized this leads to a consideration of market clearing versus non-market clearing approaches to the aggregate labour market. To the extent that the market is regarded as predominently in excess supply, two further issues become important. First, what were the determinants of labour demand? Second, what was the process by which wage rates were set? The final set of issues arises from the fact that interwar unemployment is often seen as, in some sense, structural. The discussion of this question leads directly to a consideration of migration and labour mobility. The findings overall are summarized in a short conclusion.

II. UNEMPLOYMENT AND INSURANCE

Until a few years ago, most people who thought at all about the interwar labour market would probably have agreed with Beveridge's view expressed in 1944: "The central problem of unemployment between the wars in Britain was not what it had appeared to be before the first World War. It was not a problem of cyclical fluctuation reducing demand for a time, or of disorganization of the labour market, wasting men's lives in drifting and waiting. It was a problem of general and persistent weakness of demand for labour", (p.89). However out of fashion Keynesian ideas may have become, until recently, crude unreconstructed Keynesianism was the predominant system of belief about the interwar period[2]. This then was the orthodoxy challenged by Benjamin and Kochin when they argued that: "The army of the unemployed standing watch at the publication of the General Theory was largeley a volunteer army." (1979, p.474). This, it was argued, was due to the high rates of benefit relative to wages offered by the unemployment insurance system and the liberal conditions for eligibility. As they pointed out, some contemporaries thought benefits led to high unemployment though it is not clear that most contemporaries had such a direct relationship in mind[3]. Their argument rested on three grounds. First, that the benefit system was indeed very generous; second that the analysis of time series showed that increases in the benefit to wage ratio (hereafter the replacement rate) raised the unemployment rate; and third, that benefits affected relative unemployment rates across age, sex and region in predictable ways. We will examine these in turn.

In their paper, Benjamin and Kochin argued that benefits were "more generous than ever before, or since" (1979, p.442). The ratio they used was the full weekly benefit rate for an adult male, claiming for a wife and two children as dependents relative to Chapman's (1953) index of weekly earnings. This is not an appropriate ratio since the wage rates in the denominator are not just those for adult men, but all workers including women, children and groups outside the insurance system . Taking the average wage for adult manual males alone from the wage census would reduce the peak replacement rate in 1936 from 0.57 to 0.49 and making this adjustment for the whole period 1921-38 gives an average of 0.41. Similarly, if benefit rates for different groups are weighted together to reflect the composition of the unemployed and then compared to Chapman's index, the 1936 ratio comes out at 0.41 and the average at 0.36. Alternatively, since not everyone who was registered as unemployed successfully claimed full benefit (particularly under the Unemployment Assistance shceme in the 1930s), one might simply take the ratio of total benefits paid to total number unemployed which for 1936 give 0.33 or an average of 0.24[5]. It must be concluded that on any comparison of benefits and wages, Benjamin and Kochin over-estimated the ratio.

One may still think that the ratios are high: the question is, high relative to what? Relative to the pre-war period when the only benefits available apart from the Poor Law or organized charity were the out-of-work benefits dispensed by unions to their members or under the Unemployed Workmen Act of 1905, the interwar insurance provisions were much more generous[6]. As for the post war period, the comparison made by Metcalf et.al. indicated that on various different definitions for the replacement ratio it was somewhat lower for 1951-7 than for 1932-8 and roughly equivalent for subsequent periods (1982, p.388)[7]. Compared on the other hand to an absolute poverty line such as that defined by Rowntree in his Human Needs of Labour (1937), the 1936 benefit rate for a family of four is only two thirds of this level, but close to that, defined by Rowntree in 1899 as the minimum income necessary to provide a diet necessary merely to maintain physical efficiency (Sadler, 1984, p.26)[8]. Interwar social surveys typically found unemployment to be the major economic cause of poverty, but even on Rowntree's (relatively generous) standard, it is clear that for many workers, unemployment for a proportion of the time would not necessarily plunge them into poverty[9]. Thus, one of the major dilemmas for the insurance and supplementary systems was that while benefits may have been high enough to blunt incentives for the short term unemployed, they were not high enough to provide adequate income maintenance for the long term unemployed[10].

One of the leading claims advanced was that the structure of unemployment across different demographic groups could be explained by differing replacement rates. The unemployment rate for females was only two thirds of that for males and for juveniles less than half that for adults. In 1935 the benefit rate for single males under 21 was two thirds of the adult rate while on the 1935 wage census, their wage rates were only 36% of that for adults. Similarly for females 18 and above, relative to adult males the benefit ratio was 84% and the wage relative 48%[11]. The only reason for higher replacement rates for adult males was dependants' allowances which for a family of four raises the rate by 50% over a single male in the 1920s and nearly doubles it in the mid 1930s. Even if benefits were sometimes higher for men with families one might be forgiven for thinking that family responsibilities would give rise to rather stronger preferences for income against leisure. In families where there was more than one wage earner (nearly half the total in 1931) the situation would be more complex but one might have expected non-household heads or those in the secondary employment sector to experience more unemployment.

It seems one cannot go much further without getting down to the micro level. A recent preliminary paper by Eichengreen represents an important step forward in this respect. Eichengreen drew a sample of 3000 from the record cards of the New Survey of London Life and Labour which was conducted from 1928 to 1932. Using probit analysis, he found that for male household heads, the probability of being unemployed is not very strongly related to age or marital status, but increases significantly with family size and decreases significantly with other family income and the replacement rate. Thus, higher unemployment among heads of large families does not appear to be due to high rates of benefit entitlement which has a perverse effect. For juveniles on the other hand, the probability of being unemployed depends positively on the replacement rate and negatively on other family income, but with coefficients only bordering on significance (1984, Tables 1-10). These results are tantalizing in their implications and further work along these lines holds promise for a deeper understanding of household behaviour relating to the labour market as well as comparisons with the results of studies in postwar data.

The main piece of evidence put forward by Benjamin and Kochin was their estimates for the following model on annual time series for 1920-1938.

$$U = \alpha_0 + \alpha_1 \frac{B}{W} + \alpha_2 \,(\log Q - \log Q^*) \qquad (1)$$

where U is the percentage of the insured population unemployed, B/W is the benefit to wage ratio, Q is an index of national output and Q* is its logarithmic trend over the sample period. The last term represents the demand surprise, and the constant and the B/W ratio determine the natural rate of unemployment. In most models of labour demand, output will be determined jointly with employment and therefore with unemployment. Furthermore, if the labour market clears, the wage is endogenously determined by other variables in the model. Thus, as it stands, equation (1) is neither an adequate structural equation nor a reduced form, and both the estimating technique (OLS) and the interpretation of the parameters is open to question.

Perhaps the major reason the results attracted so much criticism was that the equation was used to calculate counterfactual levels of unemployment in the absence of benefits, despite the fact that these counterfactuals were so far away from the actual values. Two different adjustments were made for the fact that output would have been higher as employment rose as a result of the fall in benefits. This led to predictions that the average unemployment rate for 1921-38 would have been between 6.7% and 9.3% instead of the 13.7% actually observed. A crucial assumption is that the benefit to wage ratio had an effect only above a value of 0.27: choosing any other arbitrary cut off point would lead to different counterfactual unemployment estimates[12].

In view of the use to which the equation was put, critics have made a number of attempts to undermine the results by rejecting the empirical estimates. The use of a weighted index of benefits in place of the original measure does not affect the results much, though if dependents' allowances are excluded or the average of benefits paid is used, the coefficient α_1 becomes insignificant (Benjamin and Kochin, 1979, pp.415-6; Metcalf, et.al., 1980, p.22-27). It has also been argued that the replacement rate is inadequate as an indicator of the "stance" of the system since the administrative rules and practices governing the admission of claims to benefit were of critical importance (Cross, 1982, pp.380-382). This being so, Benjamin and Kochin seem to have got their results despite rather than because of it[13], though the inclusion of a variable for the proportion of claims admitted adds little to the equation. (Benjamin and Kochin, 1982, p.412; Easton, 1978, p.19)[14]. A number of writers have pointed out that the parameter α_1 is sensitive to slight changes in specification such as: (a) varying the time period used, especially excluding the observation for 1920, (b) breaking the period up or including a dummy variable for the 1930s, (c) introducing a separate time trend or calculating the trend term Q* differently (Metcalf et.al. 1980, pp.20-27; Irish, 1980, p.3-4; Ormerod and Worswick, 1982, pp.402-6; Hart, 1984, pp.2-8).

In reply to some of these charges (specifically those of Ormerod and Worswick), Benjamin and Kochin have argued that the coefficient changes involved are not statistically significant. But this does not help us choose a particular point estimate in the absence of strong priors about the appropriate sample and model specification. Furthermore, when we are dealing with as few as 18 or 19 annual observations, it seems unlikely that clear inferences will be obtained and one obvious approach is to try and increase the available degrees of freedom. Collins disaggregated unemployment by region and industry and, re-estimating a variant of the model, found that α_1 was positive half the time and significant only a quarter of the time (1982, p.376)[15]. An effort to pool the data was made by Easton (1978, pp. 28-31) for five years and 22 industries. The results seemed somewhat mixed, but generally support the benefits hypothesis.

Though further tests are possible using the simple model, subsequent writers have turned away from it in attempts to build a more convincing structural model of the labour market. This material is considered in the next section. But it is worth asking at this stage what, if anything, has been learned from the studies considered so far. One thing is clear: the benefits hypothesis cannot be rejected out of hand and no thoroughgoing discussion of interwar unemployment can afford to ignore it completely. Given its prominence, it is inconceivable that the unemployment insurance scheme had no effects either at the micro or macro levels. The question is: through what mechanisms did the scheme affect economic variables and how large were the effects overall?

III. MARKET CLEARING VERSUS NON MARKET CLEARING

From the point of view of measuring the effects of different types of economic policy or potential policy as well as simply characterizing the observed facts, it is important to determine the appropriate labour market structure. Though simple paradigms are unlikely to describe the fine detail in every case, without them it is impossible to address these issues coherently at all. Labour market regimes are often described as equilibrium or dis-equilibrium, but for clarity it is better to use the terms, market clearing or non-market clearing. It is useful to characterize different approaches in a simple diagram. Fig. 2 represents supply and demand in a single market. Labour demand, D^E, is downward sloping in the wae, W, and the supply side is described by two curves which are, for convenience,upward sloping. The S^E gives the actual or "effective" supply of workers to jobs, while S^A measures the observed labour force or "apparent" supply. The difference between the two represents frictional un-employment associated with the movement of workers between jobs and their search behaviour when unemployed.

In the market clearing view, the market equilibrates at the intersection of D^E and S^E, giving rise to employment E_0 and wage W_0. Unemployment at that wage is simply the difference between L_0 and E_0. The effect of increasing labour market frictions, raising the optimal amount of

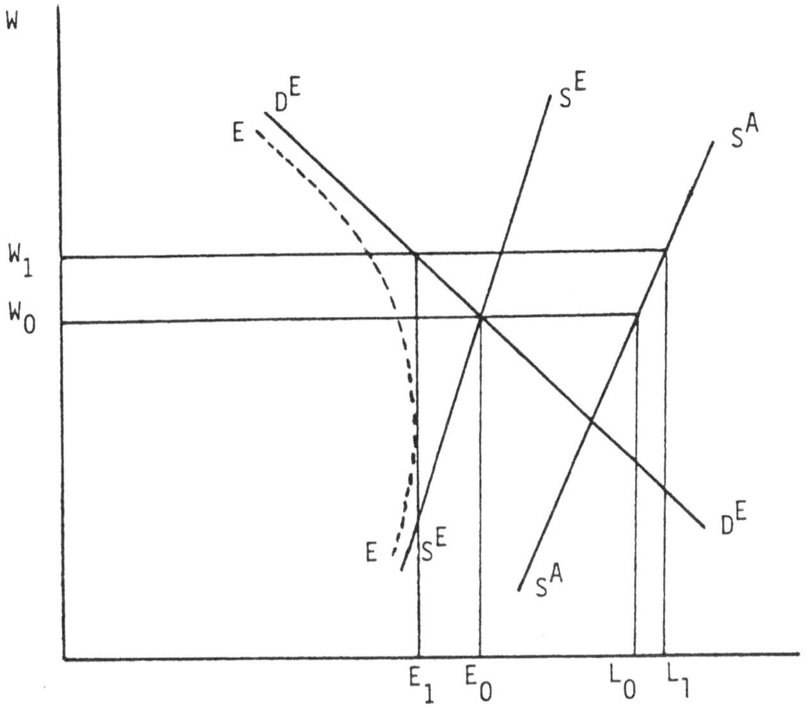

FIGURE 2 Supply and demand in a Single Market

search or increasing the leisure component of unemployment is to shift the S^E curve to the left and possibly the S^A curve to the right. This will reduce employment, raise the wage and increase the labour force. Here unemployment is all, in some sense, voluntary. The alternative is to view the labour market as non-clearing with the wage set at a level such as W_1, which fails to equilibrate effective supply and demand. In the case illustrated, this leads to employment E_1 and labour force L_1. Unemployment consists of the voluntary part between S^E and S^A and the involuntary part between D^E and S^E.

Can interwar unemployment be explained in terms of a market-clearing model? If the main reason for shifts in the gap between the S^E and S^A curves over time is changes in the benefit regime, then comparisons between different periods are instructive. Metcalf et.al. (1982) successfully argued that shifts in the benefit regime could not account for the difference between the interwar and early postwar periods. If the market cleared, or was in excess demand in the 1950s and 1960s, then the interwar period must be characterized as excess supply. Similarly, if unemployment before 1914 is regarded as having fluctuated around the natural rate without benefits, then the insurance system should account for the upward shift. In a recent paper I extended a market clearing model, with a "surprise" type supply function, which performed well on prewar data, to the interwar period. This exhibited substantial structural breaks, which were not repaired when benefits were brought into the supply equation, and the whole model performed poorly for the interwar period. (Hatton, 1984a, pp. 21-26). However, lack of comparability between the pre-war trade union data and the interwar insurance data makes it difficult to draw firm conclusions about the effects of introducing the insurance system.

Since effective supply of labour is unobserved, one can only identify the S^E curve if one knows the determinants of the gap between S^E and S^A, and under the assumption that the market clears (or that excess demand obtains). If the economy is not on the S^E curve, then it will be impossible to identify it. Broadberry, using an equation in levels on annual data, estimated equations for the D^E, S^E and S^A curves. These did not support the market clearing hypothesis: the replacement rate was insignificant and the female participation rate gave the wrong sign in the S^E equation (1983, p. 482). Using quarterly data for 1924-39, I attempted to model variations in effective supply with an equation in which the rate at which vacancies notified to exchanges were taken up depended on the replacement rate and lagged unemployment. This gave plausible results, but the replacement rate was not significant. Similarly, when this is translated into a supply and demand model for changes in employment, the supply equation does not give strong support for the model. (Hatton 1983b, p. 16).

An alternative approach is to assume, not that the market clears continuously, but that it switches between excess supply and demand along the lines of Rosen and Quandt (1978). Observed employment is simply the minimum of effective supply and effective demand, and it becomes critically important how the sample is partitioned into supply side and demand side observations. Smyth (1983) adopted this approach, specifying effective supply to depend on the real wage and the benefit to wage ratio. In addition, there is a deterministic wage equation $W_t - W_t = (1-c)(W^*_t - W_{t-1})$ where W* is the equilibrium wage. This means that whenever the nominal wage is rising the market is in excess demand, and since the degree of excess demand is known contingent upon the estimate of c, both supply and demand can be estimated on all the observations. Apart from the insignificant real wage coefficient in the supply equation, the results give strikingly precise parameter estimates and the estimate of c is significantly different from zero, indicating that the restriction of market clearing is rejected (1983, p. 46). Furthermore, simulating the model with the replacement rate at 0.27 gives results similar in magnitude to the counterfactuals of Benjamin and Kochin[16]. Some misgivings arise, particularly about the use of the simple deterministic wage equation, when these results are compared with those in a paper by Irish and Winter (1981). Using annual data for 1922-38, they tried various different methods of partitioning the data, including the use of a stochastic version of the identical wage adjustment equation. Their best results yielded a somewhat different sample separation to that of Smyth and a substantially different supply equation[17]. This supply function gave significant coefficients for the nominal wage (positive) and the price level (negative) and an upward shift dummy for 1930-8. They also performed tests on the reduced form wage equation, which failed to reject the hypothesis of market clearing. But in the light of the generally poor results for the supply equation in both versions of the model, they concluded that "it is quite possible that excess supply existed for the entire period" (1091, p. 17).

In the light of the substantial cross sectional differences in unemployment rates, it is perhaps unappealing to assume that the whole labour market switched uniformly from one regime to the other from year to year. Broadberry (1983) suggests a model in which some markets are in excess supply and some are in excess demand. Aggregating these together gives total labour demand as employment plus vacancies and total supply as employment plus unemployment. In terms of the diagram, employment is determined from the EE curve and the horizontal distance between this and the demand curve is vacancies. Unemployment is now the distance between the EE curve and the S^E curve (ignoring the distinction between the S^E and S^A curves). Changes in the wage or shifts in the demand curve will cause some markets (but not all) to switch from unemployment to vacancies or vice versa. Broadberry found that this model fitted the data for 1924-38 reasonably well, though it mattered little whether vacancies were included as part of labour demand or not (1938, pp. 478-80). Though vacancies outstanding at the exchanges were small relative to the total, even when grossed up, my best estimate for the 1920s indicates that there was on average only one vacancy for every 12 unemployed, or for every 8.5 wholly unemployed workers. Distinguishing S^E and S^A curves, the model in Fig. 1 predicts that unemployment should be inversely related to vacancies and the U/V curve should be shifted out by increases in the replacement rate. Using quarterly data for the 1920s, I was not able to find either of these effects and concluded that this was due to the predominance of excess supply in labour markets (Hatton, 1985b, p.15)[18].

In the light of this, one strategy is to estimate labour market equations under the assumption of continuous excess supply, but in addition, to provide a wage equation. My efforts to estimate a simple Phillips curve adjustment mechanism, along these lines, did not meet with great success (Hatton, 1983a, p.498). The process of wage setting is discussed further below, but the model of Matthews should be mentioned at this stage since it relates to the characterization of unemployment. Here employers are never rationed, but, for the supply side, a wage setting equation is used, which is derived from the utility maximizing behaviour of Trade Unions. Thus, the distinction between voluntary and involuntary unemployment disappears; workers collectively are not involuntarily unemployed since the wage is set by the decision of the union, but may suffer individually from involuntary unemployment as a result of the decision. One problem with such a model is that, since union variables do not enter directly, it may by observationally equivalent to that developed from a competitive framework. Thus, it becomes a matter of interpretation rather than formal statistical tests between two alternative structures.

One further issue with a bearing on non market clearing is the estimation of the S^A curve. If unemployment or potential unemployment is a constraint, then it will influence the decision to participate. The net outcome of added and discouraged worker effects is often thought to measure the impact of job rationing on labour market participation. Using annual data, Irish estimated a "Keynesian" model of participation which, while subject to some doubts about specification, supported the net added worker effect (1980, p.9). On a quarterly model for changes in the insured labour force, I obtained rather different results which indicated a negative effect of unemployment on the labour force and gave evidence of the importance of varying rates of disallowance from benefits as having influenced the flows out of insurance (Hatton, 1983b, p.24).

The issue of participation is still very much open, but is clouded by the fact that the time series data available is only for the insured labour force, and the economy wide participation rate cannot be independently measured. Further efforts to measure added and discouraged worker effects on cross sectional data from the 1931 census have so far yielded largely perverse results (Hatton, 1984b).

IV. EMPLOYMENT AND THE REAL WAGE

Little has so far been said about the specification of the demand side and, since this is of major importance, we denote separate attention to it. In the diagram of Fig. 1, if there is excess supply of labour it is because the wage is too high to clear the market. The downward sloping labour demand curve represents the marginal productivity condition for profit maximizing firms. If there is excess supply in the labour market then employment will be negatively correlated with the product wage and unemployment positively correlated with it (even if labour supply does not depend on the wage). As Keynes put it, "with a given organization, equipment and techniques, real wages and the volume of output (and hence of employment) are uniquely correlated so that in general an increase in employment can only occur to the accompaniment of a decline in the rate of real wages" (1936, p.17). In this sense the unemployment discussed by Keynes is what has more recently been discribed as "classical unemployment". Casson has recently emphasized that pre-Keynesian economists also held a non-market clearing view of the labour market and indeed anticipated much of Keynes' analysis, Keynes' criticism of "classical economists" notwithstanding. Only in the light of this, argues Casson, can the pre-Keynesians such as Cannan, Clay and Pigou be seen to have had a coherent analysis of employment.

The empirical debate about the relationship between real wages and employment is often thought to have started with the papers of Dunlop (1938) and Keynes (1939) and others which followed. In fact, this discussion was more concerned with the cyclical relation between real and money wages and produced little of direct bearing on the issue at hand[19]. The most striking piece of evidence was the relationship between the real wage and trade union unemployment for the period 1919-25, demonstrated by Rueff in the mid 1920s. Though this was originally in French, it was discussed in the Statist and by Stamp in the Financial Times and was reproduced both by Pigou (1928, pp.357-8) and Beveridge (1930, p.460). Much more recently, but still using a graphical approach, the argument has been taken up for the 1930s by Beenstock, Capie and Griffiths (1984). They argue that the major reason for the depression and recovery, which was felt primarily in manufacturing, was the rise and subsequent decline of the product wage. This is measured using both the wholesale price index and an output price index constructed as the average of investment and export price indices. As an alternative, the graph in Fig. 3 uses an index of prices of manufactures given by Phelps Brown and Browne (1968, p.405) to deflate Chapman's wage index for manufacturing. This is compared in the lower part of the graph with total man-years of employment, also given by Chapman[20]. While the product wage rose from 1929 to 1932, it rose equally fast before 1929 and only slowed down from 1933. Thus, although there is evidence of inverse movements in the later 1930's, real wage variations do not correspond to those in employment at the important turning points of 1929 and 1932. This finding is strongly supported by the recent findings of Dimsdale (1984, p.95-97) who compares several alternative deflators.

Econometric tests of the real wage employment relationship for the interwar period are a relatively recent enterprise. Casson examined several cross sections of

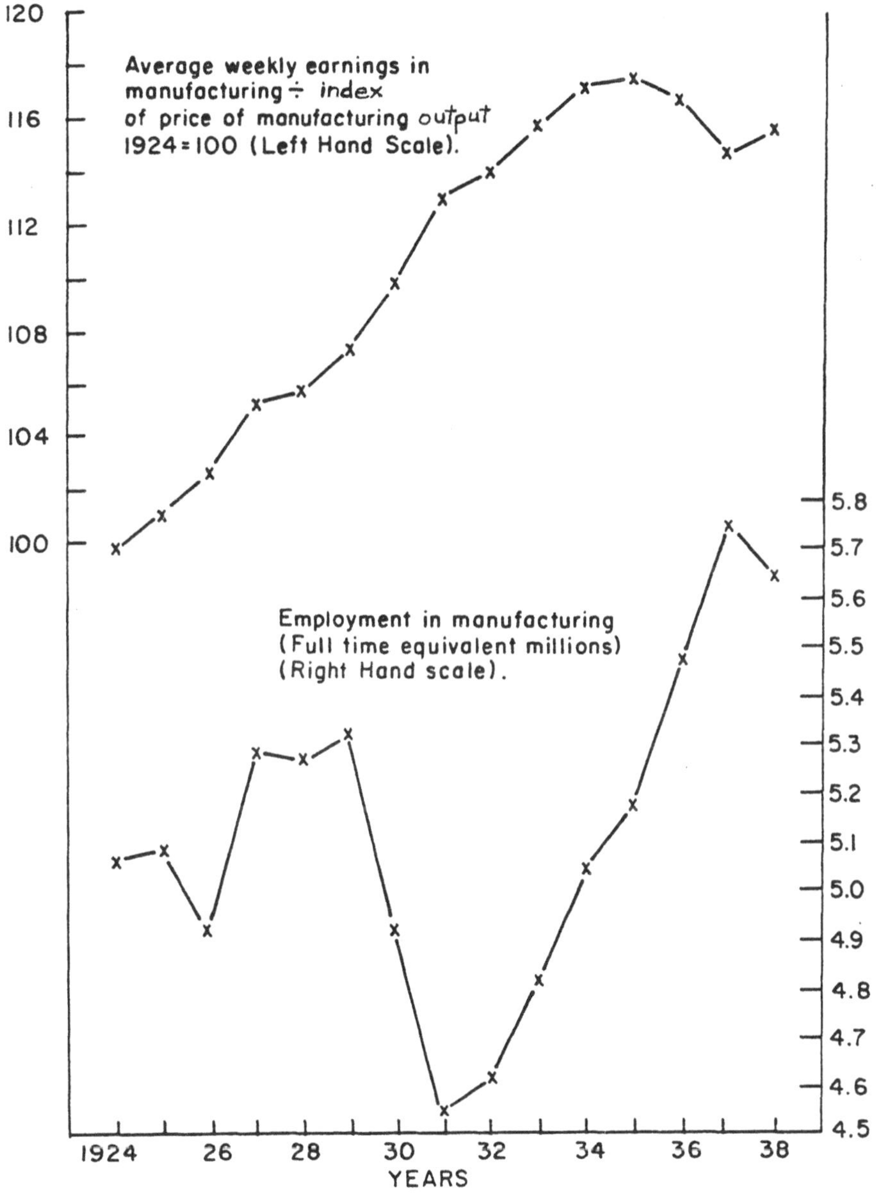
120
116
112
108
104
100
Average weekly earnings in manufacturing ÷ index of price of manufacturing output 1924=100 (Left Hand Scale).
Employment in manufacturing (Full time equivalent millions) (Right Hand scale).
5.8
5.7
5.6
5.5
5.4
5.3
5.2
5.1
5.0
4.9
4.8
4.7
4.6
4.5
1924
26
28
30
32
34
36
38
YEARS

FIGURE 3

changes in the product wage and employment in addition to estimating time series equations for five industries. The product wage always gave the expected sign in these regressions, but was significant only one third of the time (1983, pp.174,176). In common with many other empirical models, the equations included output and a time trend as additional variables. Thus, the typical specification is:

$$\log E_t = \beta_o + \beta_1 \log(\frac{W}{p}) + \beta_2 \log Q + \beta_3 t \qquad (2)$$

where E is employment, $\frac{W}{p}$ is the product wage, Q is output and t, the time trend. This model has been estimated on various data sets by Easton (1978), Matthews and Minford (1981), Matthews (1983), Irish and Winter (1980), Smyth (1983) and Hatton (1983b). It is typically derived as the first order condition for profit maximization from a C.E.S. production function when the maximized value of output is substituted back from the production function to eliminate the capital stock and give an equation linear in logs. This leads to several problems. First, even if the real wage is taken as exogenous, output cannot be, since by assumption it is jointly determined with employment. Hence, at the very least, this variable should be instrumented or some other appropriate technique used. The parameter β_1 is the substitution elasticity and β_2 reflects returns to scale, such that if $\beta_2 = 1$, there are constant returns. Though unrestricted estimates of β_2 are typically less than unity, indicating increasing returns, one solution to the endogeneity of output is to assume $\beta_2 = 1$ and take output over to the left hand side. Estimation of this model on time series for 21 industries for 1921-38 gave 7 negative coefficients for β_1, only two of which were significant. (Hatton and Seaton 1984, p.9).

Even if we could successfully estimate β_1, this will not give us the slope of the labour demand curve, which will depend on both substitution and scale effects. In theory, employment should be a negative function of the product wage when output is excluded from the equation. Alternatively, if output prices are inflexible and firms are rationed as to the amount they can sell and cannot reach the marginal productivity condition, employment just depends on the rationed level of output alone. Both Broadberry (1983) and I (Hatton, 1983a) have estimated equations which include the product wage or output, but not both. Not surprisingly, output does considerably better on aggregate data, but one cannot come down firmly in favour of a "Keynesian" regime, since through the production function, the output-employment relation would be expected to hold regardless of whether firms are rationed or not. A further difficulty is that the short run employment elasticity of output is almost always less than one, implying in this simple static framework that there are increasing returns to labour which would rule out the possibility of a downward sloping labour demand curve. One may wish to set this aside on the grounds that (among other things) there is measurement error in labour inputs due to labour hoarding or variations in hours or effort, or that variations in stocks distort the output measure. Thus, despite this almost universal finding, I had some success in estimating coefficients for 14 out of 19 industries of which 11 were significant in time series equations, which excluded output, but only in the presence of other variables including the replacement rate (Hatton, 1981, pp.16-17).

Since employment is not the only variable factor, other relative prices may also be important and the omission of these may obscure the wage employment relation. The most important of these is the relative price of raw materials, but as Dimsdale (1984) has recently emphasized, taking this into account makes it even harder to explain the depression and recovery of the 1930s in terms of relative prices. This is because the relative price of raw materials fell from 1929 to 1933 and then rose in the recovery. If labour and materials are gross complements, then the effects would be to boost employment in the early 1930s and retard it in the recovery. Dimsdale estimated the model used by Nickell and Andrews (1983), which includes the relative price of imported materials and excludes output, on annual interwar data. Neither of the relative price terms took a significant coefficient and some of the equations exhibit dynamic instability. To test for demand effects he included an index of the money stock and of world trade. These variables were both highly significant and improved the significance of the price terms. This strongly supports the view that shifts in the labour demand curve were important and suggests that one can only identify the slope when these shifts are taken into account. It should be noted, however, that though the demand terms appear as current variables, relative prices are only permitted to appear with a one year lag. Nevertheless, the results seem plausible giving long run elasticities for total employment of -0.70 for the product wage and -0.32 for the relative price of raw materials and higher elasticities for wage earners (i.e. manual workers) alone.

One may think that other relative prices may also play a role. For instance, Harrison and Hart (1984) focus on the fixed cost of employment as represented by the national insurance contribution and find some evidence that this caused substitution of hours for employment[21]. Though almost all studies have concentrated on the short run, over a period of years it might be thought that substitution between capital and other factors would take place and that the user cost of capital should also enter the equation. Under such circumstances, it would be appropriate to specify a system of dynamic interrelated factor demands to allow for differential adjustment costs. Such efforts are likely to be severely circumscribed by the fewness of annual observations and the lack of quarterly data for some of the variables. This is not to deny that demand effects would still be important, but a richer model would allow us to test whether such effects were transitory or whether they persisted in the long run. For the present, the most one can say is that there is evidence for a downward sloping labour demand curve, and for shifts in demand, though the exact magnitude of each remains open to debate.

V. WAGE RATES AND WAGE SETTING

Even if we could be secure in the belief that the main reason for high interwar unemployment was too high a real wage, one has to ask why wages were maintained at a level too high to clear the market. To contemporaries such as Pigou, the answer was very clear: "partly through state action and partly through the added strength given to work peoples organizations engaged in wage bargaining by the development of unemployment insurance, wage rates have, over a wide area, been set at a level which is too high... and the very large percentage of unemployment during the whole of the last six years is due to this new factor in our economic life." (1927, p.355). They pointed out that despite the ravages of the first World War, and the reduction in average hours in 1919, average earnings remained well above the 1913 level (Pigou, 1927; Clay, 1929b, p.140). That this was the case is illustrated in the graphs of Fig. 4 where the index of the weekly earnings

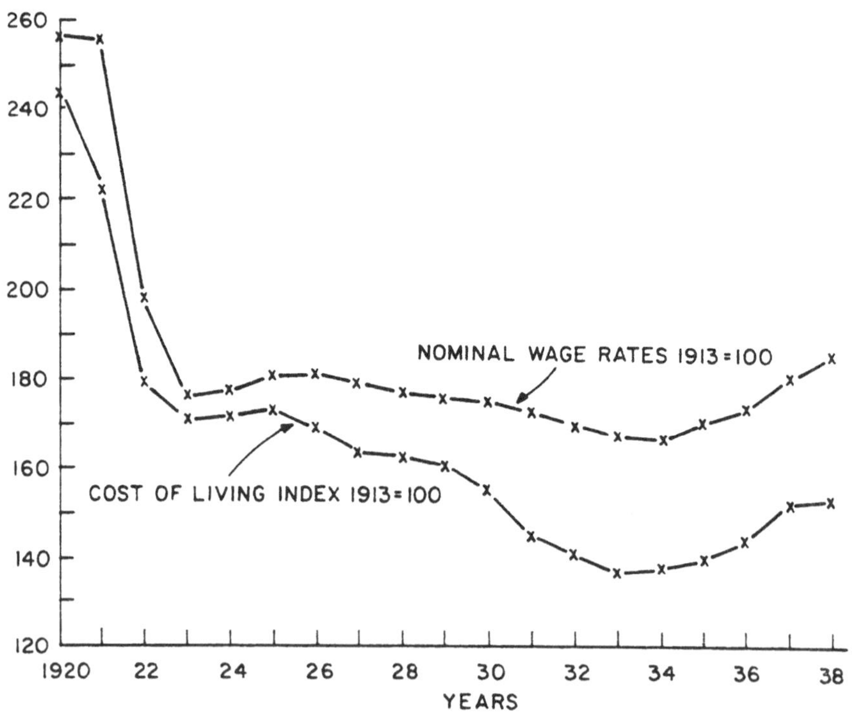

FIGURE 4

and the cost of living is shown with 1913 = 100 (Feinstein, 1972, p. T140). It also illustrates the sharp constrast between the very volatile behaviour of wages and prices up to 1922 and their stability thereafter.

Contemporaries were impressed with the increase in trade union membership, which by 1920 was double that of 1914 and treble that of 1910, but this had already fallen by a third on the eve of the general strike. Their position was not based so much on numbers as on organization, structure and incentives which fall under three heads. First, and most impressive was the change in collective bargaining between unions and employers from a local or district basis on to a national basis. This was given official support by the Whitley committe, which led to the setting up of Whitley councils with the specific objective of centralizing collective bargaining. This system was buttressed by system of Trade Borads set up under the Acts of 1909 and 1918 which determined industry-wide minimum wages in industries where organization was too weak for voluntary collective bargaining. On one estimate, such collective agreements together covered some three quarters of the labour force (Sell, 1939, p.50)[22]. Secondly, the criteria used in wage fixing no longer gave such major weight to commercial conditions in the industry as before the war. Over the period embracing the war, the principle of a living wage was reflected in the linking of wages to living costs. In a wartime setting, and in the absence of market criteria, the comparative principle also grew, not just between occupational grades in an industry as before, but across both industries and geographic areas. Thirdly, by contrast with the prewar period, wage rates set in this way could be enforced. Trade Board wage rates had legal backing and were supported by a programme of factory inspection and the prosecution of offenders in special courts. Under the unemployment insurance acts, a worker could refuse a job without forfeit of benefit entitlements if the wage offered was below that generally recognized in the locality for that type of employment[23]. Drawing attention to these features, contemporary observers developed what was essentially an institutional view of wage setting which is rather hard to capture in a simple model.

Direct estimation of wage equations developed initially with the work of Phillips (1958) and Lipsey (1960). After fitting his non-linear curve to the data for 1861 to 1913, Phillips commented on the apparent wage inflexibility of the later 1920s, that "the actual results obtained, given the levels of unemployment which were held, could have been predicted fairly accurately from a study of prewar data" (1958, p.295). Lipsey found that, for 1923-39 and 1948-57 taken together, the correlation between wage change and change in the cost of living had increased, while that between wage change and unemployment had become weaker. After 1922, the Phillips curve had become flatter and there was no level of unemployment which would case wage rates to fall (1960,pp.26-7).

Two main lines of approach were followed in the subsequent literature (insofar as it relates to the interwar period). Firstly, following the lead of Lipsey, attempts were made to incorporate a structural component into the Phillips curve, through various terms representing the dispersion of unemployment rates. Archibald, Kemmis and Perkins (1972) performed a whole battery of tests using quarterly data for 1924-38. They found that a measure of unemployment modified to take into account the regional dispersion of unemployment gave a marginal improvement over aggregate rate, but the main feature was an outward shift for the Phillips curve for the period when Britain was off the gold standard[24]. Thus, for the 1930s, stable wages could only be achieved with very high levels of unemployment (1972, pp.126-142). A similar approach was taken by Thomas and Stoney (1972) who specified, in addition, a "wage transfer mechanism". In this model the wage rate determined in one area spills over directly into the wage fixed elsewhere and the leading sector was taken to be the relatively prosperous region of London and the South East. The effect is to give rather more weight to the low unemployment areas in determining aggregate wage change, and thus increasing regional disparities shift the observed relation between wage and change and unemployment outwards. The effects for 1925-38 are striking. They found that if there had been no regional dispersion, but all regions had experienced the observed national rate of unemployment, wage rates would have fallen at 4.34% per annum instead of rising by 0.24% (1972, p.230).

The alternative approach made trade union militancy the key determinant of wage rates leaving little or no role for the direct effects of market forces. In his study, Hines found the relationship between wage change and trade union density to be particularly strong during the interwar period (1964, p.227-8). Despite a detailed empirical critique by Purdy and Zis (1972) this result still holds up on aggregate data[25]. Furthermore, it is quite strongly supported at the industry level. Burkitt examined 28 industries and found that in 21 of these wage change was significantly and positively related to the level, and/or the change in union density (1974, pp.89,90). That there is a strong correlation between wages and unionism is clear even from raw data; how it should be interpreted is not clear. The link between militancy and density is not established and union wage setting is not based on any economic model of union behaviour. Aside from this, there is the problem of causality. A more recent line of research following Bain and Elsheikh (1975) sees the growth of union membership as depending on several economic variables including wage change. Here causality runs from wages to unionism and little effort has been made to determine the direction of causality or to allow unionism and wages to be jointly and simultaneously determined[26].

The revival of interest in the role of unionism has led to renewed efforts to specify a union wage setting equation. As was indicated earlier, this approach has been adopted for the interwar period by Matthews and Minford (1981) and Matthews (1983). Here the union maximizes the expected real income of its membership (both employed and unemployed) subject to the labour demand curve, which leads to a "target" real wage. Deviations from this level are due to (quadratic) adjustment costs and errors in forecasting inflation. The results for the aggregate wage gives a significant (positive) role for real benefits, but not unemployment, as influencing the target wage and for the forecast error and lagged real wages. The results at the industry level (excluding the adjustment term) are rather varied, but generally support these findings. (Matthews, 1938, pp.17,23). Even though unionism might have been expected to appear (via the aggregation of union and non-union sectors) no role was found for this variable[27]. In the long run the model implies that the real wage depends on real benefits and unemployment and through the price equation, the nominal wage depends in addition on import prices and capacity utilization.

In his model Broadberry (1984) specifies a long run equation for the real wage, which depends on output per worker and the terms of trade. Nominal wage adjustment arises from an error correction mechanism with this long run equation embedded in it. The price equation is similarly specified with the absolute price level depending on the wage and import prices. The similarities between the models of Broadberry and Matthews makes it tempting to draw comparisons. Broadberry's wage-price system extimated on annual data for 1924-38 gives plausible results and reasonably well determined coefficients. Matthews' model on the other hand seems to do rather less well on annual data for 1921-38 but is rather more strongly motivated from a theoretical viewpoint. One important caveat however, is that the sample periods are different. Broadberry finds that extending his model back to 1922 allows significant coefficients to appear on the benefit to wage ratio or on individual dummy variables for the first two years.

We may summarize this section by saying that there is a widespread belief that institutional forces were important in determining wage rates and not without good reason. The relationship between wage change and unemployment seems weak and has led researchers to try and modify it or throw it out altogether. In the absence of a Phillips curve, there is little consensus as to what the determinants of the wage are, though it is closely correlated with both prices and unionism. Nor is there much agreement as yet on the appropriate framework in which to describe the institutional wage setting process.

VI. UNEMPLOYMENT AND STRUCTURAL CHANGE

Though recent work has focussed largely on the determinants of unemployment at the national level, there is a strong vein of opinion dating back to the 1930s that the aggregate is to be explained mainly in terms of structural factors. The pattern can be conveyed by the range of different unemployment rates. Taking the average over the years 1923-1938, industrial unemployment rates ranged from a little over 4% in groups such as Business and Financial Services and Other Road Transport to nearly 38% for Shipbuilding. Similarly, over the nine regions distinguished by the Ministry of Labour, average rates varied over the same period from close to 8% for London and the South-East to around 22% for the most hard hit regions of Wales and Northern Ireland. There is a clear ordering of regional unemployment rates which persists over time with the sourthern divisions having rates, on average, half those in the northern divisions and giving rise to the notion of Two Britains often labelled Inner Britain and the Outer Regions[28]. This pattern which appears to have been the reverse of that prevailing before 1914 is often ascribed largely to the contraction of the major nineteenth century staple industries of Textiles, Coal, Iron and Steel and Shipbuilding, to which, perhaps, Mechanical Engineering should be added. This view is, in varying degrees, the most commonly advanced text book explanation of regional variations[29]. In this tradition, Booth and Glynn have argued that "high regional unemployments differentials arose because of the geographical concentration of these ailing industries, the location and establishment of growth industries elsewhere and the immobility of the industrial work force." (1975, p.618).

Aldcroft (1984, pp.4-16) has recently drawn some interesting comparisons between the structure of changes in employment and unemployment rates in the 1930s and the 1980s. Between 1966 and 1982 there was a 37% decline in employment in industrial production, which was pervasive across all major sectors, while employment in services increased by 15%. By contrast, between 1920 and 1938, the percentage changes in employment were -2% and +20%, and though major employment loss was focussed in various parts of industry, some industrial sectors, such as vehicles, electrical goods, food, drink and tobacco and industries connected with construction, showed substantial growth. Due to the more balanced geographical location in the later period an the pervasiveness of employment loss, regional differences are not nearly as marked with the southern divisions experiencing unemployment rates about two thirds of those in the north. In spite of such findings, there has been little detailed investigation into the precise relation between industrial and regional unemployment rates with the important exception of Champernowne (1938). If labour was relatively mobile across industries, but not between regions, then, within regions unemployment rates would tend to equalize, and be higher in all industries in a depressed region as compared with a prosperous one. By contrast, if labour were largely industry specific, then regional unemployment rates would simply reflect differing industrial structure. Champernowne argued in favour of the former though he later retracted this view[30]. Employing the same industry by region data and using shift share analysis, I re-examined the issue. The region specific component of unemployment was measured by calculating how much lower (or higher) unemployment in a region would have been if each industry in that region had the national industry unemployment rate. Similarly, the industrial composition component was measured by calculating the difference between the actual unemployment rate in a region and that which emerges if the industry unemployment rates were re-weighted according to the national industrial composition of the labour force. The results of these and various other exercises indicate that both regional and industrial effects were present, accounting roughly equally for the regional diviations from the national unemployment rate in 1929 and 1932, but that by 1936 the region specific effects dominated (Hatton, 1985a, pp.6-15). Of course region specific effects are likely to be due in some measure to industrial causes, either because of labour force spillover effects between different industries in a locality or, on the demand side, the regional multipliers arising from input-output connections or income-expenditure effects. Thus these findings reflect the results rather than the causes of structural differences, but they do indicate expost some degree of both industrial and regional immobility.

It is natural to ask how much of interwar unemployment can be classified as structural, and various rule of thumb estimates have been made. Aldcroft suggests about half in the late 1930s compared with one third in the early 1980s (1984, p.29) and Glynn and Oxborrow 6 percentage points (1976, p.157) while Constantine favours 8 percentage points or 60% of total (1980, p.15). There is a severe problem of measurement, however which results from lack of an adequate definition of structural unemployment. Some writers following Beveridge have used the number unemployed for

9 months or more (1937, p.180). Alternatively, Fogarty(1945,p.5) used the excess of regional unemployment over and above that which would yield the same percentage as in London and the South East[31]. One problem is that such measures will closely reflect the overall level of demand for labour since, in cyclical depressions, owing to the volatility of certain industries and maldistribution of unemployment appears much worse. Using data for the nine Ministry of Labour divisions and for 36 industries over 1923-38, I regressed each employment rate on the national rate. Those industries and regions with high average rates typically gave coefficients larger than one (and those with low relative rates less than one) suggesting that in a sustained recovery employment growth would be greatest in the most depressed areas causing employment rates to converge (Hatton, 1985a, pp.30-34). Perhaps this is hardly surprising since the most depressed industries and areas were, in general, those associated with investment and exports - the most volatile components of demand.

Crafts, MacKinnon and Thomas (1984, Table 3) have estimated the effect on employment of the 32% fall in exports between 1929 and 1932, both direct and via inter-industry linkages. The effects of the export shock more than account for the decline in total employment, and indicate large declines in primary sectors, engineering and metals and textiles, though in some cases these were partially offset by rising domestic demand. It is clear that this decline was reflected at the regional level. In direct series estimates of the ratio of regional to national employment rates on the share of exports (and of investment) in national income, I found strong positive coefficients for the export share in the North West, North East and

Scotland and strong negative coefficients for London, the South East and South West. (Hatton, 1985a, p.36). This was largely, though not entirely, due to differing industrial structure. Using shift share analysis, I calculated industrial composition and region specific components in the deviations of regional employment growth from the aggregate for 1929-32 and 1932-36. As with the analysis of unemployment, region specific and industrial composition effects tend to work in the same direction. Industrial structure appears to have been particularly important in accounting for the low growth, relative to the national average, of employment in the North East, North West and Wales and the high relative growth of London and the South West[32].

While it is clear that time series variations in rate of employment across regions and between industries are sensitive to, and are an integral part of cyclical fluctuations, this is not the essence of the structural view of interwar unemployment. In contradistinction, the structural view focusses on the persistent differences in unemployment rates and links these to secular decline in some sectors and secular growth in others. Because of geographic and skill specificity, the gradual adjustment of expectations and the costs of adjustment, it takes time for labour displaced in one sector to be re-employed elsewhere. Because this process happens continuously, mismatch unemployment persists. It has been prominently argued that the interwar period was just such a period of long term structural change. The Edwardian growth in foreign trade and the effects of the First World War delayed structural adjustment away from the traditional staple industries and left Britain with an overcommittment of resources in these sectors given the trends in the pattern of demand and international competition which emerged[33]. Aldcroft (1966, 1967) and Richardson (1961, 1965) have argued that new industries exhibiting rapid productivity growth, expanded as the old industries contracted. More recently, Aldcroft has argued that Beenstock's "transition theory" coupled with changing tastes and technology are relevant to explaining the high unemployment of both the interwar years and recent times (1984, ch.4). This view is not without its critics and it is natural to ask whether structural change was more rapid during the interwar years than at times when unemployment was lower. Using measures of the dispersion of industry, growth rates around the mean, both Broadberry (1983, p.467) and Crafts et.al. (1984, p.2) find little evidence of higher rates of structural change in this period as compared with 1900-13 or the postwar period. Thus, measured at the industry level, there was nothing unique about structural change during the interwar period.

Crafts et.al. have taken the analysis one step futher and, following Lilien (1982), introduced the measure of dispersion directly into a quarterly model of unemployment for 1928 to 1939. In the presence of lagged unemployment, the innovation in the money supply and indices of bankruptcies and industrial production, the dispersion term takes a coefficient which is both small and insignificant (1984, p.10). Thus, the existing evidence does not point to structural change as the key to high average unemployment. One might argue from the point of view of adjustment costs that structural change should be measured at the occupational or geographical level or perhaps both. However, it seems unlikely that a different story would emerge given the dependence of these on changes in industrial structure. In order to go further, it would be necessary to explicitly model the process of search and migration and integrate this with labour demand at the disaggregated level. Though little work has been done recently in this area, the issue is worthy of further consideration.

VII. MIGRATION AND LABOUR MOBILITY

Implicit in most discussions of structural unemployment is the view that, for a variety of reasons, labour is relatively immobile. The fact of large and persistent differences in unemployment rates is evidence that labour did not flow perfectly freely between industries and regions. Booth and Glynn comment that "despite these widely differing conditions, the industrial population remained overwhelmingly immobile" (1975, p.623) and Glynn and Oxborrow that "inter-regional migration in the interwar period was much less than might have been anticipated"(1976, p.154). Nevertheless, considerable reallocation of labour did take place. Between 1923 and 1938 the proportion of the insured popultion in the southern divisions rose from 46.8% of the total to 52.3%. While the insured population of Wales remained virtualy stationary, that of the South East increased by half. By no means all of this shift was due to migration, since new entry into insurance was higher in the south than the north[34]. As the absolute differences between unemployment rates increased in the early 1930s, so did long term unemployment in the outer regions. The percentage of all unemployed who had been out of work for over a year rose from 4.7% in September 1929, to 26% in June 1936, but by this time it was 38% in Wales compared with 8.5% in the South East[35]. One might well ask why this did not engender greater migration than actually took place. In doing so, it is important to distinguish between the willingness of workers to move, given the incentives they faced, and the incentives themselves. Workers might be willing to move for relatively small net advantages, but unless there were real net benefits to migration, they would not do so[36].

The incentive to move depends on the way in which regional or industrial differences manifest themselves. This may be illustrated by applying the diagram of Fig.1 to two industries or regions (with the emphasis on the latter) placed back to back[37]. In Fig. 5, the depressed sector, j, on the right, experiences a downward shift in its demand curve from D^E_{j1} to D^E_{j2}. If wage rates remained close to market-clearing levels then the wage in the depressed sector would fall to W_1, and the differential $W_0 - W_1$ provides the incentive to move to the prosperous sector, i. On the other hand, if the relative wage were fixed at W_0 then the incentive to move would be provided by the higher probability of finding employment. In both cases, this incentive should cause leftward shifts in both S^E curves through migration which would tend to equalize wage or employment rates. If the wage in both sectors were set at the market-clearing level for the prosperous region, then the economy wide wage should fall; if not, then unemployment rates would tend to equalize. If wages were set without reference to excess supply, then there could be excess supply in both sectors or excess supply in the depressed sector and excess demand in the prosperous sector.

As Casson (1983, pp.53-61) has pointed out, there was a debate among contemporaries as to whether some or all wages were too high. Clay argued that even though wage

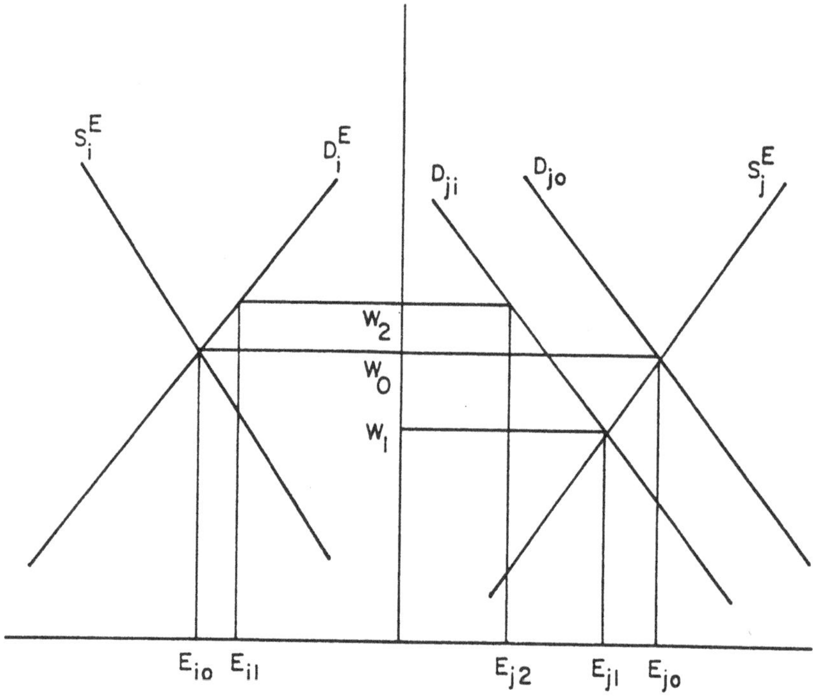

FIGURE 5

rates in depressed industries had fallen relative to others, they were still too high. Others thought that they were too high even in prosperous industries to provide vacancies for migrants though, as illustrated, there would still be an incentive to move. The stylized fact would seem to be that there was excess supply in most industries and regions, such as with the wage at W_2 in Fig. 5, but that, due to relative wage rigidity, it was much higher in some than others. Not everyone would accept this view: some might argue that there were pockets of excess demand and others that all labour markets were close to market-clearing levels. On the latter point, I have argued above that estimates of the overall level of vacancies and the evidence from econometric models militates strongly against the market-clearing view. On the former, the findings of a contemporary study by Allen and Thomas (1939) of the take-up of vacancies during 1936 in the booming London engineering trades are often cited as evidence of labour shortage . Of a sample of 2500 workers placed by the labour exchanges, 54.8% represented vacancies filled immediately and another 29.3% within four days. Though the more skilled the trade, the longer the delay, it could hardly be argued that these reflected serious labour shortages. Turning to wage rates, the variations across a given occupation or trade was relatively small, though, in London, rates were often 10-20% higher than elsewhere[39]. The distinctive pattern seems to be that established in the nineteenth century with the wage depending largely on the size of town and reflecting compensating differentials due to disamenities and, in particular, differences in the level of rents. Much of the variation in wage rates is between different industries and occupations and there is weak evidence that these were inversely related to unemployment rates[40].

Thus, both wages and unemployment differentials provided an incentive for migration, though principally the latter. But there were other factors which tended to reduce it. First, as Casson has pointed out, for given wage and unemployment rates the existence of unemployment benefits would tend to narrow the gap between the expected wage in high and low unemployment areas (1982, p.121-22)[41]. Second, since wage and unemployment rate differences were smaller within an industry, workers considering migration within an industry could expect smaller benefits than the regional aggregates would suggest. Third, for skilled and semi-skilled workers in the staple industries, the relevant alternative was often to shift both industry and location, usually to less skilled and lower wage jobs, which would further reduce the net advantage. Finally, even if the worker were willing to make such a change, it is not clear that the probability of obtaining employment would be adequately reflected in the higher relative employment rate in the receiving area. One important reason for this is the duration dependency of the probability of leaving the register. In his study of the process of unemployment, H. W. Singer (1939, p.49) found that the probabilty of leaving the register declined as duration rose, but that it declined more steeply in the relatively depressed regions. Thus, the differences in re-employment probabilities would tend to be smaller across regions for the short term unemployed.

Heim (1984) has recently argued that, given the nature of jobs in expanding industries, employers sought to recruit "new" labour, either in the form of juveniles, females or previously uninsured workers from non-industrial occupations, such as agriculture. This suggests that industrial experience in one of the declining staple industries was not just useless but a positive handicap. Workers steeped in the cultural and industrial traditions of the north would have been last in the queue for jobs in the south. In this light it is not surprising that the initiatives which were undertaken to ease the regional problems did not meet with much success. The Industrial Transferrence Scheme which was introduced in 1928 to retrain and assist in relocating workers often failed to secure them regular employment and a large proportion returned home[42]. Similarly, efforts to attract employers to "Special Areas" after 1934 had little effect since the locational advantages of the south were not outweighed by higher labour costs or labour shortages[43].

There has been very little recent study of interwar migration but there are a number of valuable studies of the pattern of migration undertaken in the late 1930s. Those of Thomas (1934, 1937) indicate that migrants tended to flow to areas where they could best use their existing skills. Skilled workers from the North East tended to gravitate to the Dagenham Motor Industry, miners often moved from the Outer Regions to the Kent coalfield and Scots to a variety of trades in London. Makower, Marschak and Robinson (1940) found that miners and textile workers tended to be more mobile than those in shipping and shipbuilding. As compared with the preceding period, during 1931-5 miners increasingly migrated to unskilled jobs in building and public works. In his study of Welsh migration to Oxford, Daniel (1939) found that for a change of location or occupation, the preceding spell of unemployment was longer than when a job change involved neither of these, and longer still if both were involved. Men with families experienced much longer pre-migration spells than those without, reflecting the higher rents in Oxford for families and perhaps the smaller advantage of the Oxford wage over unemployment benefit. Furthermore, despite the rise in the proportion of long term unemployment in the 1930s, they represented a much smaller proportion of migrants in 1933-5 than earlier. This suggests that only the more mobile and adaptable could benefit from migration in the depths of depression.

Makower, Marschak and Robinson (1938) developed a migration function which they used in a series of studies. The relative advantages between counties they found, was best represented by the differences between the rate in the sending and receiving counties as a proportion of the latter. This was found to conform with migration from various other counties (adjusted for size and distance) to Oxford and to explain much of the net gains and losses of population across counties for 1925-31 and 1931-36. For reasons indicated above, the proportionate differences in unemployment rates tended to decrease as aggregate unemployment rose. This implies that total migration would tend to move procyclically which is supported by the evidence. For 1925-31 total annual net movements between countries averaged 0.45% of the population and between Ministry of Labour divisions 0.26%; for 1931-36 the figures were 0.31% and 0.12% respectively. As a consequence, the tendency for migration to reduce unemployment differentials declined as the depression deepened in the 1930s. If migrants represented net gain in employment in the recovery areas, it would have taken 6 years to equalize unemployment rates given the pattern of unemployment and migration of 1925-31, but 32 years given the pattern of 1932-6. (1939, p.75, 83)[44]. This suggests an additional reason for the maldistribution of unemployment in the 1930s: the effect of the relative contraction of employment in the Outer Regions on unemployment rates was exacerbated by the slowing down in migration.

It can be concluded that though there was clearly immobility of labour in the interwar period in the sense that unemployment rates failed to equalize, it is not clear that it was due to inertia and the unwillingness of workers to move. The incentives for workers to move were by no means overwhelming, particularly for displaced skilled workers and those with families. Even though the rise in absolute unemployment rates was greater in the outer regions during the depression, the probability of employment for the marginal worker is likely to have decreased by more in the prosperous areas. Though potential migrants may have been marginal workers at these times, there is evidence that greater numbers would and did transfer successfully when prospects improved. Given the paucity of recent work in this area, it is easy to suggest that more light ought to be shed on the subject by further research, though not so straightforward to find sources of relevant data, particularly at the micro level.

VIII. CONCLUSIONS

What broad inferences if any, can be drawn from the body of material discussed in the preceding sections? The first is that the interwar labour market provides considerable scope for the testing of alternative hypotheses using formal techniques. This potential has by no means been exhausted, though a good deal of work has been done recently. In many instances this has not yet led to clear cut conclusions, but improved model specifications and the use of more disaggregated data holds promise for deeper insights and firmer results.

A central issue is how the working of the labour market should be characterized and here it seems that using a simple static market clearing model strains credibility as well as doing violence to the observed facts.

Variations in unemployment arose mainly on the demand side, while wage rates, at least after 1922, remained fairly stable. If one must have a crude paradigm it appears to be that on the whole, the labour market was in excess supply or at least that labour supply was very elastic. It seems likely that for the most part the unemployed would have been willing to work at the prevailing wage if they could find a vacancy. Placing the emphasis on the demand side raises the question of how different things might have been if the wage had been set at a level of say 10% lower. Unfortunately the existing evidence on labour demand is inadequate to provide us with the answer, but if labour demand were relatively inelastic then one would have to be somewhat pessimistic about the feasibility and potential benefits of lower wage rates in generating full employment.

Wage stickiness raises the question of why the process of competition did not generate different results. Here the answer suggested is that institutional forces, both formal and informal, were inimical both to the downward adjustment of wage rates and the emergence of atomistic competition in the labour market. This leads to rather a different view of the unemployment insurance system from that suggested by Benjamin and Kochin. If wages were fixed at a level where there was widespread excess supply, then even though the insurance system might induce some workers to want to supply less labour, there would always be a queue for available vacancies and employment would not be directly constrained by labour supply. But benefits may have been one of the factors taken into account in wage setting. There were other relevant comparisons as well, such as the notion of a subsistence wage, the minimum rates set by Trade Boards and customary differentials. It may never be possible to capture the subtle interplay of these forces acting through the process of collective bargaining, and in turn depending on relative bargaining strengths of unions and employers associations. A start has been made, however, and there is reason to believe that further work, especially at the disaggregated level, would yield deeper insights.

It is clear that the incidence of unemployment was closely connected with the way in which changes in aggregate demand for labour were distributed across industries and localities. Industry and region effects were reinforcing and tended to further concentrate unemployment, which ultimately emerged in the form of longer durations and increasing concentrations of long term unemployment. A key issue is why the maldistribution of unemployment remained so severe throughout the period. Clearly the answer has to do with the specificity of skills and location. The more costly it was to acquire new skill, adopt new working practises and adapt to new geographical environments the lower the mobility of labour would be. But, it is suggested that the incentives for mobility were attenuated by overall excess labour supply and that these worsened during the depression of the early 1930s. Thus is appears that structural unemployment was as much a consequence of the overall high unemployment as a cause. Here also there is scope for further research into both the structure of labour demand and, in the context of the household, of the decision to shift industry, occupation or location.

FOOTNOTES

1. For a full discussion of the available data on un-

employment form the pre 1914 era through to the post war period, see Garside (1981).

2. In one of the few papers written before the recent burgeoning of the literature, Booth and Glynn (1975) argued strongly against this view preferring a more structural explanation. This is discussed further below.
3. Most contemporary comments see benefits as setting a floor to the institutionally set wage level rather than raising unemployment directly through reducing effective labour supply. These issues are discussed further below.
4. It is not clear whether this index is higher or lower than a wage index for insured employment only. Those earning over £250 per annum were explicitly excluded from insurance, but, on the other hand, so were low wage groups such as agricultural workers and domestic servants.
5. These calculations are based on the figures in Hatton (1982, pp.4.13-4.16). For similar adjustments see also Metcalf et.al. (1982, pp.392, 396-7).
6. Trade union out of work benefits were usually about 10s before the war and generally yielded replacement ratios of about 0.3. Given that they were private schemes, eligibility was tightly controlled.
7. The criticisms made by Benjamin and Kochin of these comparisons fail to convincingly undermine the main results. They argued (1982, p.425) that Metcalf et.al. had deflated postwar benefits by a wage rate (that for manual male workers) that was too low, evidently still believing that the Chapman wage index is the appropriate one for their benefit rate. In drawing their comparisons with the postwar period Metcalf et.al. (1982, Table 2.2 p.392) confined themselves to male manual workers and adjusted the Chapman wage index upwards accordingly. This is a perfectly legitimate comparison for that particular group. Part of the problem is that Benjamin and Kochin insist on using the "population at risk" (the definition of which changes with the postwar extension of the insurance system) in their denominator while sticking steadfastly to an unrepresentative benefit rate in the numerator.
8. Other poverty lines developed by Tout, Ford and Beveridge were somewhat lower, but if extrapolated to 1981 would yield minimum incomes of between £27.4 and £35.7 or between half and two thirds of the supple-

mentary benefit scale. (Atkinson, 1984, pp.17, 25-32).

9. An average wage earning adult male with three dependents earning 64s when in work and 32s when unemployed, would have to be unemployed for three quarters of the time to reach the poverty line. On the other hand, for many workers, even full wages would not keep them clear of the poverty line.

10. For contemporary comments to this effect, see Beveridge (1937, p.10) and Burns, (1940, p.98).

11. The average benefit rate for the males aged 16-20 was taken as the average of rates over these age groups. Though the wage of the younger group will be biased down by the inclusion of workers aged 14 and 15, in the wage census it will not radically change the conclusion. In comparing the benefit rate of females 18 and above with males 21 and over, young women aged 18-20 were given a weight of one quarter. It may also be of interest to compare this with females aged 16-18 whose average benefit rate in 1935 was 44% of that of older females while the wage relative was 52%.

12. For futher discussion of the generation of these counterfactual estimates, see Hatton (1980, pp.5-11).

13. It might reasonably be argued on the other hand that the replacement rate in the equation was picking up the effect of variations in administrative and legislative rules if rules generally became more favourable at times when benefit rates were also relatively high. Thus, contributory rules conditions for benefit and duration of benefit were eased in 1928-31, and tightened in 1931-4 and somewhat relaxed again from 1934.

14. An additional measure of the stance of the system developed by Easton is for the fraction of total time for which benefits could be received. This took a significant and positive coefficient in a monthly model of unemployment for 1920-38 (1978, p.26).

15. In his model, Collins used deviations from trend of employment rather than output in an effort to pick up the pure labour force effects of insurance.

16. According to these simulations, keeping the replacement rate at 0.27 throughout the period to 1936, would have led to employment being 11.6% higher in that year even holding output constant. In Benjamin and Kochin's estimates, which allow for adjustment in output, but not in the wage, employment would have been 0.4% to 4.3% higher, thus much of their reduced unemployment comes from variation in the labour force, rather than

employment. (See Hatton 1982, pp.5.55-5.60).

17. In Smyth's estimates, the years of excess demand (when the wage was rising) are 1924-5, 1927, 1929 and 1934-8. In the case of Irish and Winter the preferred sample gave the years of excess demand as 1923-5, 1929 and 1937.

18. Steve Broadberry has suggested to me that one might do better at identifying the U/V curve if the 1930s was included. His measure of vacancies which is calculated from flow data is somewhat different from mine, which is the directly observed stock but which is only available for the 1920s. Clearly, further work along these lines would be useful.

19. It originated with Keynes' statement in the General Theory that "in the short period, falling money and rising real wages are each, for independent reasons, likely to accompany decreasing employment; labour being readier to accept wage cuts when employment is falling off, yet real wages inevitable rising under the same circumstances on account of the increasing marginal return to a given capital equipment when output is diminished" (1936, p.10). Thus, there are two questions: (1) the cyclical relation between real and money wages and (2) the relation between real wages and employment. Since Keynes had explicitly argued that these were independent, there was no ground for inferring one from the other. Yet in their examination of the data, Dunlop (1938), Tarshis (1939) and Richardson (1939) stuck almost entirely to (1). Only in a postscript to his paper did Tarshis address (2) directly, finding a strong negative relationship between monthly U.S. data on man hours of employment and hourly wages for 1932-38.

20. This price index is for final output of the manufacturing sector. Ideally a measure of the price of value added in manufacturing would have been preferred, i.e., final output price net of the component due to inputs produced elsewhere.

21. The importance of employer contributions to National insurance and local rates to employer's costs was stressed by Clay (1929, pp.96-8), but has been largely neglected in the recent debate.

22. Rowe assessed the importance of these developments as follows: "It is beyond belief that when the general level of wages in an industry is settled by agreement between a few national representatives of the employer's association and the trade unions, that the result will be the same as would have been reached

if each locality had acted independently with individual bargaining to the fore". (1928, p.195-6).

23. In addition, the unemployed worker could refuse a job which existed because of a trade dispute, or on genuine religious conscientious or moral grounds. For a full discussion of the conditions and qualifications for receipt of benefit see Hill and Lubin (1934, esp. p.153).
24. Though Phillips regarded the period 1925-31 as normal, Archibald, Kemmis and Perkins implicitly see it as deviant owing to the wage policy implied by the gold standard. Interestingly, the inverse relationship between unemployment and wage change emerges more strongly for the period when Britain was off the gold standard.
25. See Purdy and Zis (1972, p.10-13); Dogas and Hines (1975), Purdy and Zis (1976).
26. One of the few attempts to determine the direction of causality was performed by Hines in his original paper. For the inter-war period, he found that causality ran predominantly from density to wages (1964, p.234-5).
27. One rationale for this could be that as indicated, institutional wage setting was not coterminous with unionism; indeed behaviour in the non-union sector, was closely linked, by institutional means to that in the union sector.
28. The four southern divisions, London, South-East, South-West, and Midlands comprise Inner Britain, while the remaining five North-East, North-West, Scotland, Wales and Northern Ireland make up the Outer Regions.
29. Aldcroft, 1970, Ch.3, and Glynn and Oxborrow, 1976, Chs.3,5, Pollard, 1983, Ch.2.
30. Champernowne stated his argument in these terms: "It seems that the main cause of variation of unemployment percentage between industries is not so much that the percentages vary between industries within Inner Britain, or within the Outer Regions, as that some industries are mainly situtated in prosperous Inner Britain and others are mainly situated in the depressed Outer Regions", (1938, p.103). However, when challenged (by H.W. Singer) to substantiate his argument which was based on a sample of 16 industries, he retracted it conceding that the sample was unrepresentative (Champernowne, 1939, p.215).
31. These calculations have been reproduced for instance by Aldcroft (1970, p.86).
32. These results are broadly borne out by the findings of

Law (1981, p.88) who performed a similar exercise on census data for 1921-1931, though as might have been expected over a longer period, the correspondence between industrial composition and region specific effects is weaker.

33. The term "overcommittment" was explicitly coined by Richardson (1965).
34. See Dennison (1939, p.141, 153). Both Dennison (1939) and the Barlow Commission (1940) provide wide ranging discussions reflecting the contemporary concerns with migration and industrial location.
35. Beveridge (1937, p.8-9).
36. Glynn and Oxborrow discuss the incentives and impediments in terms of "push" and "pull" factors (1976, p.154-5).
37. In the discussion of Fig. 4 the demand shifts resulting from changes in wages and employment are ignored. For a discussion of two sector model with non market clearing in this context see Casson (1983, Ch.6).
38. See for instance, Aldcroft (1970, p.107).
39. Data on wage rates set by collective agreement are available in Ministry of Labour, Standard Time Rates of Wages and Hours of Labour, see esp. (1929, p.116-124 for the building trades and pp.80-81 for other trades).
40. Collins (1982, p.374-5).
41. Benjamin and Kochin tentatively suggested that the lower wage in the depressed areas yielded higher replacement rates and more benefit induced unemployment (1979, p.473). If the S^E curve were very flat in the relevant range, the market clearing wage might not fall by much in these areas, but it is hard to believe that the difference in replacement rates alone were large enough to account for such high proportions of long term unemployment in depressed areas. This is especially the case for the 1930s, when the exhaustion of stardard benefits was far more common and a large proportion of the unemployed faced effective benefit rates which were lower than the standard. Beveridge (1936, pp.384-5) for instance, reports proportions of claims to standard benefit ranging from nearly two thirds in some relative prosperous counties to less than one third in some of the more depressed counties.
42. Dennison (1939, pp.174-6) notes that both finding suitable applicants for training and the placement of transferees became more difficult after 1929. The

Barlow Commission (1940, p.150) reported that from 1928 to mid-1937 nearly 150,000 men and 40,000 women were transferred under the scheme, but that between 1930 and 1937, 50,000 men and 5,600 women were known to have returned to the depressed areas.

43. For contemporary discussions of industrial location, see Dennison (1939), P.E.P. (1939) and J.H. Jones "A Memorandum on the Location of Industry", Appendix 2 of the Barlow Commission (1940). More recently, these issues have been discussed by Heim (1983).

44. If there were excess supply everywhere, then workers who gained employment by moving would merely displace others. In this case, the time periods for rates to equalize would be 15 and 62 years respectively.

REFERENCES

D.H. Aldcroft, Economic progress in Britain in the 1920s, reprinted in D.H. Aldcroft and H.W. Richardson, The British Economy 1870-1939, London:Macmillan, (1969).

D.H. Aldcroft, Economic growth in the inter-war years: a reassessment, (1967). Reprinted in D.H. Aldcroft and P. Fearon, Economic Growth in 20th Century Britain, London: Macmillan, (1969).

D.H. Aldcroft, The Inter-War Economy: Britain 1919-1939, London: Batsford, (1970).

D.H. Aldcroft, Full Employment: The Elusive Goal, Brighton: Harvester Press, (1984).

R.G.D. Allen and B. Thomas, The supply of engineering labour under boom conditions, Economic Journal 49, 259-274, (1939).

G.C. Archibald, R. Kemmis and J.W. Perkins, Excess demand for labour, unemployment and the Phillips curve: a theoretical and empirical study, in D. Laidler and D. Purdy, (eds.), Inflation and Labour Markets, Manchester: University Press, (1974).

A.B. Atkinson, Poverty in Britain: the 1930's to the 1980's, E.S.R.C. Programme on Taxation, Incentives and the Distribution of Income, Discussion Paper #73, (1984).

G.S. Bain and F. Elsheikh, Union Growth and the Business Cycle, Oxford: Blackwell, (1976).

M. Beenstock, F. Capie and B. Griffiths, The economic recovery in the United Kingdom in the 1930's, Bank of England Panel of Academic Consultants, Discussion Paper No. 23, (1984).

D.K. Benjamin and L.A. Kochin, Searching for an explanation of unemployment in inter-war Britain, Journal of Political Economy, 87, 441-478, (1979).

D.K. Benjamin and L.A. Kochin, Unemployment and unemployment benefits in twentieth century Britain: a reply to our critics, Journal of Political Economy, 90, 410-436, (1982).

W.H. Beveridge, Unemployment: A Problem of Industry, London: Longmans Green, (1930).

W.H. Beveridge, An analysis of unemployment, Economica, 4, 357-386, and 5, 1-17 and 168-183, (1936-7).

W.H. Beveridge, Full Employment in a Free Society, London: George Allen and Unwin, (1944).

A.E. Booth and S. Glynn, Unemployment in the inter-war period: a multiple problem, Journal of Contemporary History, 10, 611-637, (1975).

S. N. Broadberry, Unemployment in inter-war Britian: a disequilibrium approach, Oxford Economic Papers, 35, 463-485, (1983).

S.N. Broadberry, Wages and prices in inter-war Britain, University College Cardiff, (unpublished), (1983).

B. Burkitt, The relationship between earnings and unionisation in the inter-war years, Applied Economics, 6, 83-93, (1974).

E.M. Burns, British Unemployment Programs 1920-1939, Washington: Social Science Research Council, (1941).

M. Casson, The Economics of Unemployment: A Historical Perspective, Oxford: Martin Robertson, (1983).

D.G. Champernowne, The uneven distribution of unemployment in the United Kingdom, 1929-36, Review of Economic Studies, 5, 93-106, and 6, 111-123, (1938-9); also The Main Cause of Variation of the Unemployment Percentage between Industries - A Correction, ibid, 6, 125-6.

A.L. Chapman, Wages and Salaries in the United Kingdom 1920-1938, Cambridge University Press, (1953).

H. Clay, The Post-War Unemployment Problem, London: Macmillan, (1929a).

H. Clay, The Problem of Industrial Relations, London: Macmillan, (1929b).

M. Collins, Unemployment in inter-war Britain: still searching for an explanation, Journal of Poltical Economy, 90, 369-379, (1982).

S. Constantine, Unemployment in Britain between the Wars, London: Longman, (1980).

N.F.R. Crafts, M. MacKinnon and M. Thomas, International trade and structural unemployment in inter-war Britain, Paper presented to the American Economic

Association Meeting (Dallas), (1984).
R. Cross, How much voluntary unemployment in inter-war Britain? Journal of Political Economy 90, 380-385, (1982).
G.H. Daniel, Some factors affecting the mobility of labour, Oxford Economic Papers, 2, 144-179, (1939).
S.R. Dennison, The Location of Industry and the Depressed Areas, London: Oxford University Press, (1939).
N.H. Dimsdale, Employment and real wages in the inter-war period, National Institute Economic Review, 110, 94-102, (1984).
D. Dogas and A.G. Hines, Trade unions and wage inflation in the UK: a critique of Purdy and Zis, Applied Economics, 7, 195-211, (1975).
J.T. Dunlop, The movement of real and money wage rates, Economic Journal, 48, 413-434, (1938).
S. Easton, Unemployment in Britain between the Wars, Simon Fraser University, Discussion Paper No. 78-5-3, (1978).
B. Eichengreen, Unemployment in inter-war Britain: a micro-economic perspective, Harvard University, (unpublished), (1984).
C.H. Feinstein, National Income Expenditure and Output of the U.K. 1955-1965, Cambridge: University Press, (1972).
M.P. Fogarty, Prospects of the Industrial Areas of Great Britain, London: Methuen, (1945)
W.R. Garside, The Measurement of Unemployment, Oxford: Blackwell, (1981).
S. Glynn and J. Oxborrow, Interwar Britain: A Social and Economic History, London: George Allen and Unwin, (1976)
A. Harrison and R. Hart, A labour market model of unemployment insurance, McMaster University Discussion Paper 85-08, (1985).
P.E. Hart, Unemployment and unemployment benefits, U.K., 1920-38, National Institute for Economic and Social Research, unpublished, (1984).
T.J. Hatton, Unemployment in Britain between the World Wars: a role for the dole?, Essex Economic Discussion Papers No.139, (1980).
T.J. Hatton, Employment functions for U.K. Industries between the wars, Essex Economic Discussion Paper No.181, (1981).
T.J. Hatton, The British labour market 1855-1939: a quantitative approach, Ph.D. Dissertation, University of Warwick, (1982).
T.J. Hatton, Unemployment benefits and the macroeconomics of the inter-war labour market: a further analysis, Oxford Economic Papers, 35, 486-505, (1983a).
T.J. Hatton, Labour supply and demand 1924-1939: evidence

from quarterly data, Essex Economics Discussion Paper No.227, (1983b).

T.J. Hatton, The British labour market in different economic eras, Essex Economics Discussion Paper No.246, (1984a).

T.J. Hatton, Explaining female labour market participation in inter-war Britain: a progress report, University of Essex, unpublished, (1984b).

T.J. Hatton, Structural aspects of unemployment between the wars, Essex Economic Discussion Paper No.196, forthcoming in Research in Economic History, (1985a).

T.J.Hatton, The British labour market in the 1920's: a test of the search-turnover approach, Explorations in Economic History, 22, pp.257-270, (1985).

T.J. Hatton and J.S. Seaton, Real wages and employment between the wars: a cautionary note, University of Essex, unpublished, (1984).

C.E. Heim, Industrial organization and regional development in inter-war Britain, Journal of Economic History, 43, 931-952, (1983).

C.E. Heim, Structural transformation and the demand for new labour in advanced economies: inter-war Britain, Journal of Economic History, 44, 585-595, (1984).

J.R. Hill and I. Lubin, The British Attack on Unemployment, Washington: Brookings Institution, (1934).

A.G. Hines, Trade unions and wage inflation in the United Kingdom 1893-1961, Review of Economic Studies, 31, 221-252, (1964).

M. Irish, Unemployment in inter-war Britain: a note, University of Bristol, unpublished, (1980a).

M. Irish, Inter-war participation in the labour market, University of Bristol, unpublished, (1980b).

M. Irish and D. Winter, Did the aggregate market for labour clear in inter-war Britain? some econometric evidence, University of Bristol, unpublished, (1981).

J.M. Keynes, The General Theory of Employment Interest and Money, London: Macmillan, (1936).

J.M. Keynes, Relative movements of real wages and output Economic Journal, 49, 34-51, (1939).

R.G. Lipsey, The relation between unemployment and the rate of change of money wage rates in the United Kingdom, 1862-1957: a further analysis, Economica, 27, 1-31, (1960).

C.M. Law, British Regional Development since World War I, London: Methuen, (1981).

D.M. Lilien, Sectoral shifts and cyclical unemployment Journal of Political Economy, 90, 777-793, (1982).

H. Makower, J. Marschak and H.W. Robinson, Studies in the

mobility of labour: a tentative statistical measure, Oxford Economic Papers, 1, 83-123, (1938).

H. Makower, J. Marschak and H.W. Robinson, Studies in the mobility of labour: analysis for Great Britain, Parts I and II, Oxford Economic Papers, 2, 70-97, and 3, 39-62, (1939, 1940).

K.G.P. Matthews, Unemployment in inter-war Britain: an equilibrium approach, University of Liverpool, unpublished, (1938).

K. Matthews and P. Minford, Estimation of a rational expectations model of the inter-war period, University of Liverpool, unpublished, (1981).

D. Metcalf, S.J. Nickell and N. Floros, Still searching for an explanation of unemployment in inter-war Britain, London School of Economics, Centre for Labour Economics Discussion Paper No.71 and (revised) Journal of Political Economy 90, 386,399, (1980, 1982).

S.J. Nickell and M. Andrews, Real wages and employment in Britain 1951-1979, Oxford Economic Papers, 35 (Supplement), 185-206, (1983).

P.A. Ormerod and G.D.N. Worswick, Unemployment in inter-war Britain, Journal of Political Economy, 90, 400-409. (1982).

E.H. Phelps-Brown and M. Browne, A Century of Pay, London: Macmillan, (1968).

A.W. Phillips, The relation between unemployment and the rate of change of money wage rates in the United Kingdom, Economica, 25, 283-299, (1958).

A.C. Pigou, Wage policy and unemployment, Economic Journal, 38, 355-368, (1927).

Political and Economic Planning, Report on the Location of Industry, London: P.E.P., (1939).

W.E.J. Purdy and G. Zis, Trade unions and wage inflation in the U.K.: a reappraisal, In D.E. Laidler and D. Purdy, (eds.), Inflation and Labour Markets, Manchester: University Press, (1974).

H.W. Richardson, Overcommittment in Britain before 1930, (1965), reprinted in D.H. Aldcroft and H.W. Richardson, The British Economy 1870-1939, London: Macmillan, (1969).

H.W. Richardson, New industries between the wars, (1961), reprinted in D.H. Aldcroft and H.W. Richardson, The British Economy 1870-1939, London: Macmillan, (1969).

J.H. Richardson, Real wage movements, Economic Journal, 49, 423-441, (1939).

H.S. Rosen and R.E. Quandt, Estimation of a disequilibrium aggregate labour market, Review of Economics and Statistics, 60, 371-379, (1978).

J.W.F. Rowe, Wages in Practice and Theory, London: Routledge and Kegan Paul, (1928).

Royal Commission on the Distribution of the Industrial Population, (Barlow Commission), Cmnd.6153, London: H.M.S.O. (1940).

B. Sadler, Unemployment and unemployment benefits in twentieth century Britain: a lesson of the thirties, in Out of Work: Perspective of Mass Unemployment, University of Warwick, Coventry, (1984).

D. Sells, British Wages Boards, Washington: Brookings Institution, (1939).

H.W. Singer, Regional labour markets and the process of unemployment, Review of Economic Studies, 7, 42-58, (1939).

D.J. Smyth, The British labour market in disequilibrium: did the dole reduce employment in inter-war Britain? Journal of Macro Economics, 5, 41-51, (1983).

L. Tarshis, Changes in real and money wages, Economic Journal, 49, 150-154, (1939).

B. Thomas, The movement of labour into South-East England, 1920-1932, Economica, 1, 220-241, (1934).

B. Thomas, The influx of labour into London and the South-East, 1920-1931, Economica, 4, 323-336, (1937).

R.L. Thomas and P.J.M. Stoney, Unemployment dispersion as a determinant of wage inflation in the United Kingdom, in M. Parkin and M.T. Sumner, (eds.), Incomes Policy and Inflation, Manchester University Press, (1972).

YOUTH UNEMPLOYMENT AND RELATIVE WAGES IN THE UK: A SURVEY OF RECENT ECONOMETRIC EVIDENCE

P.E. HART
University of Reading and National Institute of Economic and Social Research

I. INTRODUCTION

There are many possible causes of youth unemployment but this article is concerned with only one of them, namely the view that the wages of young people are too high relatively to those of adults to enable the labour market to provide jobs for all those young people who want them. We survey six recent econometric studies which measure the relationship between youth employment and relative wages in the U.K., namely Merrilees and Wilson (1979), Wells (1983), Hutchinson, Barr and Drobny (1979), (1984), Abowd, Layard and Nickell (1981), Lynch and Richardson (1982) and Rice (1984).

The first, second and sixth papers use disequilibrium methods. The disequilibrium[1] approach is most easily explained after summarising the traditional or 'equilibrium' approach in equations (1) to (3):

$$D_t = \alpha_1 p_t + \beta_1' x_{1t} + u_{1t} \quad (1)$$

$$S_t = \alpha_2 p_t + \beta_2' x_{2t} + u_{2t} \quad (2)$$

$$D_t = S_t \quad (3)$$

where D_t, S_t and p_t are endogenous variables of demand, supply and price, and x_{1t} and x_{2t} are vectors of exogenous variables. Equation (3) is an equilibrium condition. When estimating this model, it is not necessary to claim that equilibrium always existed during the sample period: but it would be assumed that there were tendencies for p_t to move to bring D_t and S_t into equilibrium[2]. It is possible to estimate this system providing there are enough exogenous variables to identify or over-identify the model. That is, D_t and S_t vary over time but only the quantity bought and sold, Q_t, is observed. If there is one predetermined variable in (1), and another predetermined variable in (2), the model is exactly identified and it is possible to estimate (1) and (2). It is also possible to estimate (1) and (2) if there is more than one predetermined variable in each (when the model is said to be 'over-identified') using an appropriate simultaneous equations estimation technique such as two-stage least squares, TSLS. In practice, identification problems are sometimes ignored by implicitly or explicitly assuming in (1), for example, that Q_t measures D_t so that separate estimation of (1) from time-series data yields a demand equation. But in the equilibrium model, supply also varies over time and unless the effects of such variations are also considered, we can never be sure that the separate estimation of (1) really yields a demand equation rather than some mongrel linear combination of both supply and demand[3].

In the disequilbrium approach, (3) is replaced by the minimum condition in (4).

$$Q_t = \min(D_t, S_t) \qquad (4)$$

where only Q_t is observed. For example, if the sample is

separated into two periods, one of excess demand with $D_t > S_t$, and the other of excess supply with $D_t \leq S_t$, then p_t is predetermined (because something is preventing it from moving to eliminate the excess demand or supply) and (1) and (2) may be estimated directly by ordinary least square, O.L.S., for each period. If there is excess supply in period 1, we may estimate the demand equation (1): if there is excess demand in period 2, we may estimate the supply equation (2).

Other disequilibrium models are sometimes used which include an additional equation relating the change in p_t to the gap between D_t and S_t. For example, if p_t is positive we should expect $D_t > S_t$, and so the direction of the movement of (relative) prices may be used to specify periods of excess demand and supply. Some disequilibrium models go further and specify that a certain proportion of the gap between demand and supply is closed by a price change in each period. But such disequilibrium models have not been used to measure the relationship between youth unemployment and relative wages in the UK if only because the recent period of probable excess supply of young labour has been accompanied by an increase in their relative wages. This perverse movement is illustrated in Table 1, extracted from Table 8 in Wells (1983), page 23, which shows an astonishing increase in the minimum wage rates of 16 and 17 year olds relatively to those of adults in the private sector. Perhaps the five percentage point increase in the relative rate for 16 year olds between October 1973 and October 1974 is linked with Stages II and III of the incomes policy then in operation which contained a flat rate increase in the guidelines. Yet the flat rate component in Stage I of the incomes policy July 1975 - July 1976 does

TABLE 1 Percentage of adult rates paid to young workers in a sample of private sector national agreements : males 1966-1982

Age	15 year old	16 year old	17 year old
1966	42.4	48.9	57.4
1967	40.9	47.2	55.4
1968	41.8	48.1	56.5
1969	42.2	48.1	59.2
1970	43.6	49.9	62.8
1971	45.7	52.5	62.8
1972	44.2	50.8	60.7
1973	45.8	51.0	61.3
1974	-	56.1	65.7
1975	-	57.0	67.4
1976	-	56.5	66.7
1977	-	58.3	68.6
1978	-	56.4	66.8
1979	-	60.2	70.8
1980	-	60.0	70.9
1981	-	60.3	71.7
1982	-	60.2	71.7

Source: Department of Employment Economic and Social Division based on analysis of 'Time Rates of Wages and Hours of Work'.

not appear to have had the same effect. Furthermore there was no incomes policy in the period October 1978 to October 1979 when there were also sharp increases in the relative wage rates of young people in the private sector.

However, this increase in the relative wages of young people is not confirmed by the time series of relative wage earnings taken from the New Earnings Survey and summarised by Wells (1983), Figures 2, 3, pages 6, 7. According to this source, the earnings of young males and females did not increase relatively to those of adult males 1974-82. Yet youth unemployment increased sharply over this period. This is important: unlike the data from the October inquiry used in the six econometric studies surveyed here, the New Earnings Survey covers services, distribution and non-manual labour and is much more representative of the earnings of young people. When the time-series of the New Earnings Survey become long enough to use for econometric analysis, these data should be substituted for the October inquiry data. Meanwhile, let us consider the econometric evidence of the relationship between youth unemployment and relative wages based on the October inquiry data.

II. MERRILEES AND WILSON (1979)

The above discussion paper issued from the Manpower Research Group of the University of Warwick has been very influential even though the authors have yet to publish it and are careful to state that it represents work in progress. In particular its disequilibrium approach and its sample separation have been adopted by Wells (1983) and underpin his important conclusion that increases in the average earnings of young people under 18 relative to average earnings of adults reduced their employment in the period 1969-81.

Merrilees and Wilson (1979) separate their sample

period 1952-78 into period 1, 1952-69 for males and 1952-71 for females, when they claim there was excess demand for young labour, and the subsequent period 2 when they claim there was an excess supply. The justification for this is discussed in the next section.

Using annual data and the first difference in the natural logarithms of variables, they estimate (1) to (3) for the market for young males and females under 20 years using two-stage least squares (TSLS) for the first period and obtain unsatisfactory results. in their Tables 1 and 2. The variable p_t in (1) is measured by the ratio of the hourly wage rate for teenagers to that of adults. It differs from the variable p_t in (2) which is real disposable teenage income defined as annual teenage employment income after tax deflated by the retail price index. In principle, the logarithmic transformation permits the decomposition of the wage variables to obtain a common value of the endogenous variable p_t in (1) and (2) to justify the use of TSLS, but this is not discussed. Again, if an equilibrium approach is adopted, TSLS estimates for the whole observational period 1952-78 should be reported because an equilibrium approach does not justify the separation of the sample into sub-periods of excess demand and supply.

Merrilees and Wilson (1974) then present OLS estimates of the supply equation for young males and females for period 1, when there was an excess demand for young labour. For males, the coefficient on wage is 0.32, with a t-value of 1.56, and is not significantly different from zero. That is, it is just as bad as the TSLS estimate. For females this coefficient is 0.18, with t = 2.18, which is significantly different from zero. Although the coefficient is small, and similar to the TSLS estimate of

0.15, it is a firmer estimate. However, their Table 2 also shows significant and perverse coefficients on current relative wages in the demand equations estimated by TSLS and by OLS, which are not discussed and which suggest that more analysis is required before the disequilibrium results can be accepted for period 1. Perhaps the most important task is to explain why the wages of young labour were not allowed to rise in period 1 to remove the postulated excess demand.

The authors then estimated an employment function for the whole period 1952-78 in which the supply variable operates only in the first sub-period and the demand variables operate only in the second sub-period. The dependent variable is the logarithm of the ratio of teenage to adult employment and the coefficients on relative wage have the correct negative sign and are significantly different from zero. These are interesting results for it is less difficult to accept the assumption that the second sub-period was one of excess supply of young labour, with trade union agreements, Wage Council regulations and other conventions preventing teenage wages from falling to remove the excess supply. For policy purposes, it is worth noting that the authors used a wage variable with a distributed lag and found that the response of relative employment to it was very slow, spreading over at least four years. Thus cutting young people's wages will take a long time to remove youth unemployment, according to these results.

III. WELLS (1983)

The Department of Employment Research Paper No. 42, together with a summary of its findings published in the

Employment Gazette, June 1983, pp. 230-237, has attracted widespread attention. It follows Merrilees and Wilson (1979) and separates the observation period into two sub-periods of excess demand and excess supply with the switching years of 1969 for young males and 1971 for young females. Let us consider the reasons given by Merrilees and Wilson (1979) and by Wells (1983) for the sample separation.

First, for the 1950s and 1960s registered unfilled vacancies for young labour exceeded their registered unemployment, whereas the opposite was the norm afterwards. However, as noted by Wells (1983), a greater proportion of the vacancies for young people are notifed. Moreover, the National Institute Economic Review (1983) November pp.39-48, shows that the upward trend in registered unemployment in the 1970s, in contrast to the trendless time-series of vacancies, was in part due to the increased propensity for the unemployed, especially women, to register. Hence, the first reason given for the switch between a regime of excess demand to one of excess supply is not entirely convincing.

Secondly, it is claimed that the increased supply of young people in the 1960-66 period, as a result of the post-war baby boom, could not have been absorbed into the labour market easily unless excess demand existed. This argument is difficult to follow; if there are an extra N entrants to the labour market there are also an extra N potential consumers with high spending habits. Providing entrepreneurs plan to increase their output accordingly, and it is not difficult for them to forecast the effects of higher birth rates 16 years earlier, the expansions in aggregate demand and supply should move in step with each other. There is no reason to suppose that an excess demand has to prevail.

Thirdly, unemployment rates were only slightly higher than those for adults until the late 1960s after which this differential began to widen. Against this, Hart (1984) shows that sequential Chow tests on forward moving regressions of the logarithm of the unemployment rate of young males on that of adult males do not confirm a switch in regimes in 1969. Nor do a series of 10 year 'window' regressions over the period 1952-81 provide any evidence of such a switch. On the other hand, Wells (1983) found that there was a structural break in his supply equation for males in 1969.

A fourth reason advanced by Wells (1983) is that two Triennial Reports of the Youth Employment Service for 1965-68 and 1968-71 allude to buoyant markets for young labour whereas a report for 1971-74 was more gloomy about the prospects for young people. But the fact that the chances of getting a job were smaller in the 1970s than in the 1960s could be explained by the general economic depression following the OPEC oil price increase and certainly does not imply that there was an excess demand for young labour in the 1950s and 1960s.

Finally, it is argued that the alternative explanation is that the market for young labour was in equilibrium, which lacks credibility. But those who use an equilibrium approach do not claim that the labour market is, or has been, in equilibrium, they merely postulate that there are tendencies to bring about equilibrium. Thus the alternative explanation advanced by Merrilees and Wilson and by Wells is simply an Aunt Sally. Perhaps the 'equilibrium' approach is a misnomer. But then so may be the 'disequilibrium' approach, for some economists would claim that a 'quantity rationing' model is a more appropriate description: it is

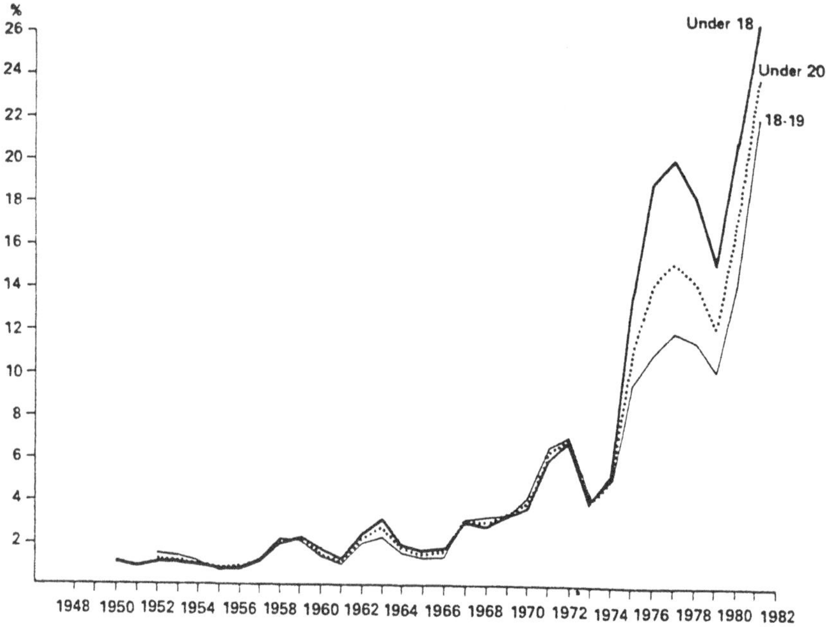

FIGURE 1 Estimated unemployment rates by age (per cent): males 1950-1981

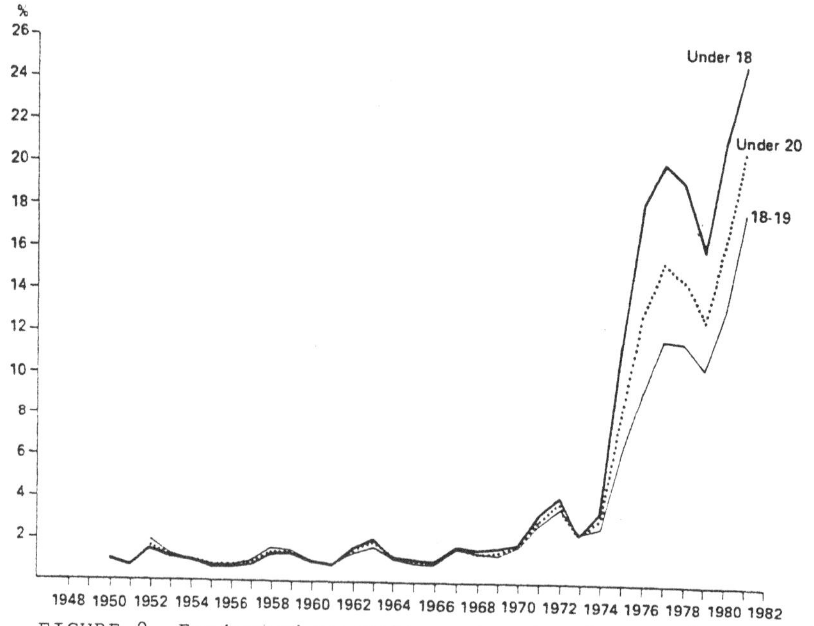

FIGURE 2 Estimated unemployment rates by age (per cent): females 1950-1981

it is possible for an under-full employment equilibrium to arise under certain conditions.

The general conclusion to draw from the evidence is that the *a priori* case for sample separation, in particular for choosing 1969 and 1971 as switching years, is not proven, as admitted by Wells (1983) p.30.

Is there an obvious choice of switching year suggested by the time series of youth unemployment rates? Figures 1 and 2 are reproductions of Wells (1983) Figures 18, 19, and show that for both young males and females unemployment became much worse after the OPEC oil price increases at the end of 1973. But even before 1973 there was a clear upward trend in the unemployment rate of young males and a slight but discernible upward trend in the unemployment rate for young females. The problem of youth unemployment may have been accentuated by the OPEC oil price hikes, but it existed before 1973. However, there is no reason to take 1969 for males, or 1971 for females, as marking a switch in regimes.

Does this mean that it is safe to ignore the regressions obtained for the earlier period, especially when apparently significant supply side coefficients have been estimated? Unlike Merrilees and Wilson (1979), Wells (1983) found significant positive effects of wages on the supply of labour for both males and females in the earlier period, which is interesting. Less interesting is the highly significant elasticity of unity of PPOP, the potential population (i.e. total young population less those in education or in the armed forces), for this only differs from the dependent variable by a relatively small amount, as shown by column c in Table 9 of Wells (1983) p.26. It is not surprising that when a variable is virtually regressed upon itself that a significant coefficient of near unity emerges which probably explains most of the relatively high values of $\bar{R}^2$ obtained for these supply equations. Thus on balance very little useful information is lost if the equations for the earlier period are omitted, especially when no convincing reasons can be found to explain why the earnings of young people were not allowed to drift upwards to eliminate the alleged excess demand.

The argument that there was an excess supply of young labour in the later epoch is less difficult to sustain; it is reasonable to accept the hypothesis that money wages are rigid downwards, as the result of trade union resistance to wage cuts. It is also easy to believe that it is difficult to reduce the relative wages of young people because differentials are jealously guarded. But it is very difficult to understand why changes in the relative pay of young people appear to have been so perverse. Perhaps the reduction in the age of majority from 21 to 18 years explains why the proportion of 18 year olds, with a maximum of two years' work experience, receiving adult rates of pay increased from 12 per cent in 1970 to 42 per cent in 1975 and 53 per cent in 1980, at a time when the unemployment rate of young people was increasing so rapidly, as shown in Figures 1 and 2. Even more striking is the perverse movement of the relative wage rates of young people negotiated in the private sector. For example, Wells (1983) Table 8, p.23, shows that this negotiated rate for a 16 year old in 1970 was 49.9 per cent of the adult wage rate and this percentage was <u>increased</u> to 57 by 1975, and to 60 by 1980. See Table 1 in Section 1 of the present paper. Why were such perverse increases in relative wage rates negotiated at a time of rapidly increasing unemployment? The answer to this question is unknown, but it is clearly important enough to merit further research. It is also clear that wage differentials were not rigid in this period: on the contrary, they moved sharply in the opposite direction required to eliminate any excess supply of young labour. On the other hand, the increased wage differential in favour of young people may have helped to preserve the jobs of adults by making it too expensive to substitute younger for older workers.

With such perverse increases in the wages of young people, it is less surprising that Wells (1983) was able to obtain significant negative coefficients on current relative labour costs in his demand equations estimated for 1969-81 (see his Tables 11, 12, 13, 14, pp.51-54), in spite of having only 13 observations (12 after first differencing) and so few degrees of freedom. For females, there were only 11 observations. He was unable to repeat this for the 18-19 year olds in his Tables 15 and 16 and concluded that the excess supply of young labour was concentrated in the under 18 years group. While some of these re-estimations of the demand equations of Merrilees and Wilson have econometric limitations, such as low $\bar{R}^2$ and possibly negative serial correlation, it would appear that the proportionate increase in the relative labour costs of young people reduced the proportionate increase in the demand for their labour over the period 1969-81. No doubt there were many factors contributing to the increase in youth unemployment, but increases in relative labour costs was one of them in the sense that they had a statistically discernible effect.

Wells (1983) then reports in Chapter 9 estimates of demand equations for the second epoch based on models formulated by Abowd et.al. (1981) and Hutchinson et.al. (1979)

considered elsewhere in this survey. He was usually unable to obtain statistically significant effects of relative labour costs on employment of the 18-19 year olds or of the under 18 females. But for under 18 year old males there were statistically significant effects of relative labour costs on employment, although the precise numerical value of the effect is uncertain. Considering the small number of observations available this uncertainty is not surprising.

IV. ABOWD, LAYARD AND NICKELL (1981)

Once again an important unpublished working paper has to be included in this survey. It is a pioneer attempt to estimate a system of demand equations for labour of different types firmly based on neoclassical economic theory. Moreover, it uses a dual cost function of transcendental logarithmic form to estimate these demand equations[4]. In order to reveal the assumptions on which it is based, it is necessary to summarise the underlying economic theory[5].

Consider a single competitive firm with an output of a homogeneous product y taking price p, with inputs x_j $(j = 1,\ldots,n)$ at input prices w_j. Profit, Π, is given by

$$\Pi = py - \Sigma w_j x_j \tag{5}$$

Hence

$$\frac{\partial \Pi}{\partial p} = y \tag{6}$$

and $$\frac{\partial \Pi}{\partial w_j} = - x_j \tag{7}$$

$$\therefore \quad \frac{\partial x_j}{\partial w_k} = \frac{-\partial^2 \Pi}{\partial w_j \partial w_k} = \frac{-\partial^2 \Pi}{\partial w_k \partial w_j} = \frac{\partial x_k}{\partial w_j} \qquad (8)$$

These symmetry conditions may be interpreted as follows. Suppose j refers to young males and k refers to young females. Then the change in the number of young males employed following a unit increase in the wage rates of young females is the same as the change in the number of females employed following a unit increase in the wage rates of young males. If $\partial x_j/\partial w_k$ is positive, j and k are substitutes. If it is negative, they are complements. Thus if young males are substitutes for young females, then young females are substitutes for young males.

Clearly this theory cannot be extended to the economy as a whole. Young males in the construction industry could be substituted for young females in retail distribution, but the latter are not substitutes for young males in construction. The symmetry conditions in (8) do not hold for the economy as a whole because aggregate output is not homogeneous. Hence it might be wrong to estimate a system of demand for labour equations from aggregate data with these symmetry conditions imposed as restrictions.

In the theoretical model, short run and long run cost curves (marginal, average, total) must rise for the firm to reach equilibrium. This rising supply curve is given by

$$\frac{\partial y}{\partial p} = \frac{\partial^2 \Pi}{\partial p^2} > 0 \quad \text{using (6)} \qquad (9)$$

Once again, this condition might not hold in the short run for the economy as a whole.

The falling factor demand curve in the model is obtained from (8)

$$\frac{\partial x_j}{\partial w_j} = \frac{-\partial^2 \Pi}{\partial w_j^2} < 0 \tag{10}$$

Thus own-price factor demand elasticities must be negative and if wage rates are increased the demand for labour falls and unemployment results. The extension of the result from the theory of a single firm to the whole economy in a time of severe economic depression has been challenged by some economists.

The relationship between changes in x_j, p, y and w_j is given by

$$\frac{\partial x_j}{\partial p} = \frac{-\partial^2 \Pi}{\partial p \partial w_j} \qquad \text{using (7)}$$

$$= \frac{-\partial^2 \Pi}{\partial w_j \partial p} = \frac{-\partial y}{\partial w_j}, \text{ all } j \text{ using (6)} \tag{11}$$

If $\partial x_j/\partial p$ is negative then j is an inferior input in the sense that the demand for it, x_j, decreases as output price (and hence output from (9)) increases. Alternatively in this case, if the wage increases, output increases. Not all inputs can be inferior and the normal case is for $\partial x_j/\partial p$ to be positive. Again (11) requires careful interpretation. By hypothesis the single competitive firm is a price-taker. If it tried to increase its price above the level prevailing in the market, y and hence x_j would fall to zero.

In the long run when all inputs are free to vary, the cost function for any given set of input prices w_j at any given output y is obtained by minimising $C = \sum_j w_j x_j$ subject to $y = f(x_1,...,x_n)$. Since the production function does not contain w_j as an argument, it follows that

$$\frac{\partial C}{\partial w_j} = x_j \qquad (12)$$

This is used by Abowd, Layard and Nickell (1981), at bottom of page 6, to obtain their demand equation for labour of the jth type (x_j) from the cost function C. They then multiply x_j by w_j/C to obtain the elasticity of total costs with respect to w_j which equals the share of the jth factor in total cost, viz.

$$\frac{\partial C}{\partial w_j}\frac{w_j}{C} = \frac{w_j x_j}{C} \qquad (13)$$

But statistical data on x_j or $w_j x_j/C$ reflect not only the demand for the jth factor, but also its supply. There is a fundamental problem of identification which is not discussed in Abowd, Layard and Nickell (1981) or for that matter in any of the standard works which use the dual cost functions to estimate a system of demand equations[6]. Since a time series of x_j is not necessarily a time series of the demand for labour the theoretical result in (13) might not apply to the observed data.

Abowd, Layard and Nickell (1981), hereinafter ALN, must be making an implicit assumption that they have identified demand equations and they proceed to estimate the required parameters by regressing $w_j x_j/C$ on the logarithmic derivative of the cost function, $\partial \log C/\partial \log w_j$. They postulate that the transcendental logarithmic (or translog) cost function holds in the aggregate[7]:

$$\log C = a_0 + a_1 \log y + \sum_j g_j \log w_j + \frac{1}{2}\sum_{ij}\sum d_{ij} \log w_i \log w_j$$

$$+ \sum_j d_{jy} \log w_j \log y + \text{remainder} \qquad (14)$$

This follows Binswanger (1974). It can be seen that if d_{ij} and d_{jy} are all zero, equation (14) reduces to a Cobb-Douglas cost function which is the dual of a primal Cobb-Douglas production function. Thus the translog cost function is more general than the Cobb-Douglas and in particular it does not imply that the elasticity of substitution between two inputs is unity, or even constant. It is an approximation to any arbitrary cost function.

ALN (1981) modify (14) by including log y, log K (quantity of capital), log M (number of non-manual workers) in a vector Z and also introduce a variable I to reflect the intensity of the pattern of labour demand across industries. For estimation, they impose the restriction $d_{ij} = d_{ji}$, thus for two inputs the fourth term on R.H.S. of (14) has the form

$$\frac{1}{2}\left\{ d_{ii}(\log w_i)^2 + 2d_{ij} \log w_i \log w_j + d_{jj} (\log w_j)^2 \right\} \tag{15}$$

Binswanger (1974) proves that the elasticity of substitution between inputs i and j is

$$\sigma_{ij} = (d_{ij}/A_j A_i) + 1 \tag{16}$$

where $A_j = w_j x_j / C$, so the restriction $d_{ij} = d_{ji}$ satisfies the requirement that $\sigma_{ij} = \sigma_{ji}$. Since

$$\sigma_{ij} = \frac{-\partial \log(x_i/x_j)}{\partial \log(f_i/f_j)}, \text{ where } f_i = \frac{\partial y}{\partial x_i} \tag{17}$$

ALN implicitly assume that for the whole economy the theoretical results for a single firm with homogeneous output y hold. However, as explained above, the fact that young males in construction may be substitutable for young females in distribution does not imply that those young females are substitutable for these young males: aggregate output is not homogeneous and the model of a single firm is not applicable in the aggregate.

Again, the cross-price elasticities are given by

$$\frac{w_i \partial x_j}{x_j \partial w_i} = \sigma_{ij} A_j = \frac{d_{ij}}{A_i} + A_j \tag{18}$$

and the own-price elasticities by

$$\frac{w_j \partial x_j}{x_j \partial w_j} = \sigma_{jj} A_j = \left\{ (d_{jj}/A_j^2) + 1 - \frac{1}{A_j} \right\} A_j$$

$$= \frac{d_{jj}}{A_j} + A_j - 1 \tag{19}$$

Since own-price elasticities are negative from (10)

$$(d_{jj}/A_j) + A_j < 1 \text{ or } d_{jj} < A_j(1 - A_j) \tag{20}$$

Thus the maximum value of d_{jj} is just below 0.25 (i.e. when $A_j = 0.5$). The minimum value is $-\sum_j d_{ij}$, $i \neq j$, because $\sum_i d_{ij} = 0$. This last result follows from the fact that if all input prices are increased by θ, $A_j = w_j x_j / C$ is unchanged. That is, using (13) and (14)

$$\frac{\partial \log C}{\partial \log w_j} = \frac{w_j x_j}{C} = g_j + \sum_i d_{ij} \log w_i + d_{jy} \log y \tag{21}$$

$$= g_i + \sum_i d_{ij}(\log w_i + \log \theta) + d_{jy} \log y \tag{22}$$

Thus $\Sigma d_{ij} \log \theta = 0$, so

$$\Sigma d_{ij} = 0 \tag{23}$$

Note that from (15) the coefficient of $\frac{1}{2}$ in (14) disappears on differentiating with respect to log w_j. Furthermore, since $w_j x_j/C$ cannot be affected by changing the units of measurement of output, y, it follows that $\Sigma d_{jy} = 0$, using reasoning similar to that when multiplying by θ in (22) and (23).

A.L.N. (1981) then estimate a system of demand equations, with cross-equation restrictions imposed, applying a generalised least squares technique known as 'seemingly unrelated regressions' to time series data[8]. The first set of results show negative own-price elasticities for men, women and youths in accordance with (10). Men are substitutes for women and for youths, but women and youths are complements. The authors then investigate alternative models with specified lags and also decompose labour into workers and hours per worker. The own-price elasticities are usually negative though not always significantly different from zero (e.g. male workers Table 5A). The own-price elasticity of hours with respect to hourly earnings is <u>positive</u> for men in Tables 4 and 6, but these elasticities are small and not significantly different from zero.

Denoting the cross-price elasticity of factor i with respect to factor price j by e_{ij}, it may be seen that e_{wy} and e_{yw} have different signs in their Tables 4, 5A, 6 which conflicts with the theory in equations (16) and (17). These perverse results might be explained by the fact that the time series data also reflect the supply of labour and the estimation methods used do not in fact identify a system of demand equations. Another shortcoming is that A.L.N.

confine their estimates to manufacturing whereas the employment of young males and females is concentrated in non-manufacturing sectors, such as construction, distribution and services.

Nevertheless Wells (1983) Ch.9 estimates labour demand equations based on the ALN approach (after 'heavy tailoring'), and on the other studies surveyed here, for the period 1969-81 when there was an excess supply of young labour to identify demand equations. In Table 17 he finds a significant negative relationship between the demand for young male labour under 18 and their labour costs relative to adult men. But no significant results emerge for other categories of young labour. His Table 18 shows significant negative relationships between the demand for young males under 18 and their labour costs relative to all females. The specifications used imply that young males are substitutes for female labour, for he does not estimate $\partial \log x_j / \partial \log w_k$ which would yield a positive coefficient if inputs j and k are substitutes, using (8). At a later stage in his Table 22, he presents positive cross-wage elasticities confirming that young male labour is substitutable for adult men and for females. These results are based on the ALN model which in turn is derived from the neo-classical mdoel of a single competitive firm with a homogeneous output so that (8) holds. Since such symmetry does not hold for the whole economy it is difficult to put much weight on the estimates of substitutability and complementarity. However, providing the period 1969-81 can be regarded as one of excess supply of young labour, and the case for doing so is very strong as explained in the previous section, Wells (1983) has overcome the major objection to the result in ALN (1981) which covered the whole period

1949-78.

V. HUTCHINSON, BARR AND DROBNY (1979, 1984)

The long time lag between the working paper in 1979 and the eventual publication in 1984 explains why so many results of economic research into the relationship between youth unemployment and relative wages are still in discussion paper form. The authors estimate a demand function for male labour aged under 20 years using annual data over the period 1952-72 and single-equation techniques. The dependent variable is L_{1t}, the actual employment level of young males in year t, and the variables on the RHS include aggregate industrial production, time-trends, average hours worked, wages relative to men and to full-time and part-time women. Time lags of up to 3 years are included in some equations.

Their preferred equation 1-9 in their Table 1 p.194, has an R^2 of 0.996 with a highly significant quadratic time trend and significant coefficients on manufacturing output (lagged 2 years), on lagged L_{1t} (1, 2 and 3 years), youths' wages relative to men, to full-time women and to part-time women (all lagged 2 years). The coefficient on wages relative to men is positive whereas those on wages relative to women are negative. Hence the authors conclude that lads and men are complements whereas lads and women are substitutes. Clearly, these results are extremely interesting, but how reliable are they for purposes of economic policy?

An immediate problem is the use of a single equation to summarise the youth labour market. As explained in the section on Merrilees and Wilson (1979), if it is legitimate to assume that there is an excess supply of labour, a single demand equation may be identified. But can it be claimed that 1952-72 was a period of excess supply of young male labour? Merrilees and Wilson (1979) and Wells (1983) argue that 1952-69 was a period of excess demand so that a demand equation cannot be identified. Moreover, their demand equations estimated for this period, admittedly using less sophisticated techniques than Hutchinson et.al., were very poor. While the assertion that 1952-69 was a period of excess demand for labour is very difficult to accept, the implied assumption of Hutchinson et.al. that it was one of excess supply is most unlikely to be true. Moreover, no evidence of excess supply is provided.

Some economists might argue that neither excess demand nor excess supply persisted throughout the period. Thus a simultaneous equations model of the supply and demand for young male labour should be estimated. For example the highly significant time trend in L_{1t} must be influenced by supply side factors such as the birth rate 16-20 years previously and should not appear in demand equations.

Nevertheless there are some interesting consistencies between their results and those of other researchers using somewhat different data and techniques. They find that there is at least a two year time lag between an increase in relative wages and a reduction in the employment of young males. This seems to be rather long, but it is consistent with the findings of Merrilees and Wilson. Again, Hutchinson et.al. find that young male labour and female labour (full-time and part-time) are substitutes which is consistent with the results of Wells (1983) and of Abowd et.al. (1981). However, their finding that young and adult male labour are complements is inconsistent with the results of the other papers.

VI. LYNCH AND RICHARDSON (1982)

Using annual data 1950-78 the authors regressed the proportion of young unemployed to total unemployed on relative employment costs and on the supply of young workers. Measures reflecting business conditions were also included on the right-hand side and the regressions were performed for young males and females separately.

When male unemployment is used to measure general business conditions it was found that the employment costs of young workers relative to older workers had no significant effect on relative youth unemployment. The replacement ratio, measuring the effect of unemployment and social security benefits, was also found to be insignificant. These results appear to confirm those of the Department of Employment (1978) which also found that measures of relative labour cost and of social security benefits had no significant effect on youth unemployment.

However, when general business conditions were measured by total vacancies, instead of the total male unemployment rate, relative employment costs had a significant effect on youth unemployment: a one per cent increase in relative employment costs produced a 1.28 per cent increase in youth unemployment relative to total unemployment. The authors prefer this result and attribute the non-significance of relative employment costs in previous regressions to collinearity between the male unemployment rate and relative employment costs.

The regressions are repeated for young females and relative employment costs have a significant effect on the relative unemployment of young females irrespective of whether general business conditions are measured by the total female unemployment rate or by total vacancies. Presumably the correlation between female unemployment and relative labour costs is not high enough to produce large standard errors of the regression coefficients in this case, but this time the problem of multi-cellinearity is not discussed. The relevant elasticity of unemployment with respect to relative labour costs is 2.52 for females compared with 1.28 for males. Thus increasing the relative labour costs of young women has an even larger effect on their relative unemployment.

The authors argue that the easiest way to reduce relative labour costs of young people, and thereby reduce their relative unemployment, would be to vary employers' national insurance contributions, lowering them for young workers and raising them for older workers. But they admit that their statistical results are 'open to discussion' and 'may well suffer to some degree from simultaneous equation bias'. This particular shortcoming is obvious from their mongrel regression equation which includes both demand and supply variables on the right hand side. Furthermore, unlike Hutchinson et.al. (1979) (1984), they make no allowance for time trends and yet their Figure 1 reproduced here as Figure 3 shows clear upward trends in relative unemployment 1950-78. The trend for females is steeper than that for males which may explain why they obtained higher elasticities for females than for males.

The sample period 1950-78 is not sub-divided into separate phases. Their time-series in Figure 3 show that the variation in the dependent variable increased remarkably after 1973. In fact, apart from a sharp rise and fall

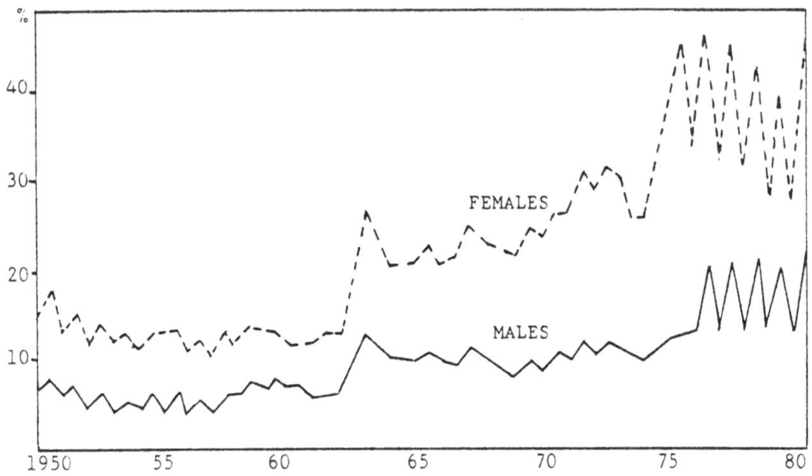

Source - D E Gazette - various years

FIGURE 3 Young (i.e. less than 20 years) to total unemployed, Great Britain 1950-78

1962-4, there appears to be too little variation in the ratio of relative unemployment to be explained by regression analysis before 1973.

VII. RICE (1984)

The above discussion paper issued from the Department of Economics, University of Sussex, uses equilibrium and disequilibrium models. The author rejects the equilibrium model in favour of a disequilibrium model. Unlike Merrilees and Wilson (1979) and Wells (1983), she does not use prior sample separation into periods of excess demand and supply of young labour, but relies on a maximum likelihood, ML, technique proposed by Maddala and Nelson (1974) to estimate both the parameters of the equations and the periods of excess demand and supply. Moreover, she correctly rejects those disequilibrium models of the 'directional' or 'quantitative' type which include changes in prices (in this case wages) in the determination of the type and period of disequilibrium. The efforts of trade unions and wages councils ensure that the wages of young labour are rigid downwards and it is reasonable to exclude negative wage changes from the model.

The author finds that there has been an excess supply of young male labour since 1972/3 and an excess supply of young female labour since 1971/2. This is consistent with the time-series in Figure 1 and is plausible enough to obtain widespread acceptance. The finding that there was an excess demand for young labour in the 1950s and 1960s, with a transitional phase in the late 1960s, is more controversial, because no reason is advanced to explain why wage earnings were so rigid upwards that the disequilibrium lasted for so long. A limitation of the particular disequilibrium model used is that no period of equilibrium can arise: there is no scope for disequilibrium in some periods and equilibrium in others. But a glance at Figure 1 shows that the important practical problem concerns youth unemployment in the 1970s and 1980s so we may confine our attention to this period of excess supply when the market for young labour was constrained by the demand from employers.

In the demand constrained regime, relative earnings were responsible for a third of the increase in unemployment of young males between 1973/4 and 1977/8, which may be compared with the effect of the general decline in demand for output which was responsible for half of this increase in this category of unemploymen . Supply side factors were responsible for less than 16% of the increase in unemployment of young males and, in particular, social security benefits had no effect.

For young females, supply factors were more important and accounted for two-thirds of the increase in their unemployment over the same period. In particular, a decline in the gap between their net earnings and benefits appears to have increased their participation in the labour force in the sense that more registered as unemployed in order to get the benefits. This increased measured unemployment.

On the demand side, relative wages were responsible for 22% of the increase in unemployment, but wages appear to have been calculated relatively to adult males. Perhaps this demand factor would have been similar to the third noted for young males, had young females wages been compared with those of adult females. The general fall in demand for output was responsible for 12.6% of the increase in unemployment compared with 50.8% in the case of young males. Presumably this difference is due in large part to the different industrial composition of the employment of young males and females with the latter concentrated in services and distribution which suffered less than manufacturing and construction from falling demand.

VIII. SUMMING UP

From a technical point of view the six econometric studies surveyed are impressive: disequilibrium models, dual transcendental logarithmic cost functions, dynamic diagnostics and many other sophisticated techniques have been used in attempts to relate youth unemployment to their relative costs of employment. The fact that the results are not always convincing is due to the inherent difficulty of measuring such economic relationships rather than to the inadequacy of available econometric techniques.

All studies suggest that increases in the labour costs of young people relative to those of adults have been associated with increases in youth unemployment relative to that of adults, particularly in the 1970s and 1980s. The precise importance of relative labour costs compared with all the other determinants of youth unemployment has not been established, but for purposes of economic policy it is useful to know that there is widespread agreement among independent research workers that increases in relative wages have been one of the factors contributing to the high levels of youth unemployment. Whether this conclusion holds when the more representative data of the New Earnings Survey are used remains to be seen.

FOOTNOTES

1. Surveys of economic disequilibrium models are provided by Quandt (1982) and Pemberton (1985).
2. Write $D^*_t = D_t - u_{1t}$, $S^*_t = S_t - u_{2t}$, then from (1), (2) and (3) $D^*_t - S^*_t = u_t$ where $u_t = u_{2t} - u_{1t}$. That is, the 'true' demand supply schedules, with an asterisk superscript, are equal when $u_t = 0$. Now $E(u_t) = 0$, since $E(u_{1t}) = E(u_{2t}) = 0$, so we should expect to be near equilibrium most of the time, assuming that D* and S* are correctly specified and that p_t is free to move to bring them nearer equilibrium. However, it is

possible that in the particular sample period chosen the average of the stochastic shocks was either positive or negative so that $u_t \neq 0$, although it could be approaching zero ('tendency towards equilibrium') most of the time. Formally, since u_t has a continuous distribution, Pr ($u_t = 0$) is zero, hence the probability of exact equilibrium is zero.

3. One formal method of identifying the demand equation is to assume that it excludes at least M-1 variables (endogenous and predetermined) where M is the number of simultaneous equations in the model after solving initially to eliminate all identities and equalities i.e. in the equilibrium model in (1), (2) and (3), M = 2, so (1) identifies a demand equation if it excludes at least one variable which appears in the supply equation (2). This would satisfy the order conditions for identification which are necessary, but not sufficient. In principle, such an assumption may be substantiated by adding appropriate variables to the supply equation, but the added variable(s) must be important, not marginal, and must be excluded justifiably from the demand equation. In practice, finding such additional variables is not straightforward and requires a careful appraisal of the supply equation, even though the primary interest may be in the demand equation. Assuming that the identification problem has been solved is tantamount to assuming that one is not estimating a mongrel equation. This may be convenient but it is difficult to justify.
4. For an exposition of duality theory, see Deaton and Muellbauer (1980). Their discussion of systems of demand equations is directly relevant to the estimation of systems of demand equations for labour by Abowd et.al. (1981).
5. Many textbooks provide good accounts of the underlying theory. The summary used in the present paper is from Intriligator (1978) Ch.8.
6. This include Christensen et.al. (1975) who claim (p.380) that their results invalidate the standard economic theory of demand. Deaton and Muellbauer (1980 p.74) correctly reject this claim, but do not discuss the possibility that their own estimates of systems of demand equations reflect variations in supply conditions as well as the demand side of the

market.

7. A very helpful discussion of translog cost functions is provided by Roy and Wenban-Smith (1983).
8. Several econometric texts explain 'seemingly unrelated regressions' estimation techniques e.g. Harvey (1981).

REFERENCES

J. Abowd, R. Layard and S. Nickell, The demand for labour by age and sex, London School of Economics: Centre for Labour Economics Working Paper No.110, (1981).

H.P. Binswanger, A cost function approach to the measurement of elasticities of factor demand and elasticities of substitution, American Journal of Agricultural Economics, 64, p.377-86, (1974).

L.R. Christensen, D.W. Jorgenson and L.J. Lau, Transcendental logarithmic utility functions, American Economic Review, 65, p.367-82, (1975).

A. Deaton and J. Muellbauer, Economics and Consumer Behavior, Cambridge University Press, (1980).

Department of Employment, The young and out of work, Employment Gazette, August, p.908-16, (1978).

P.E. Hart, Trends and cycles in youth unemployment, National Institute of Economic and Social Research, mimeo, (1984).

A.C. Harvey, The Econometric Analysis of Time Series, Oxford: Philip Allan, (1981).

G. Hutchinson, N. Barr and P. Drobny, A sequential approach to the dynamic specification of the demand for young male labour in Great Britain, Queen Mary College, London: Department of Economics Working Paper No.60 (1979).

G. Hutchinson, N.A. Barr and A. Drobny, The employment of young males in a segmented labour market : the case of Great Britain, Applied Economics, 16, p.187-204, (1984).

M.D. Intriligator, Econometric Models, Techniques and Applications, Amsterdam: North Holland, (1978).

L. Lynch and R. Richardson, Unemployment of young workers in Britain, British Journal of Industrial Relations, 20, p.362-71, (1982).

G.S. Maddala and F.D. Nelson, Maximum likelihood methods for models of markets in disequilibrium, Econometrica, 42, p.1013-1030, (1974).

W.J. Merrilees and R.A. Wilson, Disequilibrium in the labour market for young people in Great Britain, University of Warwick Manpower Research Group, Discussion Paper No. 10, (1979).

M. Pemberton, Econometric disequilibrium models: a simplified survey, Economic Perspectives, this issue, (1985).

R.E. Quandt, Econometric disequilibrium models, Econometric Review, 1, p.1-63, (1982).

P.G. Rice, Juvenile unemployment, relative wages and social security in Great Britain, Department of Economics, Univeristy of Sussex, mimeo, (1984).

A.D. Roy and G. Wenban-Smith, Trends in UK productivity: a production function approach, National Institute of Economic and Social Research, Discussion Paper No.59, (1983).

W. Wells, The relative pay and employment of young people, Department of Employment Research Paper No.42, (1983).

NON-COOPERATIVE GAME THEORY: SOME RECENT DEVELOPMENTS AND ECONOMIC APPLICATIONS

BEN LOCKWOOD
Department of Economics, Birkbeck College,
University of London.

I. INTRODUCTION

The last ten years have seen a resurgence of interest in the application of non-cooperative game theory to economics. This renewed interest is essentially due to developments within the theory itself, and in particular the fundamental refinements of the Nash equilibrium concept by Selten, and the equally important work by Harsanyi which introduced an equilibrium concept for games where players may not know the structure of the game with certainty. More recently something of a synthesis of these two contributions has been achieved by Kreps and Wilson's concept of sequential equilibrium.

These new concepts have two general applications in economics. First, Selten's perfectness criterion provides a means of distinguishing those non-cooperative equilibria based on <u>non-credible</u> threats or promises from those that are credible in this sense. Second, the concept of sequential equilibrium provides a rationalisation of reputation-building behaviour which can explain phenomena such as disagreement in bargaining as the outcome of fully rational behaviour.

Given the close connection between the theory of

oligopoly and game theory, it is not surprising that these ideas have had their greatest impact on the economics of industry and particularly, have led to a re-evaluation of such topics as barriers to entry, the relationship between market structure and technical change, and cartel behaviour. However, there has also recently been an intensive application of these ideas to the theory of bilateral bargaining and many other applications in macro as well as microeconomics.

In addition, the perfectness idea has stimulated a good deal of recent research into the "pure" theory of repeated games, in an attempt to establish a general characterisation of those cooperative agreements which can be credibly sustained as non-cooperative equilibria, and some results of fundamental importance, (particularly Abreu's (1982) work) have emerged.

Because of the breadth of the subject, any survey must necessarily be selective. Therefore, we restrict ourselves here mainly to the theory and applciations of games with complete information. We begin by surveying refinements of Nash equilibrium, and also some recent work on rationalisable strategies which suggest, by contrast, that Nash equilibrium is too strong. Next, we discuss some of the implications of imposing the perfectness criterion in economic games round two unifying themes. The first is strategic choice of actions at the early stages of a game in order to influence other player's later moves, sometimes known as strategic precommitment. The second is the phenomenon of the threat of credible preemption, which emerges in games of timing, such as adoption of a new technology. We illustrate these themes with discussion of recent work in the "new industrial economics" and bargaining theory. We conclude by a survey of recent developments in repeated games and the theory of cartels.

II. NORMAL AND EXTENSIVE FORMS

There are several, ways of varying degrees of abstraction, of formally representing games. Two possibilities are the normal and extensive forms, introduced by Von Neumann and Morgenstern. The former is a "shorthand" representation, and just defines the list of players, the set of strategies available to each player, and the payoff of each player as a function of the strategies chosen by all players. The latter, by contrast, is a complete description of any game; it also specifies the move order of play (i.e. who moves when), the choices available to a player whenever it is his/her turn to move, the information a player has when it is his/her turn to move, and the initial conditions that begin the game.

The standard formulations of the extnesive form (e.g. Owen (1982), Shubik (1982)) are based on Kuhn's game tree model. While this is undoubtedly a useful and powerful way of thinking about extensive forms (and we shall use game trees in what follows) the formal model is notationally complex, and for this reason, we adopt an alternative formalisation of the extensive form based on Harris (1985).

We suppose play takes place over a sequence of dates, possibly infinite; $t = 0, 1, \ldots, T$. At each date, t, player $i = 1, \ldots, n$ can choose an <u>action</u> a_{it} from a set A_{it} of available actions which may depend on the previous <u>history</u> of play. The history of play is defined as follows. Let $a_t = (a_{1t}, \ldots, a_{nt})$ be the actions chosen at time t, and let $h_t = (a_0, a_1, \ldots, a_t)$ so that h_t is a history of actions chosen up to and including t. We suppose that A_t may depend upon h_{t-1}, the previous history of play.

A strategy for i is simply a decision on which feasible action to take at each date, conditional on the information available to him. We suppose that the information available to any player at t is h_{t-1} itself. Although this apparently imposes the condition that all players must act in ignorance of each other's actions at the same date, this is no real restriction, as we are free to specify which players can make non-trivial moves at each date[1] - i.e. the players for which $A_{it}(h_t)$ is non-empty. Formally, a <u>strategy</u> for f_i, is simply a sequence of maps $\{f_{it}\}_{t=0}^{T}$ where f_{it} associates with each h_{t-1} an element of $A_{it}(h_{t-1})$. For this definition to be consistent, we require that h_{t-1} be the history actually generated by the decisions of the players in periods 0 to t-1. Finally, let the space of all possible strategies for i be F_i.

To complete description of the extensive form, we need to specify payoffs over "terminal nodes" of the game. We suppose that player i has a payoff associated with each complete history of play, h_T or $U_i = U_i(h_T)$. For example, this may be the discounted sum of payoffs from action at each date. Now call any such complete history of play an <u>outcome</u>. Associated with any strategy n-tuple, $(f_1, \ldots, f_n) \equiv f$, is a single determinate outcome (i.e. there is a map, σ, from the space of strategy n-tuples, $F = \times_{i=1}^{n} F_i$ to the space of outcomes H_T). Therefore, one can define induced payoffs over strategies as follows;

$$U_i^*(f) \equiv U_i(\sigma(f)). \tag{1}$$

Then the game with payoffs U_i^* (f), and strategy spaces F_i is in normal form.

Note that this model allows us to distinguish sharply between strategies as a whole and the actions at each stage that the strategies prescribe (the tactics!). This means that we can think about an equilibrium strategy n-tuple, f^*, also in terms of the equilibrium outcome, $\sigma(f^*)$, or sequence of actions, that it generates and in terms of equilibrium payoffs associated with those actions, $U_i^*(f^*)$. These distinctions will be crucial to an understanding of recent developments in the theory of repeated games (see Section V below).

We conclude this section with an example of a game of entry-deterrence which will hopefully bring to life these concepts. Consider a market with two firms; A, the incumbent, and firm B, the potential entrant. At date 0, firm B decides wether or not to enter. If he does, it incurs set-up costs of F. At date 1, if B has entered, both firms choose quantities simultaneously. We suppose for simplicity, each firm can choose only two outputs, a monopoly output M and a smaller output S. The game tree is as in Figure 1, where nodes are labelled by the player whose turn it is to move at that node. Note that neither firm knows what the other's output level is in period 1 (i.e. the game is a simultaneous move one) so B's information set, indicated by the dotted line, encloses both possible output choices by firm A.

This game can be expressed in our notation as follows. Let A_{0B} be the empty set, as A does not move at time 0, and let $A_{1A} = \{E,N\}$ as B can choose either to enter or not. Then $A_{1A} = A_{1B}(E) = \{M,S\}$ and $A_{1B}(N)$ is the empty set, as B cannot choose an output if he has not entered.

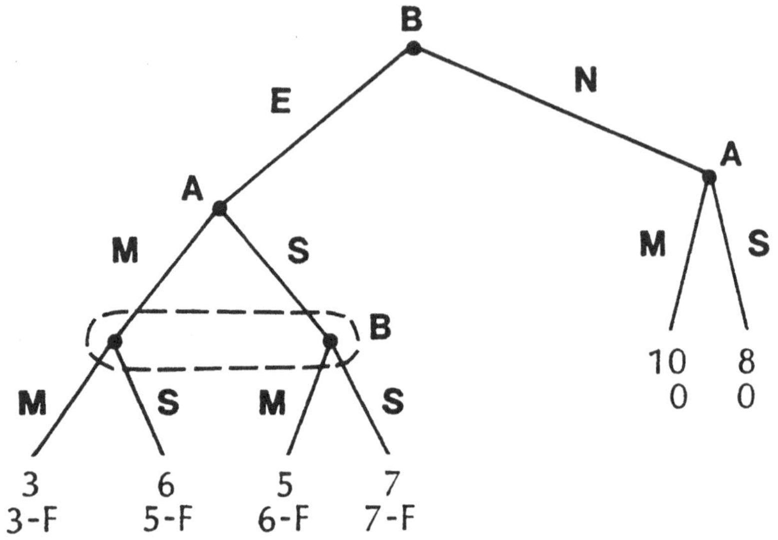

FIGURE 1

Now, the information that A has at date 1 is simply whether B has entered or not. Hence, a strategy for A, f_A is a function mapping $\{E,N\}$ into $\{M,S\}$ i.e. a pair of output levels chosen contingent upon whether B has entered or not, $(f_{1_A}(E),\ f_{1_A}(N))$. For B, a strategy is a decision whether to enter or not, and an output level form $\{M,S\}$ chosen contingent upon entry. Hence, f_B is either simply N or a pair $(E,\ f_{1_B}(E))$. Payoffs over histories are simply as given in Figure 1.

III. EQUILIBRIUM CONCEPTS - SOME NEW DEVELOPMENTS

(a) Nash Equilibrium

The best known and most important equilibrium concept is that of Nash equilibrium[2]. The Nash idea is that in equilibrium, strategies must be mutual best replies. Formally, $f^* = (f_1^*, \ldots, f_n^*)$ is a Nash equilibrium if and only if player i can do no better than to choose f_i^* given that players $j \neq i$ have chosen f_{-i}^*, where $f_{-i}^* = \equiv (f_1^*, f_2^* \ldots f_{i-1}^*, f_{i+1}^*, \ldots, f_n^*)$.

It is used constantly and unreflectively by many economists, but it has also long been realised that in many cases, multiple equilibria can arise, and this has led to many refinements of the Nash concept. The most important of these, due to Selten, is (subgame) perfect equilibrium, which starts from the observation that some Nash equilibria are imperfect in that they rely on threats to take actions contingent upon histories which do not actually arise in equilibrium, which the players would not want to carry out if called upon to do so. Selten proposed a definition of equilibrium which eliminated these imperfect equilibria, which we discuss below.

First, however, I will discuss some recent criticisms of the Nash concept (Bernheim (1984), Pearce (1984)) which suggest it is too strong an equilibrium condition. Pearce argues that if there is no pre-play communication, the case for Nash equilibrium "asserts that a player's strategy must be a best response to those selected by other players, becuase he can deduce what these strategies are". A good example, due to Schelling, is that of two individuals who want to rendezvous in a large city with a single train station. Each player could reasonably deduce that the other will go to the train station.

Pearce goes on to say that this justification "takes for granted that there is a unique rational choice for j to make; this uniqueness is not derived from fundamental rationality postulates, but simply assumed".

To illustrate this point, consider a generalisation of the train station example, where there are not two stations, East and West. We many formalise this as a matrix game;

	E	W
E	(2,1)	(0,0)
W	(0,0)	(1,2)

Here if both players choose the same action (i.e. rendezvous at the same train station) they get a postive payoff, and if they miss each other, they get nothing. The game has two pure-strategy Nash equilibria where both players choose E or choose W, and a mixed strategy one where 1 plays E with probability 1/3, and 2 plays it with probability 2/3. Pearce's point is that if we merely suppose that the players are rational, we cannot reasonably eliminate strategy pairs such as (W,E) although they are not Nash equilibria, because they conceivably represent rational choices by players based on incorrect, but not "irrational" beliefs about the choice of the other player - for example, player 1, knowing 2's preference for W, might try to "second-guess" him by going there, whereas 2 might go to E for the same reason.

Pearce and Bernheim suggest a sequential elimination proceedure for constructing all such possible strategy n-tuples, based only on two minimal assumptions. First, it is supposed that players are rational, both in the sense that they are expected utility-maximisers, and that their prior beliefs about the probability that their opponent will play any strategy do not conflict with their information. For example, a rational player would not suppose his opponent would play a strongly dominated[3] strategy. Second, all features of the game - the payoffs, strategy sets, and the fact that players are rational - are assumed to be common knowledge.

The end result is that for each i, there is a well-defined subset R_i of F_i of "non-eliminated" strategies such that for any f_i in R_i, there exists a g_{-i} in R_{-i} such that f_i is best response to g_{-i}. Pearce calls any strategy n-tuple f in $R = \overset{n}{\underset{i=1}{X}} R_i$ <u>rationalisable</u> Clearly, any Nash equilibrium is rationalisable but generally R is bigger than this. For example, in the rendezvous game, <u>any</u> strategy pair is rationalisable. Pearce also introduces additional criteria to refine rationalisability, based on the "trembling hand" idea, which is discussed briefly below.

(b) <u>Refinements of Nash Equilibrium</u>

We now turn to the major refinement of Nash equilibrium, subgame perfection. Consider again the entry-deterrence game of Section II. For some values of F, it may have two equilibria. The first is where B enters and in the event of entry, both firms choose output S. This will only be an equilibrium if B can make non-negative profits from entering i.e. $F \leq 7$. The second is an equilibrium where A announces that he will choose the higher output, M, whether B enters or not, and B decides not to enter because $F > 5$.

However, there is something wrong with the second kind of equilibrium, which is that it relies on a <u>threat</u> by A to produce a large output, M, in the event of entry, which is not credible in the sense that in the event in entry <u>actually</u> takes place, A would rather produce an output which is a best reply to whatever B produces and vice versa, so both would produce S. But these latter outputs are actually the Nash equilibrium of the subgame which starts when B has entered.

Thus, the obvious refinement of Nash equilibrium to eliminate non-credible threats would seem to be to require all strategies to be best replies starting in <u>any</u> subgame, especially those subgames that are not reached in equilibrium. This is precisely Selten's concept of subgame perfection. However, while the visual meaning of subgame is obvious, we need to express it in our notation. First, observe that each history h_t indexes a node in the game tree. Furthermore, as all players can distinguish between different histories, <u>every</u> node corresponding to h_t (and only these nodes) must be the initial node of a subgame. Finally, define "the strategies f contingent upon h_t" to be the strategy n-tuple which generates h_t over the first t periods and follows f thereafter. Then

Definition

The equilibrium f* is subgame perfect if, for all h_t and all t, the strategies f* contingent upon h_t are in Nash equilibrium.

There is a unique perfect equilibrium in our entry game. Because strategies have to be in Nash equilibrium in each of the two subgames, both firms must choose S in the event of entry and firm A must produce M in the event of no entry. Most importantly, B will choose to enter if and only if it is profitable to do so, given what happens next i.e. $F \leq 7$. Note that this equilibrium is characterised by working backward through the game tree. This method that always generalises to finite horizon games: as long as they possess subgame-perfect equilibria, at least one of them can be found by such dynamic programming arguments. This undoubtedly accounts for some of the popularity of the subgame perfection criterion.

However, it has its limitations, in that the intuitive

sense of the definition may also apply in games that lack proper subgames. For example consider the game tree of Figure 2 taken from Kreps and Wilson (1982). This game has no proper subgames as player 3 cannot distinguish between 1 moving L and 2 moving L. It has two Nash equilibria in pure strategies; (R, R, L) with payoffs (1, 1, 1) and (L, R, R) with payoffs (3, 2, 2). The second equilibrium suffers from the problem that if player 2 were to arrive at the node where he moves with even the smallest probability (he never gets there in equilibrium) it would be better for him to play L, taking 3's strategy to play R as given. This exhibits the same kind of problem as the entry game - actions presecribed by strategies at unreached information sets would not actually be carried out, given the equilibrium strategies of other players.

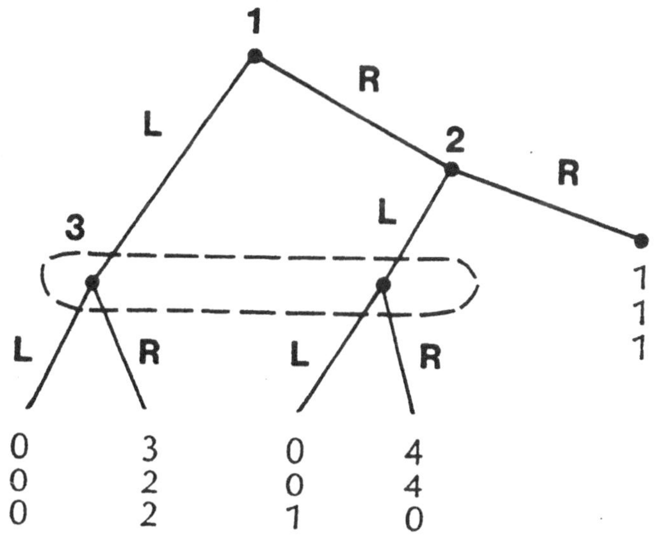

FIGURE 2

Selten's solution to this (see Selten (1975)) was to offer a refinement of subgame perfection, known as "trembling hand" perfection, which required equilibria perfect in this sense to be limits (as $\varepsilon \to 0$) of some sequence of equilibria where the actions chosen at each information set are probability measures on pure actions, where each pure action must be chosen with at least some positive probability ε - hence the "trembling hand". While this solves the problem, the criterion is very difficult to use, because it is constructive - one has to show that any candidate for a perfect equilibrium is in fact the limit of some "trembling hand" equilibrium. Nevertheless, Myerson (1978) has proposed yet another refinement, proper equilibrium, which is in the same spirit.

However, as long as complete information is assumed the games where subgame perfection fails to eliminate "imperfect" Nash equilibria are, from the point of view of economics, mere curiosities. The situation is completely different with incomplete information. Since Harsanyi, we know that such games can be thought of as games of imperfect information, where "nature" moves first in choosing player types. In this case, at each date, each player must have well-defined beliefs about the type of his opponents, and these should be part of the definition of equilibrium. Such an equilibrium concept, <u>sequential equilibrium</u>, has been successfully developed by Kreps and Wilson (1982) but its discussion is beyond the scope of this survey.

IV. SOME APPLICATIONS - GAMES OF TIMING AND STRATEGIC PRECOMMITMENT

As already observed, much of the appeal of the subgame-perfection criterion lies in the fact that "credible" or subgame-perfect equilibria can usually be derived by dynamic programming arguments, i.e. by working backwards through the game tree (although, as we show in Section V, there are subgame-perfect equilibria based on "punishment" strategies that cannot be characterised in this way). Therefore, the implications of imposing "credibility" on Nash equilibrium can be quickly and easily checked in a wide variety of models.

What these implications are, of course, depends on the game in question. We can distinguish two types among the many that are in frequent use. The first is a multi-stage game where the actions to be taken at each stage are exogenously specified. Models of entry-deterrence, vertical product differentiation, choice of location - to name but a few - naturally fall into this class (the stylised entry-deterrence example analysed above is of this type).

For this type of game, the picture that emerges is that in perfect equilibrium, players will often take "strategic" actions in the early stages of a game, in order to induce other players to choose more favourable actions later on. Some authors call the choice of such actions strategic precommitment.

In particular economic applications, such "strategic" actions imply departure from short-run cost minimisation or profit maximisation, and may lead to (additional) social inefficiency in the allocation of resources. This type of inefficiency seems to be conceptually different from inefficiencies due to externalities or imperfect competition, and so we term it strategic inefficiency. The strategic inefficiencies arising from entry-deterrence have been extensively analysed (see Fudenberg and Tirole (1984) for a useful synthesis), so in this section we consider some other examples.

The second type of game is where the timing of an action is determined endogenously. For example, technological innovation in an oligipoly can be modelled in this way (Reinganum (1981), Fudenberg and Tirole (1985)). For such games, the force of subgame perfection is rather different - it can provide a systematic analysis of the degree to which the threat by a rival of "pre-emption" affects e.g. the time of adoption of a new technology, and hence ultimately help to pin down the relationship between market structure and speed of diffusion.

(a) Strategic Precommitment and Strategic Inefficiency

(i) Investment and Delegation

It is a commonly accepted idea, going back at least to Marshall, that certain strategic variables such as quantities or prices are more easily variable in the "short run" than factors of production such as labour or capital or expenditure on R and D. Recently, there has been a small explosion of papers[4] exploring the implications of this idea, the first of which was Brander and Spencer (1983).

The basic idea is as follows. Consider a two stage game played between two duopolists where capital stocks are determined before the duopolists choose outputs or prices, but where other factors of production are chosen simultaneously with the latter.

The Nash equilibrium in the second stage or subgame

(which we term the "market" subgame) will be determined by each firm's short-run cost functions and hence by capital stocks. Hence, in the first stage, when capital stocks are chosen, there are two considerations for each firm. First, the firm will wish to choose capital to minimise the cost of producing a given amount of output in the market subgame. Second, there is the strategic consideration that a small change in the firm's capital stock will induce his opponent to change his output or price, and this latter effect will normally cause the firm to choose a different level of the capital stock to that required by short-run cost-minimising i.e. what we are calling strategic inefficiency. (Such inefficiency is also known as factor bias (Dixon (1985a)), or under- or over-capitalisation). However, the direction of the inefficiency will in general depend on the nature of the market subgame: whether it is prices or quantities that are chosen, whether the goods are substitutes or complements, and so on. It turns out that the precise answer in the case where quantities are chosen depends on whether the quantities are what Bulow et.al. (1985) call strategic substitutes or complements, as well as substitutes or complements in the ordinary sense. Two products are strategic substitutes or complements depending on whether an increase in output by firm i decreases or increases j's marginal profits, i,j = 1,2. Bulow et.al. argue that many developments in strategic entry deterrence are also best uunderstood using this distinction.

To illustrate this, suppose that the revenue function of firm i can be written $R^i(x_i,x_j)$ where x_i is the output of firm i, and the short-run cost function $C^i(x_i,k_i)$, where k_i is the level of precommited capital. We assume $R^i_{ii} < 0$, $C^i_{xx} > 0$. Now the equilibrium outputs in the equilibrium outputs in the market subgame are characterised by the conditions

$$R^i_i\ (x^*_i,\ x^*_j) - C^i_x\ (x^*_i,\ k_i) = 0 \qquad i,j = 1,2 \tag{2}$$

as by assumption, the second-order conditions are satisfied. Therefore, the equilibrium x^*_i depends on k_1, k_2.

Now suppose the cost of capital is r. Then in the first stage of the game firm i chooses k_i to maximise

$$R^i\ (x^*_i,\ x^*_j) - C^i\ (x^*_i, k_i) - r.k_i \tag{3}$$

taking as given k_j and taking into account the dependence of x^*_i on k_i. This leads to the first-order condition

$$R^i_j \cdot \frac{\partial x^*_j}{\partial k_i} = r + c^i_k \tag{4}$$

where the term on the left-hand side of (4) reflects the strategic effect on firm i's profits of a small change in k_i. Now under the condition that $c^i_{kk} > 0$ there will be over (under) capitalisation if $r + c^i_k > (<) 0$.

Now assume that $R^i_j < 0$, i,j = 1, 2, so that x_i and x_j are substitutes in the ordinary sense. Then, under a standard uniqueness/ stability condition (e.g. Brander and Spencer's equation (6)) $\frac{\partial x^*_j}{\partial k_i}$ will be positive or negative as R^i_{ij} is positive or negative (i.e. as x_i and x_j are strategic complements or substitutes). It follows from this and equation (4) that there is over-capitalisation with strategic substitutes and the opposite with strategic complements.

Whether or not output and investment are higher or lower in this two-stage equilibrium than in the equilibrium where capital and output are chosen simultaneously is a more delicate question, but Brander and Spencer are able to show that there will be greater output and investment and lower profits with strategic substitutes.

An obvious limitation of the analysis so far is that the set of factors of production which can be precommited is assumed fixed. Dixon (1986) suggests a three-stage equilibrium, where the set of factors to be precommited (either both capital and labour, or just capital, or neither) is determined endogenously in the first stage. In the case where the costs of precommitment are zero, the result is that commitment of both factors is the only equilibrium. The reason for this is simple. Consider a duopoly for example, where firm 2 does not precommit (or only partially precommits); full precommitment by 1 effectively allows him to choose output before 2 and hence act as Stackelberg leader, and so full precommitment is always a dominant strategy.

In a quantity-setting model, of course, the full- precommitment equilibrium is identical to the no-precommitment equilibrium - both are the familiar Cournot-Nash equilibrium in "quantities", where in the first equilibrium the "quantities" are actually capacities - so that we have the paradoxical result that allowing for unrestricted precommitment changes nothing. But this is only the case if the costs of precommitment are zero, a highly unreasonable assumption under uncertainty, where a natural cost arises from loss of flexibility. It seems likely that with enough uncertainty (e.g. about demand) partial or non-precommitment equilibria will arise, and a start in investigating this has been made by Dixon in the same paper.

The idea of strategic precommitment is not limited

to factors of production in the conventional sense. For example, as Vickers (1985a) has shown, there is, in general, a strategic advantage to the owners from delegation of control of firms to managers with different preferences. For example, imagine a two-stage game where owners choose managers in the first stage, and then managers choose outputs in the market stage. In such a game, any profit-maximising owner prefers a manager that also cares about sales, even if all other firms are run by profit-maximising managers. In effect, by choosing such a manager, the owner can shift his "own" reaction function outwards in the market subgame, and by doing so increase profits.

Vickers also shows that this principle of strategic delegation implies, in a simple case, the undesirability of vertical integration (Vickers (1985a) p.146). The same sort of arguments would seem to imply the undesirability of horizontal integration; there may be a strategic advantage to "tailoring" managers to markets. Furthermore, it seems to be the case that a certain amount of horizontal decentralisation is desirable on efficiency grounds e.g. the M-form firm. Whether the strategic and efficiency considerations determining firm structure tend to go the same way, or whether they conflict is a fascinating and open question.

(ii) Wage Bargaining without Binding Wage Contracts

Inefficiency from strategic precommitment can also arise in investment and employment determination if wages, or the division of the surplus between firm and union, cannot be determined simultaneously with the choice of factor inputs. In a series of papers, Grout (1984, 1985) showed that in a two-stage bargaining game where employment and investment are determined first, and then given these, the wage is determined, there can be inefficiently low investment. The crucial condition which ensures this is the presence of sunk costs i.e. the resale value of capital lower than the purchase price. He did not model the bargaining game explicitly, but appealed instead to the generalised Nash bargain as a solution concept. However, as Binmore has shown (see Binmore (1980)) the generalised Nash bargain is the outcome of a bargaining game of the Rubinstein kind with sequential offers, where the bargaining strengths are determined by discount factors, so the model can easily be given firm game - theoretic foundations. More recently, Manning (1985) has shown that the underinvestment result depends crucially on the assumption that the bargaining strengths of both parties are the same in the two stages.

We briefly present a simplified version of Grout's model. Suppose there is a fixed labour force of size unity, which can produce revenue $r(k)$ with k units of capital. Capital has a cost of c and a resale price of q, and $c > q$ so there are sunk costs. Hence, given that capital has been installed, the surplus from a wage agreement w for the firm is $r(k) - w - qk$ and the surplus for the union is $w - b$, where b is the reservation wage. The wage bargain struck maximises $(r(k) - w - qk)^{1-\alpha} \cdot (w - b)^{\alpha}$ where α indexes the bargaining strength (inversely related to the discount factor) of the union. The solution wage satisfies

$$w(k) = b + \alpha(r(k) - q \cdot k - b). \tag{5}$$

Now suppose, for simplicity, that when k is bargained over in the first stage the union has no bargaining power. Then the firm will choose k to maximise

$$r(k) - w(k) - c \cdot k \tag{6}$$

Substituting from (5), we find the firm's choice, k* satisfies

$$r'(k^*) = \hat{c} = \frac{c - \alpha q}{1 - \alpha} . \tag{7}$$

As $\hat{c} > c$, there is obviously underinvestment. The reason for this is clear from (6); at the optimal k*, a small increase in k will not only have a direct cost, c, but also a strategic cost, $w'(k^*) > 0$ in raising the wage slightly.

Furthermore, the two-stage equilibrium may be Pareto inferior to the binding contract equilibrium, where capital is chosen efficiently i.e. $r'(k^{**}) = c$, and the wage is $w(k^{**}) = b + \alpha(r(k^{**}) - ck^{**} - b)$. To see this, observe that from (7), as $\alpha \to 1$, the capital stock chosen in the two-stage equilibrium, k* and hence the total surplus tends to zero, so that for α large enough, the two-stage equilibrium must be Pareto-inferior.

(b) Timing and Preemption

When a firm is considering adoption of a new technology in an oligopolistic environment, it must consider not only the benefits from early adoption as weighed against the costs, but also the adoption times of its competitors. Reinganum (1981) showed that in a symmetric but otherwise quite general duopoly model, the only possible pure strategy Nash equilibria in adoption times involved the two firms adopting at different times, T_1^* and T_2^* ($T_1^* < T_2^*$), so the industry equilibrium was characterised by diffusion.

Moreover, there are two equilibria - that is, firm i may adopt at either T_1^* or T_2^* - but any firm does better by innovating earlier i.e. at T_1^*.

Fudenberg and Tirole (1985) argue that given that the early innovator does better than the late one, these equilibria are not subgame- perfect. Unless theleader can precommit to adopting at T_1^* at time 0, the "follower" can do better than adopting at T_2 by adopting at $T_1^* - \Delta$ (where Δ is the time intervale between moves, and it is assumed that Δ is small), given that the "leader", having been pre-empted, will then switch to a later adoption time.

Therefore, Reinganum's Nash equilibria can only be understood as precommitment equilibria. Fudenberg and Tirole's view is that the precommitment story is highly implausible, given the symmetry of the model; "the firm which is able to precommit itself to adopt first does best, yet any firm can precommit first in equilibrium. The strategic interactions supressed by precommitment would re-surface in a competition to be the first to precommit".

What Fudenberg and Tirole do is characterise the sub-game perfect equilibria of Reinganum's model, thus taking into account credible preemption. It turns out that a diffusion equilibrium still emerges, but one where the profits from both firms, or the rents from innovation, are equalised (although this need not be the case with three or more firms). More importantly, the earliest date at which any firm innovates, T_1^{**}, is earlier than T_1^*, so the threat of preemption does indeed lead to earlier innovation. Indeed, as one might expect, T_1^{**} is the earliest date at which payoffs from innovating first and innovating second are equalised[5].

The exact form that the (perfect) equilibrium

strategies take, however, depends on whether the model is specified in discrete (i.e.$\Delta > 0$) or continuous time ($\Delta = 0$). In discrete time, it is possible to show that in equilibrium both firms will randomise between adopting and not at each date between T_2^* and some $T_1^{**} \leq T_\Delta \leq T_1^*$. It is possible to show that T_Δ goes to T_1^{**} as Δ goes to zero, and furthermore that the probability of adoption at any date t between T_Δ and T_1^* goes to 0 with Δ, so that the probability of "mistakes", or simultaneous adoption, at any given date is of order Δ^2. It follows from this that the overall probability of mistakes goes to 0 with Δ, so in continuous time, simultaneous adoption will never be observed - with probability 1/2, firm 1 will adopt at T_1^{**} and firm 2 at T_2^*, and with equal probability the roles will be reversed.

The entire analysis rests critically on Reinganum's original assumption that the present value of costs of adoption at T is viewed from t are independent of t. This is a very strong assumption as it does not allow for any flexibility in allocation of resources over time to R and D. The consequences of endogenising allocation of R and D expenditure over time have been explored by Harris and Vickers (1985) and Fudenberg, Gilbert, Stiglitz, and Tirole (1983). To keep things tractable, they both work with very stylised models. Both assume that there is no gain to adopting second. Harris and Vickers restrict themselves to a perfect information game with alternating moves, and Fudenberg et.al. are able to analyse the simultaneous move case only at the cost of imposing a very simple discrete R and D technology.

In both cases, the findings are quite striking; in

perfect equilibrium firms that have even quite small initial cost disadvantages drop out of the "race" to adopt at the beginning, allowing the leader to adopt at a cost-minimising pace. If initial cost disadvantages are very small, what happens depends critically on the information structure. With sequential moves (Harris-Vickers) the firm which moves first adopts, and the first mover's behaviour is still only affected by the presence of a potential rival in the initial period. With simultaneous moves, however, both firms invest intensively in R and D and tie the race if they are not too far from the finishing line so eventual winners are in this case substantially affected by the presence of a rival. This latter outcome corresponds to the equilibrium outlined above, which is as it should be, because the Reinganum model has identical costs and simultaneous moves.

V. INFINITE HORIZON GAMES - COOPERATION AND INDETERMINACY

The problem of indeterminacy of equilibrium has already been touched upon - indeed, this provided a major rationale for the introduction of the perfection criterion. Recent research has made clear however, that in many types of infinte horizon games the imposition of the perfection requirement may do little to reduce the set of equilibrium outcomes[6]. To put it another way, many apparently co-operative agreements can, with an infinite horizon, be the outcomes of non-cooperative (perfect) equilibria.

This has been shown most strikingly by Aumann, Shapley, and Rubinstein for the case of repeated games[7], where without discounting, perfection imposes <u>no</u> restriction on the set of outcomes (see e.g. Rubinstein (1979)). Furthermore, more recent work has shown that even in the finite-horizon case, if the constituent game has multiple equilibria, then similar kinds of indeterminacy can arise - in fact, a similar result to the Aumann/Shapley-Rubinstein one it true if the constituent game is repeated often enough (Benoit and Krishna (1985)).

But this is not all. Even small amounts of incomplete information can lead to indeterminacy, in that a game with a unique perfect equilibrium may exhibit a large number of sequential equilibria (see Fudenberg and Maskin (1983), or Rubinstein (1983)).

A closely related and pertinent question is, of course, the nature of structure of perfect equilibria in infinite horizon games. In an important paper Abreu (1982) has provided an answer for the case of repeated game for discounting, which makes possible a characterisation of the set of equilibrium outcomes for such games. Furthermore, his approach clearly generalises to dynamic games, and to repeated games with imperfect monitoring (i.e. games where the history of play can be only observed up to a random error term - see Abreu, Pearce, and Stacchetti (1984)). These results have important implications for the theory of cartels between oligopolists. In this section, we review all these new developments, concentrating on the case of repeated games with complete information.

(a) Characterising Equilibria in Repeated Games

Our starting point is the observation that infinitely repeated games[8] admit a large number of Nash equilibrium outcomes. Futhermore, the set of equilibrium outcomes can easily be described by considering Nash equilibria of a special sort, those involving so-called trigger strategies. These strategies prescribe that at each date, t, player i play a_i^* unless and until precisely one player (possibly himself) deviates and plays $a_j' \neq a_j^*$. If $j \neq i$, then i switches to an action that punishes j, a_i^j and plays this for ever; if on the other-hand, it is himself that has deviated, he switches from then on to playing his best reply to the punishment a_{-i}^i which he expects to ensue.

We might as well consider punishment actions that punish players most severely, i.e. punishments, that yield players only their security levels v_i in the constituent game, where v_i is defined as

$$v_i = \min_{a_{-i}} \max_{a_i} u_i(a_i, a_{-i}) \tag{8}$$

Let any vector of actions that achieves v_i be denoted $m^i = (m_1^i, m_2^i, \ldots, m_n^i)$.

Now suppose that all players $j \neq i$ announce that they will play trigger strategies. What is the best that i can do in reply? If i is considering deviating, the best he can get with discounting (see footnote 7) is a payoff of $(1 - \delta).\max_{a_i \in A_i} u_i(a_i, a_{-i}^*) + \delta.v_i$, because once he has deviated from a^* once, he can get at most v_i from then on. Hence a^* is the equilibrium outcome of a Nash equilbrium (in trigger strategies) if and only if $u_i(a^*)$ is greater than this i.e. a^* satisfies

$$u_i(a^*) \geq (1-\delta).\, u_i^*(a_{-i}, a_i') + \delta.v_i, \text{ all } a_i' \in A_i, \text{ all } i \tag{9}$$

Note in particular that as $\delta \to 1$, we find that any a^* that yields each player more than his security level v_i (i.e. is strictly individually rational for that player) is a Nash equilibrium outcome. This is one version of a result as the "folk" theorem for repeated games. Without discounting (i.e. with long-run averaging) we get the essentially identical result that any weakly individually rational outcome is an equilibrium outcome.

We illustrate all this with an example from Fudenberg and Maskin (1983) of a matrix constituent game;

	U	D
U	1,1	0,-2
D	-2,0	-1,-1

In this game, player i minimaxes player j by playing D with probability 1, and j's best response is to play U with probability 1, so $v_j = 0$ for j = 1,2. Then without discounting, any mixed strategies (a_1^*, a_2^*) (where a_i denotes the probability that i plays U) which yield each player at least 0 can be sustained as an equilibrium outcome, using strategies where any defection by i is punished by j switching to D for ever.

Is such an equilibrium perfect, however? The answer is that for almost all games[9] it is not, the reason being that in the event that some player i deviates (a subgame never reached in Nash equilibrium, of course) the players who must than minimax i for ever will in general not wish to do so. For example, in our matrix game 1 minimaxes 2 by playing D, but given that 2 responds by playing U, 1 can do better by switching to U himself. To put it another way, 1's threat to minimax 2 is not credible.

In a series of papers, Aumann, Shapley, and Rubinstein tackled this problem for the case without discounting. Their insight was to point out that in order to make trigger strategies credible (i.e. perfect) players must also be punished for refusing to cooperate in the punishment of another player. Moreover, they showed exactly how this could be done.

A natural first attempt at modifying the trigger strategies would be to declare that players who fail to carry out minimax punishments should themselves be minimaxed for ever. However, this will not work in our example, as punishing one's opponent for ever is extremely costly, yielding a payoff of -2, so that each player would rather be punished for ever than punish for ever.

Rather, the key to constructing credible punishment strategies is to make punishment periods <u>finite</u> (play always returning to the original a^* at the end) and depend on the number of previous deviations by any particular player for whatever is prescribed by his equilib um strategy. Suppose that player i is punished for τ_n periods after his nth deviation. Then, as punishment periods are finite, with limit averaging it costs nothing for a player to carry out a punishment. Similarly, no player i can gain or lose by a finite number of deviations from playing a_i^* the original cooperative agreement. Hence, to establish that any individually rational a^* can be sustained as a perfect equilibrium it suffices to show that no player i can do strictly better than $u_i(a^*)$ by deviating an infinite number of times. Now, the average gain from any sequence of deviations over T periods is bounded above by

$$\frac{n(T)}{T}.b_i + \frac{T - n(T)}{T}.(v_i - u_i(a^*)) \qquad (10)$$

where b_i is an upper bound on $u_i(a)$, and n(T) is the largest number of complete periods of punishment that can be fitted into T periods (i.e. n(T) is the largest integer n such that

$\sum_{i=1}^{n} \tau_i \leq T$).

It is clear that as long as the τ_n increase fast enough with n so that $n(T)/T \to 0$ as $T \to \infty$, the limit average gain from deviation as $T \to \infty$ will be $v_i - u_i(a_i^*)$ which is non-positive as long as a_i^* is individually rational. This can be achieved, for example, by making τ_n a geometric series i.e. $\tau_n = a^n$, $a > 1$.

We have therefore proved;

Proposition (Aumann-Shapley-Rubinstein)
Without discounting, any individually rational payoff of the constituent game is the payoff of some perfect equilbrium of the repeated game.

The validity of this result depends both on no discounting of the future and the repeated game structure. For example, it does not carry over to dynamic games without discounting even when (long-run) security levels are well defined: for a counterexample, see Lockwood (1984)).

More importantly, however, with discounting, the device of geometrically increasing punishments fails, as arbitrarily long punishments are not arbitrarily severe, because far-off punishments are relatively unimportant, so one would expect the imposition of perfection to have some real force.

In fact, we require, roughly speaking, any subgame-perfect equilibrium outcome a^* to satisfy (9) where v_i is replaced by w_i, the worst payoff that all players can credibly impose on i (and we expect that $w_i > v_i$). However, this raises a thorny problem; unlike the Nash case, where v_i is exogenously defined, w_i is endogenous. In fact, w_i must be the "worst" payoff for i associated with a perfect equilibrium (if such a worst payoff exists).

The reason for this is as follows. Let A^P be the set of outcome paths associated with perfect equilibria of the repeated game, and let f^* be any perfect equilibrium whose outcome path is a^*. Then w_i is simply the payoff to i from the continuation of f^* from t + 1 onwards contingent upon the history where i deviates from a^* at t. By the perfectness of f^*, this continuation must also be a perfect equilibrium and w_i must therefore satisfy only

$$w_i > \inf_{a \varepsilon A^P} \sum_{t=0}^{\infty} \delta^t . u_i(a_t) \qquad (13)$$

Futhermore, it seems impossible to break into this circular definition of the w_i. For example, we do not know whether A^P is a closed set - i.e. whether worst credible punishments exist. Even if they do, we have no constructive means of finding them.

Abreu (1982) showed how this circularity could be overcome by restricting attention to what he calls <u>simple</u> strategy n-tuples. These are defined as follows. Let a^i be an outcome path. Then a simple strategy n-tuple $f(a^*; a^1, \ldots a^n)$ prescribes that each player i play a^*_{it} at each date until one player (say i) deviates at τ in which case all players start playing $a^i = (a^i_0, a^i_1 \ldots .)$ at τ + 1, τ + 2 and so on. If j ≠ i deviates from this punishment, then a^j is started from the beginning, and most importantly, if i deviates from his own punishment, a^i is started ov<u>er again</u> from the beginning[10]. Note that unlike the trigger punishments, a^i_{it} <u>need not</u> be a best reply to $a^i_{-i,t}$ or in other words, the possibility that players cooperate in their own punishments is allowed for. Note also the dimensional simplification - a simple strategy is entirely characterised by n + 1 outcome paths, $(a^*, a^1, \ldots, a^n)$.

The key property of a simple strategy n-tuple is that it is perfect if and only if one-shot deviations from it, contingent upon all histories, are not profitable for any player. The conditions which ensure this are, assuming a^* is stationary (i.e. $a^*_t = a^*$, all t);

$$u_i(a^*) \geq (1-\delta)\, u_i(a^*_{-i}, a'_i) + \delta \sum_{t=0}^{\infty} \delta^t u_i(a^i_t) \tag{12}$$

all $a'_i \in A_i$, all i;

$$\sum_{t=\tau}^{\infty} \delta^{t-\tau} \cdot u_i(a^j_t) \geq (1-\delta)\, u_i(a^j_{-i,\tau}, a'_i) + \delta \cdot \sum_{t=0}^{\infty} \delta^t \cdot u_i(a^i_t)$$

all $a'_i \in A_i$, all i, j, all τ. (15)

(12) ensures that deviations from the original outcome path are not profitable for any player, whereas (13) ensures that deviations from any ongoing punishment $(a^j_\tau, a^j_{\tau+1} \ldots)$ is not profitable for any player.

The second fundamental property of a simple strategy n-tuple is that $f(a^*; a^1, \ldots a^n)$ is perfect if and only if the associated "punishment" strategy n-tuple $f(a^i; a^1, \ldots a^n)$ is also perfect, i = 1, 2...n. To see this, note that (13) is precisely the condition for $f(a^i; a^1 \ldots a^n)$ to be perfect, all i as (12) is implied by (13) if $a^* = a^i$. (Abreu calls the n-tuple of "punishment" simple strategy n-tuples $\{f(a^i; a^1, \ldots a^n)\}_{i=1,\ldots n}$ a <u>simple penal code</u>.) Therefore, (13) is satisfied if and only if a^i is a perfect outcome path, all i. This fact enables us to prove that there exist "worst" punishments, or equivalently, that A^P is closed.

Let $(a^1_v \ldots a^n_v)^{\infty}_{v=1}$ be a convergent sequence[11] of n-tuples of outcome paths such that $a^i_v \in A^P$ all i, all v and

such that the payoff from a_v^i converges to $\inf_{a \in A^P} \sum_{t=0}^{\infty} \delta^t . u_i(a_t)$
We know that (13) is satisfied for all v
as the a^i are perfect equilibrium outcomes, so (13) is also satisfied in the limit as $v \to \infty$ by the continuity of payoffs. Let the limit of a_v^i be $\underline{a}^i$; then the strategy n-tuple $f(\underline{a}^i; \underline{a}^1,....\underline{a}^n)$ is also perfect for all i and yields i the "worst" credible punishment - i.e. the infimum on the RHS of equation (11) above. Abreu calls $\{f(\underline{a}^i;\underline{a}^1....\underline{a}^n)\}_{i=1..n}$ an <u>optimal</u> simple penal code.

However, what is most interesting about (13) is that it provides a set of necessary conditions that optimal penal codes must satisfy. First, it is apparent from (13) that (as already remarked) optimal penal codes may not have the "best reply" property, but players can credibly be persuaded to cooperate in their own punishments only if punishments are more severe at the beginning of the sequence - they must have something to lose by going back to the beginning.

Second, subject to this "stick and carrot" requirement, optimal penal codes may have a very simple form, as Abreu himself has shown for an oligipoly game. In fact, Fudenberg and Maskin (1983) have constructed a class of "simple" simple penal codes which are approximately optimal as the discount factor tends to unity in the sense that the payoff to i from a^i tends to his security level v_i as δ tends to 1. This enables them to prove a "folk" theorem with discounting[12], which states that (subject to a regularity condition in the n-person case) for any strictly individually rational payoff vector, there exists a δ^* such that this vector is the payoff of a perfect equilibrium for all δ such that $\delta^* \leq \delta < 1$. (See Fudenberg and Maskin (1983) Theorems 1 and 2).

The simple penal code involved is particularly "simple" with two players. Choose any a^* such that $u_i(a^*) > v_i$, i=1,2. Then the F/M simple penal code prescribes that in the event of any deviation both players should play the strategy m_i^j that minimaxes the other for k periods, and then revert to a^*, so that

$$a^i = (\underbrace{m,m,\ldots,m}_{k\ \text{times}};a^*,a^*,\ldots,), \text{ with } m = (m_1^2,\ m_2^1);\ i=1,2 \tag{14}$$

To prove the F/M "folk" theorem, (for the 2-person case and stationary outcome paths) we simply show that for any such a^*, there exists an integer k^* and number δ^* such that (12) and (13) are satisfied given (14) whenever $1 > \delta \geq \delta^*$. For convenience, normalise payoffs so that $v_i = 0$, i = 1,2. Then it is easily verifed that (12) and (13) become

$$u_i(a^*) \geq (1-\delta)\ u_i\ (a^*_{-i},a_i') + \delta.w_i,\ \text{all } a_i' \in A_i,\ \text{all } i, \tag{15}$$

and

$$w_i = (1-\delta^{k^*+1}).u_i(m) + \delta^{k^*+1}.u_i(a^*) > 0,\ \text{all } i \tag{16}$$

As $u_i(a^*) > 0 \geq u_i(m)$, a k^* and δ^* satisfying (15) and (16) can certainly be found.

Next, we turn to the question of indeterminacy in finitely repeated games. First, it is well-known that if the constituent game has a unique Nash equilibrium, the only perfect equilibrium of the constituent game is repeatedly played. The argument is a simple backward induction one; in the final period, the only possible outcome is Nash equilbrium. Knowing this, no player can be induced to play anything other than his Nash equilibrium strategy in the penultimate period, and so on.

With multiple equilibria, this no longer holds true. Players can be threatened by the imposition of "bad" Nash equilibria in later periods to play strategies in earlier periods that are not mutual best replies - in other words, there may be some perfect equilibrium outcomes of the repeated game that are <u>not</u> entirely composed of Nash equilibria of the constituent game. This point has been made recently and independently by Benoit and Krishna (1985), Friedman (1985), and Moreaux (1985).

For example, consider the following matrix constituent game, due to Benoit and Krishna.

	B	C	D
B	5,3	0,0	2,0
C	0,0	2,2	0,0
D	0,0	0,0	0,0

This has <u>two</u> Nash equilibria - a "good" one (B,B) which Pareto-dominates the "bad" one, (C,C). Suppose now the constituent game is played twice, and players do not discount. Then the trigger strategies which prescribe that both players play D in period 0 and B in period 1, unless precisely one player deviates in period 0, in which case C is played by both players, are in perfect equilibrium even though (D,D) is <u>not</u> a Nash equilibrium of the constituent game.

Benoit and Krishna have exploited the potential of this simple idea remarkably fully. Under the assumptions of no discounting and that there are "enough" equilibria in the constituent game so that each player can be punished by switching from one equilibrium to another, they show that given any game repeated T times with associated "worst" perfect equilibrium payoffs, w_i^T, for each player, one can find a longer game T^*, with strictly lower "worst" perfect equilibrium payoffs for each player. Hence, in the limit, w_i^T tends to v_i for each i, although, surprisingly, it may not do so monotonically (see Benoit and Krishna, p.913). It follows immediately from this that under the stated assumptions, any strictly individually rational payoff can be sustained as the perfect equilibrium payoff of a game repeated often enough.

The argument is an ingenious one, and involves constructing three-stage punishments for each player i, using the w_i^T. The outcome path of the three- stage punishment involves a first phase where all other players minimax player i, a second reward phase where $j \neq i$ are rewarded for doing this (which is essential if the original T-period punishment w_j^T is preferred by any j to minimaxing i) and a third phase where play cycles through a finite sequence of constituent game Nash equilibria. Deviations by any player from the first two phases of this outcome path (say at time t) are punished by as many repetitions of the original T-period punishment as can be fitted into the remaining $T^* - t$ periods, "topped up" with playing j's "worst" constituent game Nash equilibrium in the remaining $T^* - t - T + 1$ periods at the end of the game. By construction, these latter punishments are themselves credible - i.e. perfect equilibrium outcomes. Finally, by appropriate choice of the lengths of the various phases, the new punishments can be made more severe than the old.

Note that subject to the constraint imposed by the finite horizon, these punishment strategy n-tuples are simple in Abreu's sense. Therefore, one can view Benoit and Krishna's results as complementary to the work of Abreu and of Fudenberg and Maskin - they exhibit simple penal codes which are "approximately" optimal in finite horizon games, if the horizon is long enough. Apart from these limiting results, however, the central question raised by Abreu's work - the characterisation of optimal penal codes - remains largely unanswered, and it is probably unreasonable to expect any general results, although the recent paper by Abreu, Pearce, and Stacchetti does suggest a general method for finding them.

These recent developments seem very far removed from potential applications, such as theories of cartel behaviour. There are two reasons for this. The first is that the focus has been on optimal punishments (which are potentially very complex) rather than on the implications of simple credible trigger punishments, such as reversion to constituent game Nash equilibrium. The other, easily forgotten in all the technicalities, is that with perfect information, one would never actually observe a cartel carrying out a punishment.

Green and Porter (1984) present a model of a cartel where past outputs of other firms are imperfectly observed - in fact, each firm only observes its own output and the market price. In this circumstance, punishments can only be triggered by prices. They also considered the punishment of reversion to Nash equilibrium for T periods. Within this framework, the objects of interest are the reversion period and the trigger price, and Green and Porter discuss how these could be estimated from the data generated by such cartel behaviour. It is worth noting that Abreu, Pearce and Stacchetti (1984) have shown that all symmetric perfect (or more properly, sequential) equilibria of the Green-Porter model have a similar structure. Only two outputs -

a cooperative and a reversionary output - are ever produced by each firm, and the choice between them depends on a generalised trigger-price rule.

(b) The Problem of Indeterminacy

These developments should not obscure the fact that in many infinite-horizon games, subgame-perfection fails significantly to resolve the indeterminacy of Nash equilibrium. One way out of this impasse would be to impose plausible simplicity conditions on strategies. For example, in the oligopoly context, one may restrict strategies to depend only on the opponent's past actions, to capture the idea of reaction functions (Maskin and Tirole (1983), Kalai and Stanford (1985)). Unfortunately, such restrictions do not produce uniqueness unless firms choose outputs sequentially, and are committed to these for several periods at a time.

Another approach to simplicity is to model bounded rationality explicitly. For example, Rubinstein (1984) supposes players playing the Prisoners Dilemma can be described by finite automata. Preference for simplicity is embodied in the solution concept, which requires that each player wishes to minimise the number of active states of the machine, and that all states must be used infinitely often. A striking conclusion is that no Pareto-efficient outcome can be sustained as an equilibrium outcome, but this is due to the fact that the simplicity requirements rule out trigger strategies.

Two more possibilities in the spirit of bounded rationality have been mooted, by Binmore (1985) and Selten (1985) among others. First, Selten briefly discusses modelling individual learning processes. The second concept is one that captures "learning" by a species; that of an evolutionary equilibrium, a concept taken from biology. Here, players are drawn from a known distribution of types, and each player is an automation in the sense that his strategy is fixed, not optimally chosen. The population distribution changes over time as the result of a survival process which increases the proportion of types who are successful in this game, and an equilibrium is a fixed point of this process. While research in these areas is in its infancy, given the impasse that fully rational game theory faces, (see especially Binmore (1985) p.53-56) they will undoubtedly prove to be important.

VI. CONCLUSIONS

It is certain that the systematic use of the perfect and sequential equilibrium concepts will continue to spread to all areas of economics where strategic interaction is important and the credibility of behaviour and reputation are issues. We have already touched upon two areas where systematic applications of these ideas has to some extent changed the subject; industrial economics, and behavioural theories of bargaining. For example, in industrial economics, the causàlity running from structure to conduct to performance is being replaced by the view that the structure (e.g. the number and sizes of firms, and their cost structures) is determined endogenously, by strategic interaction.

However, applications of these ideas to other areas are not appearing - for example, recent work by Backus and Driffill analyses reputation building by governments using the sequential equilibrium concept;

they show that even a government that cares about unemployment may wish to require a reputation for "toughness" by adopting (with some probability) a deflationary fiscal stance, in order to moderate private sector wage demands (Backus and Driffill (1985), (1985a)).

By contrast, "pure" non-cooperative game theory is beset by problems of indeterminacy. We have examined this problem in repeated games with complete information in some detail in Section V above. Rather different problems occur in the case of incomplete information - here, indeterminacy arises because different equilibria can be supported by differing beliefs by players over information sets that are unreached in equilibrium. The problem is that there seems no general way of selecting particular beliefs; plausible consistency conditions (such as that of Kreps and Wilson (1982) p.872) do not ensure uniqueness. One solution is to abandon the search for general criteria and use in particular (economic) arguments to support particular belief systems in particular cases, but even this is typically not enough to ensure uniqueness (see e.g. Fudenberg and Tirole (1983)).

We have already touched upon some responses to the indeterminacy problem. These involve either severely limiting the optimising behaviour of individual players (a la Rubinstein) or dispensing with it altogether, in favour of satisficing, or natural selection, or the explicit modelling of actual decision- making procedures. Selten (1985, p.86) concludes "perhaps many descriptive theories for specific contexts will finally grow together into a coherent theory of limited rationality."

FOOTNOTES

1. For example, if only one player can make a non-trivial move at each date, there are no simultaneous moves - the game is one of so-called complete information.
2. This was due to Nash in 1950-51 but has antecedents in Cournot's work in the 1830's.
3. A strongly dominated strategy f_i is one such that there exists a g_i in F_i which is a strictly better response to all f_{-i} in F_{-i} than f_{-i} i.e. $U_i(g_i, f_{-i}) > U_i(f_i, f_{-i})$ all f_{-i} in F_{-i}.
4. Much recent work (e.g. Dixon (1985), (1985a), Yarrow (1985) inter alia) has investigated the question of factor bias in the case where the market "subgame" solution concept is either a competitive or a rational conjectural equilibrium. While neither of these concepts can be formally reconciled with Nash equilibrium in the subgame, these analyses are certainly in the spirit of perfect equilibrium.
5. Fudenberg and Tirole also show that in the continuous time case, there may be a continuum of "late adoption" equilibria where both firms hold back from innovating until at least a date $S > T_2^*$. These equilibria cannot arise in the discrete time model, no matter how small the time grid, for reasons discussed by Fudenberg and Tirole p.391. It is worth noting in passing that Fudenberg and Tirole adopt a completely different method of anlysis than the one sketched here. Instead of analysing continuous-time equilibria as limits of discrete-time equilibria, they adopt the much more elegant approach of specifying "enlarged" strategy spaces in the continuous time game directly, which allows the subgame perfection requirement to be imposed directly in continuous time.
6. This is not always the case. For example, in bilateral bargaining games, with an infinite horizon, the perfection criterion is spectacularly successful, reducing a continuum of Nash equilibrium outcomes (i.e. any partition of the "cake" between the two players) to a

single determinate partition (see Rubinstein (1982)).

7. A repeated game is a constituent game in normal form, with action spaces A_i and payoffs $u_i(a_1,\ldots,a_n)$, played repeatedly. It has natural applications to the theory of cartels between firms. We deal with both repeated games with and without discounting. In the former, payoffs are given by

$(1-\delta)\sum_{t=0}^{\infty}\delta^t u_i(a_t)$ and in the latter by

$\limsup_{T\to\infty} \frac{1}{T}\sum_{t=0}^{T} u_i(a_t)$. In the case where the limit average exists, the former converges to the latter as $\delta \to 1$.

8. This is also true of finitely repeated games, and the demonstration of this involves similar sorts of "trigger" strategies. Of course, the equilibrium outcomes will be affected by "end-game" considerations, for example that the outcome in the final period must be a constituent game Nash equilibrium.

9. The exceptions are games where the payoffs of some Nash equilibrium of the constituent game coincide with the minimax payoffs for all players e.g. the Prisoner's Dilemma.

10. To complete the description of the strategy, we suppose that if two or more players deviate simultaneously, play returns to a* from the beginning.

11. By the compactness of the space of outcomes and the continuity of the payoffs (in the product topology) such a sequence exists.

12. Such a result does not seem to hold if the past history of play can only be imperfectly observed by each player. Radner, Myerson and Maskin (1985) present an example of a repeated two-player "partnership game" where each player can only imperfectly monitor the other's effort and show that there is a discontinuity in the set of perfect equilibrium payoffs as $\delta \to 1$.

REFERENCES

D. Abreu, Repeated Games with Discounting: A General Theory and an Application to Oligopoly, mimeo., Princeton University, (1982).

D. Abreu, D. Pearce and E. Stacchetti, Optimal Cartel Equilibria with Imperfect Monitoring, Harvard Institute of Economic Research Discussion Paper No. 1090, (1984).

D. Backus and J. Driffill, Inflation and Reputation, American Economic Review, 75, p.530-538, (1985).

D. Backus and J. Driffill, Rational Expectations and Policy Credibility Following a Change in Regime, Review of Economic Studies, 52, p.211-221, (1985a).

J. Benoit and V. Krishna, Finitely Repeated Games, Econometrica, Vol.53, p.905-923, (1985).

D. Bernheim, Rationisable Strategic Behaviour, Econometrica, Vol. 52, p.1007-28, (1984).

K.J. Binmore, Nash Bargaining Theory II, ICERD Discussion Paper, London School of Economics, (1980).

K.G. Binmore, Equilibria in Extensive Games, Economic Journal, Vol. 95, Supplement, p.51-59, (1985).

J. Brander and B. Spencer, Strategic Commitment with R & D; the Symmetric Case, Bell Journal of Economics, Vol. 14, p.225-35, (1983).

J. Bulow, J. Geanakoplos, and P.D. Klemperer, Multimarket Oligopoly: Strategic Substitutes and Complements, Journal of Political Economy, 93, p.488-511, (1985).

H. Dixon, Strategic Investment in an Industry with a Competitive Product Market, Journal of Industrial Economics, 33, p.483-499, (1985).

H. Dixon, Strategic Investment with Consistent Conjectures, Birkbeck College London Discussion Paper No.176, (1985a).

H. Dixon, Cournot and Bertrand Outcomes as Equilibria in a Strategic Metagame, Economic Journal Conference Supplement, forthcoming, (1986).

J. Friedman, Cooperative Equilibria in Finite Horizon Non-Cooperative Supergames, Journal of Economic Theory, Vol. 35, p.309-399, (1985).

D. Fudenberg, R. Gilbert, J. Stiglitz and J. Tirole, Pre-emption, Leapfroging, and Competition in Patent Races, European Economic Review, Vol.22, p.3-31, (1983).

D. Fudenberg and E. Maskin, The Folk Theorem in Repeated Games with Discounting and Incomplete Information, mimeo. (1983).

D. Fudenberg and J. Tirole, Sequential Bargaining with Incomplete Information, Review of Economic Studies, Vol. 50, p.221-247, (1983).

D. Fudenberg and J. Tirole, The Fat Cat Effect, The Puppy-Dog Ploy, and the Lean and Hungry Look, American Economic Review, Papers and Proceedings, 74, p.361-366, (1984).

D. Fudenberg and J. Tirole, Pre-emption and Rent Equalisation in the Adoption of New Technology, Review of Economic Studies, Vol. 52, p. 383-402, (1985).

P.A. Geroski, L. Phlips and A. Ulph, Oligopoly, Competition and Welfare: Some Recent Developments, Journal of Industrial Economics, 33, p.369-386, (1985).

E. Green and H. Porter, Non-Cooperative Collusion under Imperfect Price Information, Econometrica,Vol.52, p.87-100, (1984).

P.A. Grout, Investment and Wages in the Absence of Legally Binding Labour Contracts, Econometrica, Vol. 52, p.449-60, (1984).

P.A. Grout, A Theoretical Approach to the Effect of Trade Union Immunities on Investment and Employment, Economic Journal, Vol. 95, Supplement, p.96-101, (1985).

C. Harris, Existence and Characterisation of Perfect Equilibrium in Games of Perfect Information, Econometrica, Vol. 53, p.613-629, (1985).

C. Harris and J. Vickers, Perfect Equilibrium in a Model of a Race, Review of Economic Studies, Vol.52, p.193-209, (1985).

J. Harsanyi, Games with Imcomplete Information Played by Bayesian Players, Parts I, II and III, Management Science, Vol.14, p.159-182, 320-334, 486-502, (1967-8).

E. Kalai and W. Stanford, Conjectural Variations Strategies in Accelerated Cournot Games, International Journal of Industrial Organisation, Vol. 3, p.133-53, (1985).

D. Kreps and R. Wilson, Sequential Equilibria, Econometrica, Vol. 50, p.863-894, (1982).

B. Lockwood, A Characterisation of Equilibrium Paths in Dynamic Games, Birkbeck College Discussion Paper No. 165, London, (1984).

A. Manning, Integration of Trade Union Models in a Sequential Bargaining Framework, mimeo, Birkbeck College, London (1985).

E. Maskin and J. Tirole, A Theory of Dynamic Oligopoly, 1: Overview and Quantity Competition with Large Fixed Costs, Technical Report No.409, IMSSS, Stanford University, (1983).

M. Moreaux, Perfect Nash Equilibrium in Finite Repeated Games and Uniqueness of Nash Equilibrium in the Constituent Game, Economics Letters, Vol.17, No.4, (1985).

R. Myerson, Refinements of the Nash Equilibrium Concept, International Journal of Game Theory, Vol.7, p.73-80, (1978).

G. Owen, Game Theory. Second Edition, New York: Academic Press, (1982).

D. Pearce, Rationalisable Strategic Behaviour and the Problem of Perfection, Econometrica, Vo.52, p.1029-1050, (1984).

R. Radner, R. Myerson, and E. Maskin, An Example of a

Repeated Partnership Game with Discounting and with Uniformly Inefficient Equilibria, mimeo, (1984).

J Reinganum, On the Diffusion of New Technology: A Game-Theoretic Approach, Review of Economic Studies, Vol.48, p.395-406, (1981).

A. Rubinstein, Equilibrium in Supergames with the Overtaking Criterion, Journal of Economic Theory, Vol.21, p.1-9, (1979).

A. Rubinstein, Perfect Equilibrium in a Bargaining Model, Econometrica, Vol.50, p.97-109, (1982).

A. Rubinstein, A Bargaining Model with Incomplete Information about Time Preferences, Institute for Advanced Studies, Hebrew University, Jerusalem, (1983).

A. Rubinstein, Finite Automata Play the Repeated Prisoner's Dilemma, ICERD Discussion Paper 85/109, London School of Economics, (1985).

R. Selten, Re-examination of the Perfectness Concept for Equilibrium Points in Extensive Games, International Journal of Game Theory, Vol. 4, p.25-55, (1975).

R. Selten, Comment on R.J. Aumann in Frontiers of Economics, (ed. K.J. Arrow and S. Honkapohja), Oxford:Basil Blackwell, (1985).

M. Shubik, Game Theory in the Social Sciences, MIT Press, (1982).

J. Vickers, Strategic Competition Among the Few - Some Recent Developments in the Economics of Industry, (forthcoming), Oxford Review of Economic Policy, (1985).

J. Vickers, Delegation and the Theory of the Firm, Economic Journal, Vol.95, Supplement, p.138-147, (1985a).

G. Yarrow, Welfare Losses in Oligopoly and Imperfect Competition, Journal of Industrial Economics, 33, p.515-529, (1985).

AUTHOR INDEX

SUBJECT INDEX